W9-CKD-073

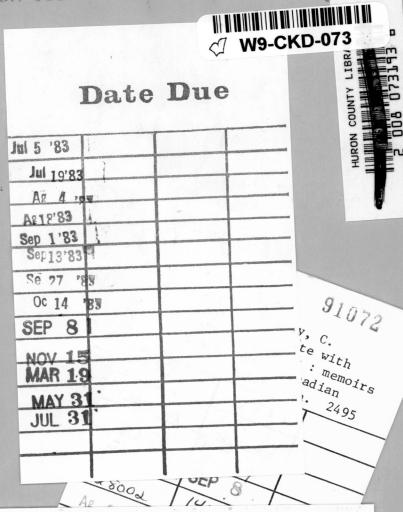

Date Due

Jul 5 '83		
Jul 19'83		
Ag 4 '83		
Ag 18'83		
Sep 1 '83		
Sep 13'83		
Se 27 '83		
Oc 14 '83		
SEP 8		
NOV 15		
MAR 19		
MAY 31		
JUL 31		

91072

91072

Stacey, C. P. (Charles Perry), 1906-
A date with history : memoirs of a Canadian
historian / C.P. Stacey. Ottawa : Deneau,
[1983].
293 p.
Bibliography: p. 276-282.

1. Stacey, C. P. (Charles Perry), 1906-
2. Historians - Canada - Biography. I. Title.
0888790864   1827685

6/90

This book has been published with the help of a grant from the Social Science Federation of Canada, using funds provided by the Social Sciences and Humanities Research Council of Canada.

A Date with History

C. P. STACEY

Memoirs of
a Canadian Historian

A Date with History

DENEAU

PUBLISHED BY
DENEAU PUBLISHERS
281 LISGAR STREET
OTTAWA, CANADA K2P 0E1

© C.P. Stacey

Printed in Canada
First Printing

CANADIAN CATALOGUING IN PUBLICATION DATA

Stacey, C.P. (Charles Perry), 1906-
A date with history
Includes index.
ISBN 0-88879-086-4

1. Stacey, C.P. (Charles Perry), 1906-   2. Historians—
Canada—Biography.   I. Title.
FC151.S72A3   971'.007'2024   C83-090051-9
F1024.6.S72A3

For
HELEN

"I suppose history never lies, does it?" said Mr. Dick, with a gleam of hope.

"Oh dear, no, sir!" I replied, most decisively. I was ingenuous and young, and I thought so.

The Personal History of David Copperfield

Contents

Preface

This is not really an autobiography, for I have omitted many things that would have interested only me and my friends. It is an account of my life as an historian, and particularly as an official war historian.

Doing that job brought me many experiences, and contacts with many people, which may perhaps have enough interest to justify setting them down in print. I learned some things which would not have been suitable for inclusion in an official history, and others which could not decently be revealed during the lifetimes of the people concerned, but which nevertheless ought to be somewhere recorded. I have accordingly put them down here. I might perhaps have called the book *Unofficial History*; but the late Field-Marshal Lord Slim got to that title first.

I owe debts to many friends who have helped me in various ways: particularly Fred Azar, Michael Bliss, Robert Bothwell, Hugh Halliday, Norman Hillmer, Murray Hunter, Desmond Neill, Mrs. J.M. White and, as in so many other books, Barbara Wilson. Jack Granatstein was the first person who suggested that I undertake this task. I am grateful to the Historical Division of the Department of External Affairs, and particularly to D.P. Cole. I have to thank Patricia Kennedy for her marvellous typing. Finally, the book owes a great deal to the perceptive editing of Diane Mew.

Massey College, Toronto,   C.P.S.
October 1982

Chapter 1

And Quiet Flows the Don

In the year 1889 the University of Toronto relinquished its right to levy tolls on vehicles using two important streets adjacent to the university — College Street and University Avenue. In return, the City of Toronto conveyed to the university one-foot-wide strips of land adjoining the sidewalks on College Street between Beverley and Yonge streets and on University Avenue between College and Queen streets. The purpose of this arrangement was simple and practical; it was to enable the university to prevent the establishment of houses of ill-fame in its close vicinity.[1]

The object was fully achieved. A few years later, when William Lyon Mackenzie King and his contemporaries at the university went in search of such establishments, they had to go far afield; the future prime minister's diary indicates that the centre of activity was King Street, over a mile to the south. And as one would expect, the area covered by the city's grant became very respectable. In particular, the south side of College Street opposite the university grounds (the word "campus" in the modern American sense had not yet arrived in Canada) became a sort of Doctors' Row. For two blocks, almost every house was a doctor's residence and office. One of these physicians was my father, Dr. Charles Edward Stacey; and thus it was that I came to be born at 161 College Street, just across the road from the university.

1

My family were south Irish Protestants on both sides. My father's father, William Stacy (my father seems to have been the first to insert the "e" in the family name) came to Manvers Township, Durham County, Canada West, in 1853. He brought with him letters of recommendation from the Church of Ireland (that is, Anglican) rector of Kilmaganny, County Kilkenny, stating that he had been employed as parish clerk and schoolmaster there but had resigned "as I hope, to improve his prospects in America." How many millions of immigrants to North America across the centuries have nursed that hope! The improvement in William's case was fairly modest. He settled in Fleetwood, a hamlet which now exists only as a name on the map, and in due course opened a store. By 1858 he had sufficient status in the community — certainly not much was required — to be appointed an ensign in the Fifth Battalion of Durham Militia. (I have his commission; it hangs beside my own.) He and his wife, Maria Adams from Kilmaganny, raised a large family.

My father, the only one of the family to get to university, financed his education by teaching school, and graduated from Trinity Medical School, Toronto, in 1885. He practised for a time in Acton, Ontario, and then took the plunge and decided to hang up his shingle in the big city, the provincial capital. It was in 1891 that he first appeared in the Toronto City Directory, his home and office being at 396 College Street. It was there that he brought his bride, my mother, Pearl Perry of Cannington, Ontario, after their marriage on 6 September 1898. Perhaps it was my mother who encouraged him to move at the turn of the century to Doctor's Row. At any rate, by 1901 they were installed at 161 College Street. For this respectable three-storeyed, semi-detached red brick house my father paid $2,000.

My mother's family had been in Canada a little longer than the Stacys. One of her maternal great-grandfathers, Matthew Cowan, had arrived from Tipperary in 1827. He had been a lieutenant in the yeomanry there (which marks him down as a supporter of the establishment), and when the rebellion of 1837 broke out in Upper Canada he ran true to form. A diary of the crisis kept by one of his neighbours, a rather captious lawyer, reveals that my great-great-grandfather, who was a local magistrate, made himself rather objectionable, arresting people right and left. I don't know that I find his performance very attractive; but perhaps it's not a bad thing to be able to prove that one's family was against that rather unpleasant little man William Lyon Mackenzie, who led the rebellion, just as I am glad to have that commission of my other ancestor's which describes him as "William Stacy, Gentleman." It's nice to have documentary evidence that we had one in the family once.

What brought my mother and father together I never knew. Music may have had something to do with it, for they were both musical. He sang in Toronto's Mendelssohn Choir, and she both sang and played. She played the organ in the Anglican church in Cannington, and I remember her telling me, with amusement and also I think a little modest pride, of how she was once introduced at a local concert as "the nightingale of the North." I have a feeling that the introducer was the Catholic priest, who doubtless had a touch of the blarney with him.

What I think must be one of my very earliest memories concerns the appearance of Halley's Comet in 1910. I was then four years old. I remember being held up on the back porch of our College Street house so I could see the comet; my family were properly anxious that I should not miss this historic phenomenon. They asked me if I saw it, and I replied quite truly that I didn't. They kept on asking, and I kept on not seeing it. Finally, to put an end to the interrogation, I shamefully lied and said I saw it. But the fact is that I never did see Halley's Comet; and it isn't due again until 1986. Another very early memory is of the same year. I am quite sure it is of a memorial service for King Edward VII, who died in May 1910. I recall the scene in front of the Parliament Buildings, quite close to our house; it was raining, and there was a sea of black umbrellas, and in the midst of them a phalanx of red coats.

Red coats were always prominent in public ceremonies in those days, and they seem to have been important in my life from a very early time. The Garrison Church Parade, held on or near Victoria Day, was a great occasion for me and a considerable occasion for the community at large. I soon learned to distinguish between the Governor General's Body Guard in their silver helmets, the Royal Grenadiers in their scarlet and bearskins, the Queen's Own Rifles in their dusky green, and the 48th Highlanders in their tartan. (The technical corps, I am afraid, were beyond me.) Ah, that river of bright uniforms flowing down University Avenue to the sound of martial music in those years before 1914! A good few years later I marched in that parade myself two or three times, though not in a bright uniform. The Garrison Church Parade is still held annually in Toronto, but the glory is departed.

Just what sort of urge it was that pushed me towards the military life I find it hard to say. Long ago, General Otter, a sort of patron saint of the Canadian militia, wrote that a man's motive for joining up might be "patriotism, military ardour, a passion for display, or a desire for recreation." I find it hard to fit myself into the general's pattern. There was no real military tradition in my family, for neither the lieutenant of Irish yeomanry nor the ensign in the Durham Militia (a largely paper force) seems a very martial figure. Perhaps those gay uniforms marching down University Avenue appealed to a youngster who was later to have an interest in the drama. I would be sorry to think that I was merely a victim of a "passion for display"; but possibly that was it. At any rate, I seem to have been hooked, and have remained hooked ever since.

My family, not to put too fine a point upon it, was poor. Nowadays doctors are thought of as affluent, but in those days, long before medicare, things were different. There were what I heard referred to at home as "fashionable" doctors, and there were specialists, notably surgeons, who did well; but the rank and file of general practitioners worked hard for very small rewards. House calls of course were the universal rule; doctors were regularly called out of bed in the middle of the night, sometimes, it turned out, because of quite minor complaints; and much was done for poor patients on a basis of mere charity. The doctor's bill often got a very low priority when it came to payment; people were known to grumble that it was too much; and there were many bad debts on my father's books.

Life in our household was always dominated by the need for economy in everything, not excluding diet. We learned to appreciate modest dishes (I can still eat pork and beans with comparative relish). Things did not improve with the passage of time; if anything, they got worse. There was a time when my mother was able to keep a maid, but that time ended, I think, when I was quite young. Long afterwards, when I found myself reading the record of the struggle of Mackenzie King's family to "keep up appearances" in Toronto, I suddenly felt that I was on familiar ground, and I wondered how many "professional" households went through such experiences.

During his time in Acton, my father covered his rounds with a horse and buggy. But there was no accommodation for a horse at 161 College, and after moving there he rode a bicycle. August 4, 1914, was a notable date in our family for two reasons: the British Empire went to war with Germany, and the Staceys acquired their first motor car, a Model T Ford. To me, at the age of eight, I think the second event was the more important. After that I often went with my father on his rounds, waiting in the car while he visited his patients. The greatest medical emergency of the period was the epidemic of "Spanish influenza" in 1918. It put a great strain on the country's doctors, the more so as many of the younger ones were still on service overseas. Doctors' cars in those days were distinguished by a green cross sticker on the windshield. When my father stopped to attend one patient, people poured out of nearby houses begging him to come and see members of their families too, and of course he had to do so. There was no rest day or night. It was a time of tragedy. One of the other doctors in our block had a son, also a doctor, who had served through the war overseas without suffering a scratch. He arrived home during the epidemic and died the following week of influenza. I have always thought that the experience of those terrible days may have shortened my father's life.

In the days before my sister Dorothy and I started to school, and also in holiday times, my mother was very clever at organizing interesting (and cheap) little expeditions to amuse and incidentally to instruct us. One objective was the zoo, located in those days in Riverdale Park on the edge of the valley of the River Don, in what was then the east end of Toronto. People nowadays complain that the Don is dirty, and assume that this pollution is recent. I can assure them that in my boyhood the Don, which may have been a bright and shining stream when Ernest Thompson Seton roamed the valley, was at least as dirty as it is today. The zoo was not much of an institution compared to the one maintained today by Metropolitan Toronto, but it was rather wonderful to us. Another attraction in those parts was the Don Valley Brick Works, where we were charmed by the little cars running up the hill and coming down with their loads of clay. We picnicked on the grass at Reservoir Park, where the city waterworks intelligently provided an urban beauty spot. We went to High Park, which the pioneer architect John Howard had presented to the citizens of Toronto, and saw his house, Colborne Lodge, whose greatest attraction was the enormous wooden snake on the veranda. And we went to the Old Fort ("Historic Fort York" today), then unrestored and much run down, but the scene of a bloody episode of the War of 1812 and well calculated to provide a small boy with a lesson in history. In 1913, on the centenary of the

Battle of York, C.H.J. Snider of the Toronto *Evening Telegram* published *In the Wake of the Eighteen-Twelvers*, a very vivid piece of fictionalized history which tells the tale of that episode of the city's past. My aunt Anne Anderson Perry gave me the book, which probably did something towards making me in due course a student of Canadian history. But it didn't occur to me then that one day the Toronto Historical Board might label me Honorary Curator of Old Fort York.

The necessity for formal education, however, caused problems. The district behind our house had, as the contemporary phrase went, "gone down." McCaul Street had once been a "good residential district" (another contemporary phrase); but things had changed, and the residences had passed into the hands of "Jews and foreigners" (how often I heard those words!).* With the children of such people, young WASPs like my sister and me could not be allowed to mingle — I suspect they wouldn't have wanted us anyway. The local public school had been taken over by the immigrants, and was considered impossible for the young Staceys. For my sister, four years older than I, the problem was solved by sending her as a day girl to a private school for girls called Glen Mawr, which had been established by a respectable English lady. After my sister went to school, I was a rather lonely little tyke. I remember that when very young I cheered my solitude by inventing two imaginary playmates, little boys named, improbable as it may seem, Bommie and Geekie.

The family was rather slow in solving my school problem, and in fact I didn't go to school until I was nine years old. In the meantime I was "taught at home," with the unfortunate consequence that I made good progress in subjects I liked, and very little in those I disliked. I learned to read very early, and became an omnivorous reader; I shouldn't like to attempt a guess as to my age when I read *Ivanhoe*, but I was young. On the other hand, I was no good at arithmetic, and figures still tend to defeat me; I am one of the people to whom the invention of the pocket calculator has been a great boon. It was a misfortune for me that my school wasn't found sooner. It was the Normal Model School on Gerrard Street East (it is now defunct, and the Ryerson Polytechnical Institute occupies the site). Model

---

* McCaul Street has lately passed into still another phase. The street sign at the corner of College Street is now bilingual — English and Chinese. How, I wonder, does one translate "McCaul Street" into Chinese?

was an adjunct of the Normal School, which today would be called, American-fashion, a Teachers' College; my schoolmates and I served as guinea pigs for the student teachers to practise on, though luckily this was usually only for a small part of the day. We became connoisseurs of these novices' efforts, and the universal opinion among us was that the best teachers were the nuns. We sagely concluded that they had nothing to take their minds off their work.

There were both boys and girls at Model, but it was not co-educational: never the twain did meet. There were in fact two separate schools, united in the middle by a gymnasium which both sexes used, but at different times. The whole school body met together only on ceremonial occasions in a common assembly hall, and these were very rare. This seemed to us boys a perfectly satisfactory arrangement.

Because of my age and supposedly advanced state of learning, I went into the Second Form, missing kindergarten and First Form, and a good deal of academic and other knowledge that I would have picked up there. (I am not sure that I have ever fully caught up.) This must have been in the autumn of 1915, when the country was deep in the First World War. Model was a good school, and the teachers were competent and humane. One I particularly remember was Thornton Mustard, a lively and humorous man who taught the Fourth Form. I recall him taking us on a hike in the valley of the Humber, Toronto's western river, the counterpart of the Don in the east. We came to a spot where an old rusty road-roller stood apparently abandoned on the edge of the cliff above the river. Mustard, to my considerable astonishment, said, in an unschool-masterly way, "Let's push it over," and push it over we did, running away thereafter, led by Mustard, lest someone should pursue us and charge us with destruction of property. Thornton Mustard later became principal of the Normal School, and in 1939 I was saddened when I heard that he had lost his life in the sinking of the *Athenia*.

Raymond Massey in his memoirs tells how he attended the lowest forms of Model considerably before my day (the fact that a member of Toronto's Methodist nobility went there suggests that the school had a good name). In the Second Form, he was taught by M. A. Sorsoleil, whom he calls "a burly, ebullient mustachioed French Canadian." By my time the mustachios were a thing of the past and the Frenchness was not much in evidence; but Sorsoleil was still burly and ebullient and the "gifted teacher"

that Massey remembers. He was then headmaster and taught the Fifth
Form, the highest form in the school. Massey's contemporaries called him
"Sorcy"; mine invariably called him "Sorehead." The nickname was not
really deserved, but I suspect that Sorsoleil made something of an affecta-
tion of fierceness.

The war, of course, was always with us during my time at Model. I
remember the old gentleman who taught us singing in the lower forms
commenting out of a clear sky on the German philosophy. Did it, he asked
us, derive from Christ's teachings or Nietzsche's teachings? None of us had
ever heard of Friedrich Nietzsche, and we thought he said "Nature." Just
where Nature came in was not clear, but he obviously didn't want the
answer "Christ's teachings," and we were anxious to please; so we all with
one accord said "Nature's teachings." He then told us about that bad man
Nietzsche, who was clearly closely allied to Kaiser Bill, a well-known
abomination. Sorsoleil had a son flying overseas, and he sometimes read us
Jack's letters. Curiously enough, the only one I now remember relates
to the misdeeds of a squadron — not Jack's — whose members inflated the numbers of German aircraft they shot down. The headmaster
said with emphasis. "They *lied* for each other!" We were properly
shocked.

The war news reached us through the newspapers, for as yet of course
there was no radio. At special crises, one bought newspaper "extras" from
boys crying them through the streets, or went downtown and read the bulletins posted in the windows of newspaper offices. I have no recollection of
the news of Vimy Ridge or Passchendaele or Amiens; but I do remember
the impact of the Canadians' first battle, in April 1915, before I was going
to school. That was the Second Battle of Ypres, when the Germans first used
gas; the newspapers were full of names like St. Julien and Langemarck,
there was a communiqué about the Canadians saving the situation, and
suddenly there were long casualty lists. We got used to those. My parents
were glad they had no son of military age. There were recruiting campaigns; going home from school one day, I met a party of soldiers from a
mounted unit leading a riderless horse with a placard on it: "Who will fill
the empty saddle?" Conscription came, and during summer holidays with
relatives in the country I was scandalized by stories of farmers hiding their
sons in the bush to keep them out of the army. And then there was a rowdy
Armistice Day, and it was over.

I went on from the Model School to another similar establishment: the University of Toronto Schools, which was (were?) intended to do for student teachers at the secondary school level just what the Model did at the primary one. Why the plural, Schools? One theory is that there was an intention to set up a second school, for girls, alongside the boys' school which I attended; but this was never done. U.T.S. was, and I think still is, a school with high intellectual standards and a fine corps of teachers. As at the Model, we paid to attend — more than at the Model, but still not much. This situation has lately been drastically altered by authorities who feel that quality should be paid for.

I cannot remember a master at U.T.S. in my day who could be called either incompetent or disagreeable (with perhaps one exception, which I shall mention). There was Tommy Porter, a famous figure who spoke to all new boys and made some attempt at imparting a little sex education (in my whole educational career, this was a unique experience). There was W. J. Lougheed, who was very patient with my utter hopelessness in algebra, and "Johnny" Workman who was equally considerate in geometry. Norman Murch taught us German, and sang *Die Lorelei* to us. (I was grateful to him long afterwards, when confronted with a mass of German documents after the Second World War; it was useful to have at least enough knowledge of the language to relieve me from total reliance on the experts.) Curiously enough, I have no recollection of being taught history, except, I think, some Canadian history in the lowest form, and ancient history, imparted by another famous school personality, J. O. Carlisle ("Jock"), who cultivated an incisive style that kept the class on its toes, always expecting and rather hoping for another explosion at the expense of some laggard. Physics was taught by George Cline, who had commanded the Canadian Corps Signal Company in the war, was a major and later a lieutenant-colonel in the militia, and became a special friend and mentor, and something of a hero, of mine.

And then there was the head. H. J. Crawford was a "character" and known to the boys as the Bull. He marked himself off from the rank and file by wearing an academic gown, and was always out and about the school, limping on a game leg. The appreciation of him published in *The Twig* when he died said, "Perhaps his most outstanding trait was his vividness. Everything he did, he did with all his might."[2] Like Sorsoleil, I think he rather cultivated a formidable exterior, and small new arrivals were sometimes more than a little frightened when he suddenly addressed them, particularly as he was apt to lard his remarks with historical or literary allusions utterly strange to them. But he was essentially warm-hearted, and they soon realized it. He was a good classical scholar. He had been head since the school was established in 1910, he had made it and was proud of it; and it, I think, was rather proud of him.

School journalism took up a good deal of my time at U.T.S. At the Model there had been at one time an outbreak of wall newspapers, in which I was involved: large sheets of paper covered with supposedly witty articles and pictures, posted up in the classroom. Now at U.T.S. a self-appointed group had the idea of launching a printed school magazine. The authorities were not altogether warm to the project, but they did not forbid it. We persisted, and the *U.T.S. Monthly* duly appeared. My main contribution to its birth was prevailing on the neighbouring merchants to buy advertising space, my first venture into the world of business. Once the thing had actually appeared, it became more official, and the head suggested a change of name. The motto of the University of Toronto is *Velut Arbor Aevo* — "As a tree, by lapse of years" (I have always thought that it doesn't make much sense). Our school, an offshoot of the university, had as its motto *Velut Arbor Ita Ramus* — "As the tree, so the branch." The head, who had undoubtedly composed this motto, suggested that the magazine should be called *The Twig*; and so it was. The magazine still exists. Throughout my time at the school it remained at least approximately a monthly; now, however, it is a hardy annual.

There was considerable military activity at the school. The cadet corps was not wholly unpopular (I must admit it was quite popular with me), and it had quite a good band of its own. We used to have our annual inspection on the university's front campus, the stretch of greensward in front of University College which had once been called more elegantly the South Lawn. One year we turned up for it in the middle of the university spring examination period, which apparently no one had thought of. We formed our line, the inspecting officer arrived and the band cheerfully and noisily struck up the general salute. The front door of Simcoe Hall, the administration building, opened, and from it emerged, as if shot from a gun, Jimmy Brebner, the university registrar, gesticulating wildly and screaming like a demented banshee. No doubt he had visions of hundreds of students petitioning on the ground that their trains of thought had been interrupted in the middle of an examination by the noise of drums and trumpets. The sound of the band died away in a long disconsolate wail, and the inspection was completed without benefit of music.

The cadet corps had a "Signal Corps," which I joined. It was under the wing of Major Cline, and from it a good many boys passed out in due course into his militia unit. *The Twig* contains a photograph of the signallers of 1922. I am in the rear rank, along with my two best friends, George McClellan and Stephen Dale. On display are the tools of our trade: Lucas lamps, wartime field telephones, and numbers of little blue and white flags. The Signal Corps was also into wireless in quite a big way, but not me; I was no technologist. George McClellan and I both ended up wearing the badges of the Royal Canadian Corps of Signals in the Second World War, he as a genuine signaller and a lieutenant-colonel, I doing something quite different but maintaining a sentimental connection with the Corps.

We came back from vacation in the autumn of 1922 to the news that H. J. Crawford had died at the beginning of August. The tribute to him which appeared in the December *Twig* was unsigned, but my memory is that it was written by Jock Carlisle. Certainly no schoolboy could have done it. But it was I who suggested putting at the beginning of it the verse from Kipling, "... praise we famous men, From whose bays we borrow...."

The responsibility for appointing a new headmaster presumably rested with the provincial government, since U.T.S. was an adjunct of the Ontario College of Education. We, in our simplicity, assumed we would get some member of the existing school staff to carry on the work on the lines already well laid down. But this was not what happened. I have always suspected that some influential people were jealous of the school, disliked what they thought its pretensions, and were disposed to put its masters in their place.* At any rate, the person appointed was an outsider, J. G. Althouse, the principal of the Oshawa High School. Althouse was undoubtedly an able administrator (he ended up as Chief Director of Education for Ontario), but he seemed to me a little short of charm. No doubt

---

*That same attitude may underlie the recent decision to change the title "headmaster" to "principal." No doubt it also reflects the growing Americanization of Canadian education.

he expected to encounter hostility in his new appointment, and this led him to be more aggressive than he might otherwise have been. Not long after his arrival *The Twig*'s board of strategy had a discussion with him. What the point at issue was I don't now remember; what I do remember is the harsh way in which Althouse laid down the law, brusquely tolerating no dissent. I suppose all Althouse really lacked was grace, the quality his predecessor possessed in such abundant degree. The fact is that H. J. Crawford was, as they say, a hard act to follow. But I am afraid that the new regime made me a little less sorry to leave U.T.S. than I would otherwise have been.

In the fall of 1923 I entered University College at the University of Toronto. I had made at least one decision about my future: I was not going to follow my father into the medical profession. I felt no vocation for it. Tommy Porter had urged me to think of medicine: "The finest profession in the world; think of all the good you can do." When I told my father about this he replied a trifle grimly, "He didn't mention the harm a doctor can do if he isn't fitted for the job." I had briefly considered the Royal Military College and the profession of arms; but all my advisers, including George Cline, were unenthusiastic, and I have never regretted putting the idea aside. (I was always certain that I would be a soldier, even if not a professional one.) With good marks in most things, and a painfully characteristic "condition" in mathematics, I went into the Faculty of Arts, uncertain where my studies there might lead me.

Chapter 2

Undergraduate

For me, going to university merely involved crossing the street. The Staceys still lived at 161 College Street, and from my little hall bedroom at the front of the house I could look out at one of the University of Toronto's buildings — the Mining Building, still extant. I was just seventeen when I made my formal crossing and became a part of what all Torontonians in those days called simply "the University." If I was too old when I went to school, I was a bit too young when I went to college; but I survived. And I properly appreciated, I hope, the privilege of being a member of University College, whose lovely old stone building is one of the chief monuments of the growing Canadian culture (and prosperity) of the 1850s.

I enrolled myself in the honour course called English and History. The specialized honour courses were in those days considered the glory of Toronto's arts faculty, and the source of its reputation. More recently, reformers abolished them in favour of what is called a "less structured" curriculum, with unlimited freedom of choice for the student. The result, many people thought, was disaster, and at last report, a movement in the direction of the older system was observable. The honour courses in my day were less narrow in scope than might be supposed; although mine was called English and History, of the fourteen examination papers I wrote in

13

my freshman year, six were in Latin! I also did a good deal of French, although it must be said that the French Department of University College in those days was notably undistinguished. Its brightest spot was Baron St. Elme de Champ, a bearded and lively old *boulevardier* (so at least I think of him), with a definitely roving eye. He taught conversational French, and really did teach it. I bow to his memory, and as I bow I smile.

The English Department was better. I don't know why English should be taught by Scots, or people with Scottish names — Malcolm Wallace, J. S. Macdonald, R. S. Knox — but that was the way it was, and very competent they were. As time passed, however, my interest seemed to centre more and more in history, and the Department of History was well calculated to maintain it. In 1923 the "old chief," George M. Wrong, the modern founder of the study of Canadian history, was still head, and as a freshman I attended his lectures. I remember more about his mannerisms, and particularly his firm way of dealing with latecomers, than about his scholarship. Wrong lectured for the first term; for the second term we had Stewart Wallace, who in those distant and simple times doubled as lecturer in history and university librarian, and who certainly held our interest. I find it curious that the freshman course was the only university course in Canadian history I ever had, though in due time I was to make a career in that field.

The History Department of those days did not produce many books, but it excelled in teaching. One of the best lecturers was Hume Wrong, a son of the department head and an able if not an especially endearing man. His lectures were elegant performances, meticulously staged. But he gave an impression of snobbery that tended to repel students, and he seemed to have a rather uncertain temper. On one occasion an unfortunate young woman wandered into one of his lectures very late. Wrong suspended his discourse and with an angry and dramatic gesture, his voice rising to something like a scream, ordered her out; she fled, overwhelmed. Less edgy, and on the whole, I think, the best lecturer in the department, was G. M. Smith, who became a good friend of mine. George Smith had served through the war in Princess Patricia's Canadian Light Infantry and had rather enjoyed the military life; I remember him describing himself in a lecture, with a twinkle, as "a plain, blunt soldier." His lectures were carefully prepared, although on occasion he would apologize for giving "an old lecture" not having had time to prepare a fresh one.

These were the stars; not all our preceptors shone so brightly. Ralph Flenley was a delightful man, but of his lectures the less said the better. Of the juniors, the one I knew best was Bartlet Brebner, a son of the famous and disagreeable registrar who had disrupted the U.T.S. inspection parade. I had him as my teacher in tutorial groups in two successive years, and enjoyed the association. The department, however, was indisposed to encourage him. He went off south to do graduate work at Columbia and never came back, though he made great contributions to the writing of Canadian history. We were friends to the end of his life.

We had among us, though few would have suspected it, a future prime minister of Canada. Lester B. ("Mike") Pearson was an interesting lecturer (it was only as a lecturer that I knew him) and he had a cheerful sort of adolescent charm which stayed with him and certainly had something to do with the success of his career. But even second-year students, I think, realized that he was no massive scholar. He had other interests — notably coaching both the hockey and football teams — and it was sometimes evident that he had not done his homework with much care. On one occasion when he was supposed to be lecturing on the period of the English Civil War he arrived with no lecture notes, but a copy of John Drinkwater's then current play *Oliver Cromwell*. He read it to us, and we enjoyed it. It was not a scholarly performance; but over half a century later, this is one of the few of the hundreds of lectures I attended at the University of Toronto that I remember with any clarity.

About the time I graduated, the Department of External Affairs in Ottawa was undergoing its first great expansion; and both Hume Wrong and Mike Pearson went off to join it, Mike freighted with his abilities and his charm, Hume with his probably greater abilities and his certainly lesser charm. Both achieved eminence, Wrong as a brilliant official and adviser on foreign policy to politicians, Pearson finally reaching the highest political office in the state.

In those days extra-curricular activities were as important in the process of education as what went on in classrooms; and for me, it was natural to continue to be involved in journalism. The U. of T. student paper, *The Varsity*, possessed respectable antiquity, having been founded as a mainly literary journal in 1880. In 1923 it was just a daily newspaper, published five days a week. I had known about it through my sister, who was on its staff, and I thought this was for me. I lost little time in enrolling myself as a freshman cub reporter.

One of my first assignments brought me moderately close to scooping the world. In October 1923 the University of Toronto achieved its first and, so far, its only, Nobel Prize. It was in medicine, for the discovery of the insulin treatment of diabetes, and it was awarded jointly to Dr. (later Sir) Frederick Banting and Professor J.J.R. Macleod. Banting had been the leader in the active research; the Toronto *Globe* reported, "It is understood that the prize was awarded jointly, in view of the fact that Professor MacLeod [*sic*], as head of the Department of Physiology at the University of Toronto, directed the work in the laboratories where Dr. Banting conducted the investigations which led up to the discovery of insulin."[1] It was Macleod's laboratory, but Banting's idea. Recent research suggests that Banting in fact owed much to Macleod's experience, guidance and encouragement, but it's clear that Banting was disinclined to acknowledge this.

The Varsity gave me the job of interviewing the two new laureates. Naturally, I was thrilled. I went first to Macleod, who received me kindly; he was, I think, in a rather euphoric mood. I asked him (foolish question No. 999) whether he intended to retire on the proceeds of the prize, and he replied smilingly that he might have if they were a little bit larger. I passed on to interview Dr. Banting, and it was there that my seventeen-year-old simplicity received a rather severe shock. I did not see Banting (in fact, I never met him); he had retired into purdah, and was using his brilliant young research associate, Charles H. Best, as front man and public relations officer. Best, an agreeable young man, immediately revealed to me that Banting was extremely angry that Macleod had been included in the award. He was considering issuing a public statement expressing his feelings, and if he did so he would issue it through *The Varsity*. Best would let me know later. I went away, more thrilled than ever by the prospect of a story that would hit front pages around the planet, and also I think a little thoughtful. Men of science, it seemed, might not be quite the selfless dedicated creatures we laymen (and particularly seventeen-year-olds) had been taught to venerate.

When I went back to see Charlie Best again he told me that Dr. Banting had decided not to issue any statement. This of course was a sad disappointment to me, though it was certainly an act of wisdom on his part. I reported to *The Varsity* editors. Naturally, nobody thought of betraying

Best's confidence and printing the story anyway; we on *The Varsity* had high standards, aiming to maintain the practices of the best metropolitan newspapers. But I think the episode made some contribution to my education. It is interesting that the University of Toronto has contrived to forget Macleod almost entirely. He is in the British *Dictionary of National Biography*, and I hope he will be in the *Dictionary of Canadian Biography* when it reaches his time.

Being on *The Varsity* was serious business, and it certainly interfered to some extent with the formal aspects of education. (Among the editors-in-chief of my day, I was regarded as somewhat unusual, since I managed to graduate.) For every day's issue there were, as a rule, two "night editors," who had the job of making up the paper and seeing that it was ready for the press. Other members of the staff, particularly the senior ones, were often there too. In those days the paper was printed at the University of Toronto Press plant, on the campus. In the small hours of the morning we newspapermen would take a break and go over to Spadina Avenue for a hot beef sandwich at the Goblin restaurant; then we went back to the Press to put the paper to bed. Finally, a little before the east grew grey, I would go home (just across the street, remember) to catch a little sleep before going to a nine o'clock lecture. How I managed to do this — and I did it night after night for years — I now haven't the faintest idea. Youth, youth!

Our proclaimed aim was "that of being *a good newspaper*, a faithful and accurate chronicle of events."[2] In particular, we impressed on neophytes that the place for editorial comment was the editorials; opinion was sedulously excluded from the news columns. It was a shock to an elderly alumnus to come back to the University of Toronto at the end of the 1950s and find how *The Varsity* had changed. There was nothing except opinion — radical, leftist opinion — to be found anywhere in it. The youngsters of 1960 would have thought the undergraduate attitudes of my generation merely bovine. Our social consciences were not active. I fear that, lapped in the peace and prosperity of the mid-twenties, we had little awareness of wrongs to be righted, either our own or other people's.

The Varsity staff was a pleasant and comradely band of brothers (and sisters), the pleasanter because it recruited from all the faculties of a large and scattered university. A good many students were drawn to it because it seemed to offer a good apprenticeship to the profession of journalism, and in fact a fair number of my contemporaries went on into the newspaper world. Two of them have been elected to the Canadian News Hall of Fame (the only *Varsity* products, I think, to be so recognized): two close friends, as it happened, Phyllis Griffiths and Helen Allen. Both had long careers on the old Toronto *Telegram*. Phyl was primarily a sports reporter. Helen had the imagination and the heart to see how sensitive newspaper publicity could be made to serve a high humanitarian purpose: finding adoptive parents for children suffering from disadvantages that might have prevented them from ever getting homes.

I went through the ranks on *The Varsity*, as night editor, dramatic editor, news editor, and finally in my last year, editor-in-chief. I too thought of becoming a newspaperman, but finally abandoned the idea. But I think my experience on the paper taught me something about the business of writing — at least as much as I learned from my various excellent courses in English.

The Varsity office in my time was in Hart House, the magnificent Gothic students' union building — that seems the only generic term for it — which the Massey Foundation had presented to the university. (But since Hart House was then a purely male preserve, the women of *The Varsity* had a separate office in the basement of University College.) It was mainly my *Varsity* connection, I think, that brought me into frequent contact with John Burgon Bickersteth, the warden of Hart House. In the twenties the life of the university centred to a very great extent on Hart House, and the focus of life in Hart House was its dynamic and engaging warden. Bickersteth was very English, but he made himself totally acceptable to young Canadians of my generation. He had worked in western Canada before the war (his experience there is recorded in a book of letters called *The Land of Open Doors*), had served in the war with distinction, and had been recruited for Hart House by the Masseys in 1921.

The position Bickersteth made for himself was reflected in the party the members of Hart House gave for him on his thirty-eighth birthday in 1926. It was a surprise party ("the first event that has taken place in Hart House during his tenure of his position of which Mr. Bickersteth had no knowledge"). The warden was kept occupied in a meeting of one of the House committees while the company assembled in the Great Hall. When all was ready one of the conspirators burst into the committee to announce that a riot had broken out in the Great Hall over complaints about the food;

violence seemed about to erupt; would the warden please come at once and quell the disturbance? Bickersteth, pale-faced, hastened to the hall, to be faced not with an *émeute* but with one of the largest birthday cakes in history and 550 people, including the chancellor, the president, and great numbers of the faculty, graduates and students, all vociferously singing "For He's a Jolly Good Fellow." I don't know of any other demonstration quite like it in the history of the university.

Bickersteth's reputation spread beyond the University of Toronto. One of the people who heard about him was Mackenzie King, then playing with the idea of finding somebody to organize the work of the cabinet in Ottawa as Maurice Hankey had organized that of the cabinet in London. In 1927 King offered Bickersteth an appointment as his executive assistant. Bickersteth was tempted but cautious. He consulted Hankey and came to the conclusion that a job like his could not be done on the basis of an appointment to the prime minister's personal staff; he declined with thanks. King recorded that Bickersteth would have been willing to take the post of Clerk of the Privy Council, "but it cannot of course be arranged" (apart from all other aspects, there already was an incumbent Clerk of the Privy Council, who was certainly no Hankey). When Bickersteth finally told him that he had decided to stay at Hart House, King wrote in his diary, characteristically, "I think it a wise decision & feel relieved."[3] This brush with greatness left Bickersteth with a strong taste for contacts with the mighty, and as time passed he delighted in making himself a go-between for confidentialities between Ottawa and London. He kept in touch with King, whose feelings for him were a mixture of admiration and annoyance; he particularly disliked Bickersteth's habit of inviting himself to stay with King at Laurier House when he came to Ottawa. On one such occasion he wrote in his diary, "These damn Englishmen are infernally cheeky in this country. . . a feeling of superiority and patronizing ways."[4]

The end of the story is rather sad. Bickie went to England in 1940, and after the disaster in France that year he evidently felt obliged to stay on (though over military age) and do what he could. Perhaps his feelings were the keener because he had been, I am told, an eminent appeaser of the Nazis in prewar days. General McNaughton apparently found him sitting on a roadblock in Home Guard uniform, and invited him to come to Canadian Corps headquarters and run his education program for the troops.

From there Bickersteth went on to the British War Office and the important appointment of Director of Education. After the war he came back to Hart House; but things had changed. The postwar generation of students had never heard of him; some probably saw in him merely an elderly Englishman with a funny accent and out-of-date ideas. When he tried to enforce pre-1939 standards of dress and deportment he got into trouble. On a visit from Ottawa I met him on the campus and he told me something of his difficulties, saying tragically, "You know, Stacey, I was *hissed* in the Great Hall!" Perhaps he was remembering the birthday party; I know I was. Shortly he retired, with an honorary degree from the university, and spent the rest of his long life in his family home at Canterbury. When in 1974 he was appointed to the Order of Canada, it was to the lowest class. There had been a time when nobody would have dreamed of making him anything less than a Companion. He died in 1979.

I have said nothing of the drama; but the drama, in some of its humbler manifestations, was important in my life in those undergraduate days. University College had an organization called the Players' Guild. I find it difficult to convince modern students that we actually did a show every week. We operated in the rudimentary little theatre in the building of the University College Women's Union and there we held weekly afternoon meetings at which one-act plays, or fragments of longer plays, were presented by various teams of members, people taking turns as directors, cast and crew. After the presentation there was a discussion. Needless to say these shows were often crudely presented and greatly under-rehearsed, but we learned quite a bit about dramatic literature and had a lot of fun.

Once a term we did a more ambitious full-length evening show. I have the printed programs of two of these of 1926. In February, there was Sheridan's *The Critic*, in which, I find, I played Sneer. Doris Shiell, who later became my wife, spoke the Prologue, and Eleanor Barton (later Woodside) was an enchanting Tilburnia. Then in December we did James Elroy Flecker's *Don Juan*. The title role was done by Nat Benson, whom I remember more prominently as presiding over *The Varsity*'s funny column "Champus Cat," which under Nat was genuinely funny. I was Lord Framlingham, the Prime Minister, the Commander of the Don Juan legend, in addition to coming on among the "Strikers, Seamen, etc." Stephen Dale appeared, not unsuitably, as "Robert Evans, a Radical-

Socialist leader." At least twice we tried Gilbert and Sullivan: scenes from *The Pirates of Penzance*, with me trying to function as the Pirate King, and, in March 1927, nearly the whole of the first act of *The Sorcerer*, in which I enjoyed myself as John Wellington Wells, and Helen Allen, who among her other talents could sing, played the heroine, Aline. She, too, very much later, became my wife.

"Faculty advisers" were rather prominent in our lives in those days (the term is now, I think, unknown), and notably so in the Players' Guild. Ernest Dale, a professor of Classics, was our honorary president. He was enormously knowledgeable about the theatre, and his advice was invaluable. He was a fine actor himself, and I remember the gusts of horrible offstage laughter he contributed as the curtain closed on the last scene of Lord Dunsany's *The Laughter of the Gods*.

In my third year I picked up an academic honour for which I worked hard. The university possessed a prize called the All Souls Historical Essay Prize, which the calendar stated had been set up by two fellows of All Souls College, Oxford: Sir Keith Feiling, a prewar member of Toronto's History Department, and the Honourable Edward Wood, later Lord Irwin and Viceroy of India and later still Lord Halifax and Foreign Secretary. The topic prescribed in my year was "Carlyle as a Historian." I determined to go in for it. I think I was already beginning to have historical ambitions; besides, the prize was $150 — big money in 1926. No doubt it was largely Wood money, generously donated to encourage culture in the colonies (I pulls my forelock to your lordship).

The drawback was that I had to read the works of Carlyle, and this I proceeded to do. I was already acquainted with *The French Revolution*, and I think with *Letters and Speeches of Oliver Cromwell*; but there was something called *History of Friedrich II of Prussia, called Frederick the Great*. It was in an indefinite number of volumes (in the "Shilling Edition" of 1888, which I later bought as a souvenir of the prize, there are actually ten). I read them, and I am prepared to take legal action against anyone who questions this statement; but I have never advised anybody else to read them. Having done the reading, I wrote the essay. I doubt whether it was a very good essay, the more so as I finished typing it only just in time to meet the deadline for submission. I turned in the essay and never saw it afterwards; I hadn't kept a copy. It got the prize — I imagine I was the only competitor. And with the money I bought something expensive I needed for my equipment as a militia officer: a sword, infantry pattern, as prescribed for officers of the Corps of Signals. I carried it on various ceremonial military occasions for decades and I have it still. The other permanent memorial of the incident so far as I was concerned was a lasting antipathy for the writings of Thomas Carlyle.

That I used that historical prize to buy a sword perhaps symbolizes the union of two elements in the life I was going to lead: writing history, and soldiering. At any rate, the episode brings me back to my career as an amateur soldier. In my first year at the university I joined its contingent of the Canadian Officers' Training Corps. It was a flourishing organization, owing its prosperity largely to the fact that its members were excused the compulsory physical training to which undergraduates were normally liable. In my second year, however, I joined the militia proper, enlisting, along with George McClellan, in the local signal unit, which was then No. 2 Signal Company of the 2nd Battalion, Canadian Corps of Signals. George Cline, our friend from U.T.S., commanded first the company and afterwards the battalion. George McClellan and I became lance-corporals together, and before long rose to the dizzy height of commissioned rank as lieutenants. At one intermediate stage I was for a brief moment a staff-sergeant, acting, and, of course, unpaid (theoretically there was pay for parades, but we signed it over to the unit to enable it to continue to function); and I think I was prouder of my three stripes and crown than I ever was of the various insignia on my shoulder that I achieved in later years.

Militia soldiering, in our unit, involved chiefly Friday night parades, and the amount of practical training that could be done was limited. The government of the day didn't provide enough money to enable us to go to summer camp; and in my time the most the Toronto company contrived in the way of field training was a weekend under canvas at the city's jail farm, whose governor was a militia colonel himself and sympathetic.

Signal units were mounted troops: that is, we wore riding breeches and spurs, and rolled our puttees from the top down instead of from the bottom up. But of course we had no horses, just as no militia units had any motor vehicles, though in case of mobilization they would need great numbers of them. There was, however, some slight provision for training in riding, and a group of us took an evening course, using the regulars' troop horses, in the old Stanley Barracks riding school. There I acquired such skill in horsemanship as I ever came to possess, which was not much. The sergeant instructor was a pleasant young man and good at his job, quite different from the tough regular non-commissioned officers, many of whom made it their business to make life as unpleasant as possible for their pupils. There were regular officers who played that game too; I encountered one when trying an Officers' Training Corps "practical" examination in the old University Avenue Armouries. It was a bitterly cold winter day, and the building was like a refrigerator. In these conditions an intelligent man keeps his troops on the move. Our examiner was not intelligent; he kept us stationary all morning, steadily fixing and unfixing bayonets. I am sure a good many of the people on parade spent the next week in bed, nursing colds and a newly acquired dislike for regular soldiers and for the military life.

Is this, perhaps, the place to tell the story of my "document commission"? As I have already said, it hangs on my wall alongside my grandfather's, signed by Lord Willingdon in the name of King George V and dated 1 June 1927. Down the middle of it there is a crease; and thereby, it may be said, hangs the tale.

In 1958, when the moment for my retirement from the regular army was approaching, it occurred to me that I had been in the Sovereign's Canadian forces, boy and man, for quite a time; and I had never had a "parchment" to prove I was an officer. I telephoned my friend Bill Anderson, then a brigadier in the Adjutant-General's Branch at Ottawa, which in those days looked after such matters. Could he, I asked, please start the machine grinding to produce the requisite piece of paper? I thought it would be nice to have a commission dated 1958 to hang beside my grandfather's, dated 1858. Bill made inquiries. The first reaction was that I *must* have had a commission. The second was that they couldn't prove it. The third was that nothing could be done now because King George V was dead. I gave up, and retired in 1959 without any piece of paper.

Back at the University of Toronto, I resumed as an "associate officer" a connection with my old militia unit, now called the Toronto Signal Regiment. In 1967 the unit moved from the highly unsuitable building at 185 Spadina Avenue, where I had acquired my tincture of military knowledge, to Fort York Armoury. By way of preparation they embarked upon the operation known as "stripping the files," which was undertaken by a public-spirited former commanding officer. One day he telephoned me and said, "What do you think I have found in your personal file?" It was my commission. It had evidently arrived at the unit after I had left to go to Oxford, and had simply been neatly folded up the middle and put in the file, where it remained for precisely forty years. It was presented to me in the mess, after an evening when everybody had attended the Centennial Tattoo; and the then commanding officer, who was about half my age and the son of a man who had served with me, kindly told me that if I needed any advice on how to behave I should apply to the senior subaltern. The whole affair, I felt, was the sort of thing that gives one confidence in the military forces; it sometimes takes them a little while to get results, but in the end...

The military value of the prewar Canadian militia was limited. Government parsimony meant that we had little chance to learn the real business of soldiering. We in the junior ranks were an ignorant lot, though our seniors, of course, having been through the war, were far from ignorant, and a little of their knowledge probably rubbed off on us. But we were laying a foundation on which something important could be built in a crisis. That crisis came in 1939. Long afterwards I quoted in a book words used by "a distinguished Canadian professional soldier" (who was in fact my friend General Maurice Pope): "We had a citizen volunteer Army. It was that Army we mobilized and it was that Army and nothing else that fought our war."[5] Looking back in sentimental moments (perhaps when I have had a drink or two) I almost feel disposed to quote someone else — Edmund Burke: "the unbought grace of life, the cheap defence of nations, the nurse of manly sentiment and heroic enterprise." Certainly the nation in those days was defended cheaply; it was done in great part at private expense. It still is.

In our family we continued to be only too conscious of slender means. I wanted to make a contribution, and summer jobs were common form among the undergraduates of my time. The first such job I took was a small one: working at registration when the British Association for the Advancement of Science met in Toronto in 1924. My chief memory of this is registering Julian Huxley and automatically calling him "Professor." He gently explained that that imposing title was less common in England than in North America. (I imagine his actual appointment was something like "Junior Demonstrator.") The following summer I found myself in a quite different milieu. Inquiring at the university employment office, I was referred to a respectable local firm called the Belle Ewart Ice Company, which had an urgent problem. Toronto, early in June 1925, was in the midst of a heat wave, and everybody was shouting for ice. Within an hour or so I was answering a telephone and attempting to appease customers whose perishable foods were perishing.

When that immediate excitement was over I stayed on with the Belle Ewart, and in fact worked there for three summers. I should explain that the ice business was still largely unmechanized. The electric refrigerator was still virtually unknown; everybody had an ice-box, filled with ice from time to time by an employee of the Belle Ewart (or of a competitor which we considered inferior) who delivered it in a horse-drawn wagon. Technology had raised its ugly head to the extent that the ice thus brought to the public was chiefly produced by mechanical means in a plant behind our Gerrard Street offices. I discovered, however, that there were customers who insisted on "natural ice" — ice cut in winter from the frozen waters of Lake Simcoe, near the community of Belle Ewart where once the company had obtained its whole supply.

I rode the wagons. When my stint in the office was over, the company gave me a job as a checker. This involved accompanying each driver in turn, checking the addresses of the customers on his list and making certain that he was not selling ice on the sly to unofficial customers of his own. Since he was unlikely to do this on the very occasional days when I happened to be with him, the job seemed to me rather unproductive; but as long as the company paid me I didn't complain. What the job did for me in a larger sense was to give me a first-hand glimpse of the relations between capital and labour. I was, in my humble way, in touch with both; I was an agent of the bosses, and I was constantly in close and quite friendly contact with the workers. I was thus regularly exposed to the workers' opinion of the bosses. I am sorry to say that it was pretty uniformly unfavourable.

The end of my undergraduate career at the University of Toronto was marred by something that I thought, and still think, a piece of dirty business on the part of the university. In June 1927 I was ready to graduate, with first-class honours in my course. However, my pleasure at the prospect was marred by the sad fact that my father was dying. He had had a stroke some years before, and though he had gone on practising (I am sure he couldn't afford not to) it was on a restricted basis. Now there had been another stroke and it was obvious the end was close. Within a few days of Convocation there was a telephone call from the office of the bursar of the university. The staff of *The Varsity* had held its annual party some time before. The University Press had printed the programs. There was a bill for some six dollars which the committee in charge had so far neglected to pay. I knew nothing about it; but the bursar or his underling now calmly said that if it was not paid at once I would not be allowed to take my degree.

I greatly doubt whether the bursar had any right to make such a threat. As it was, I simply asked the committee to get busy and pay the bill, they did, and I got my degree on 10 June. My father died five days later. *The Varsity* had ceased publication for the year, but I drafted an adequately stinging editorial and passed it to my successor as editor-in-chief; and in the following October he published it. It pointed out incidentally that, while no one defended non-payment of bills, student organizations might be wise to give their printing jobs to commercial printers who were not in a position to use academic blackmail to collect their accounts.[6] I am sure that neither the bursar nor the Press liked this much, and I believe that Jim Robson, the new editor, had some trouble over it; but by then I was in England.

By this point I had reached a further decision about my future. I wanted an academic career, and one in history. The friendships I had formed among the University of Toronto's teaching staff influenced me in both matters. They were a pleasant society, I thought, the sort I would like to belong to, and while I should never grow rich pursuing such a career, riches was not what I was after. The combination of teaching and writing appealed to me. Undertaking this vocation involved further education. In terms of the Toronto historians of the day, one thought automatically of Oxford; they were almost all Oxford men. Getting to Oxford involved money. Automatically, again, one thought of a Rhodes Scholarship, an award which in those days carried great prestige. I duly applied for a Rhodes, went through the selection process, and didn't get it.

I got a solid consolation prize, a Parkin fellowship, provided by the generosity of an English lady, Mrs. Marian Buck, who lived near Ledbury in Herefordshire and had been an admirer of Sir George Parkin, the

Canadian imperialist (I am using that word in its innocuous Canadian sense, a man who believed in the British Empire and in maintaining the British connection) who was the first secretary of the Rhodes Trust. She was a pleasant, if rather formidable, old woman, whom I visited more than once in her fine house at Bosbury. Her money took me to Oxford for two years. The next problem, in Oxford terms, was to find a college. My History friends at Toronto tended to be Balliol men, but Balliol had no room for me. The kindly intervention of another friend, Oswald Smith, the classicist who was registrar of University College, got me into his old college, Corpus Christi, the smallest in the University of Oxford. I have always been rather grateful to Balliol.

In April 1927 my sister Dorothy had married Harcourt Brown, another University College man who was to have a distinguished academic career in French and the history of science. My mother sold the family house on College Street for $6,000 and went to stay with her mother, long a widow, in Victoria, British Columbia. My mother was left quite poorly off, and she now began perforce a new career of administering her own affairs; I doubt whether until my father died she had ever so much as written a cheque. It is a tribute to her natural ability and shrewdness that, after weathering the storm of the Depression, she died in 1964 leaving an estate about four times as large as the one my father left her. The College Street house went down and down, until it hurt me to see it when I visited Toronto; it was like meeting an old friend begging in the street. I was actually glad when it was demolished to make room for the headquarters of the Toronto Board of Education.

The autumn of 1927 found me setting off across the Atlantic on my first sea voyage. My travelling companion was E. K. Brown, who had graduated a year or two ahead of me and was returning to studies at the Sorbonne. Ed was to become a leading Canadian literary critic before his career was cut off by a tragically early death. We travelled by way of New York, where we caught the *Minnesota*, a one-class ship of the Atlantic Transport Line. Aged twenty-one, I had never been in New York (or indeed in the United States) before. Ed and I, walking the streets of the big city, obvious country cousins, were accosted by a man who asked us if he could do anything to help us. We were suspicious; was he about to try to sell us the Brooklyn Bridge? He went on to say that he was a member of an organization that made it its business to assist visitors to New York. We breathed more freely, and asked if he could direct us to a decent cheap restaurant. He did so, and we parted with mutual expressions of goodwill. I like to remember that tiny incident as my first introduction to the great republic. I know now that it was not uncharacteristic.

The ship did not sail until after midnight, so we were able to take in a theatre: Jane Cowl in *The Road to Rome*. Thus the first page of the diary I was starting in recognition of the dignity of study abroad contains a severe piece of dramatic criticism: "Not a terribly good play, and risqué beyond good taste."

Chapter 3

Oxford, and Some Other Places

Britain was in poor shape in 1927. She had emerged from the ordeal of the General Strike the year before, and outsiders admired the manner in which she had come through it without serious violence. But the economy was sick, unemployment was rife in the old staple industries; war debt payments to the United States were heavy and bitterly resented, for it was considered that the Americans had exacted Shylockian terms. Nevertheless the old imperial structure still stood up proudly. In the south as distinct from the industrial north there was some degree of prosperity, and a young Canadian like myself, prepared by heredity to be impressed, had no difficulty in finding much to impress him.

Certainly I was prepared to be impressed by Oxford. No university, not even Cambridge, has ever had such good notices. The sentimental poets have served her well.

> Know you her secret none can utter?
> Hers of the Book, the tripled Crown?

I knew about the Scholar-Gipsy, I was aware that Oxford was the home of lost causes and impossible loyalties, and I was acquainted with the snapdragon growing on the walls opposite Newman's freshman's rooms at

Trinity — that passage is sidelined in my copy of the *Apologia Pro Vita Sua*, bought in 1926. And when I actually arrived at Oxford in mid-October of 1927, I *was* impressed, at least up to a point. I set down in my diary that the beauty of the place had not been exaggerated. I was also duly impressed with the intellectual standard of the university as I met it, though I added that it seemed to me "at variance with the many mildewed regulations that hem the undergraduate in, as well as with the inadequate provision made for his creature comfort in the matter of plumbing and the like"! There spoke the good North American. I did not change my opinion of the mildewed regulations, and looking back it seems to me that by treating grown men as though they were children the university invited them to act like children, which they often did. Now, no doubt, there has been improvement.

I found myself living in the little front quadrangle at Corpus — staircase VII, "two pair up." This quadrangle is notable for the "Pelican," the famous sundial of 1581 which is reputed to tell, among other things, the date of Easter. My rooms, I once inaccurately convinced myself, had been those of Richard Hooker (scholar 1573), author of *Of the Laws of Ecclesiastical Polity*, a rather typical Corpus worthy. (The college's only notable man of action seems to have been General James Oglethorpe, founder and defender of Georgia.) Everyone had "rooms" at Oxford; the idea of sleeping and studying in the same chamber, as practised in North American universities, was socially unacceptable. My little rooms were on the grim side, but being short of cash I didn't propose to spend much on cheering them up. One decoration I did acquire, which doubtless amused my contemporaries then and rather amuses me now, was a Canadian Red Ensign. In my second year, the college being able to accommodate me no longer, I moved into modest "digs" on Newton Road, beyond Folly Bridge.

Corpus was a very pleasant little college. Its president in my day was P. S. Allen; he and his wife Helen were great authorities on Erasmus. They invited me to lunch immediately after my arrival — a special kindness to a new student from overseas, I now suspect — in the President's Lodgings, a modern house, and one of the loveliest I have ever been in. The history tutor at Corpus when I matriculated was R. B. Mowat, of whom I have very amiable memories. I have always felt that he was a better scholar than readers of his books would believe. It was a college joke that since the Mowats produced a child a year, it was important for Raby to produce a book a year to meet the bills. His book on Anglo-American relations, as I realized when I got seriously into that field myself, is really not very good. But he gave me a very useful working-over on English history.

I should explain that I was not doing graduate work in the modern sense; I was doing what Oxford termed "Schools"* — the ordinary undergraduate course, which would give me a second B.A. degree in two years out of deference to my Canadian degree. This was the usual thing for Canadian and American graduates at Oxford in those days. I visited my tutor once a week and read him an essay, and I must say I found producing that weekly essay a considerable effort, but it did me good. The curriculum of the Oxford Honour School of Modern History was antique but thorough. Generations of undergraduates had been brought up on Bishop William Stubbs' *Select Charters and Other Illustrations of English Constitutional History*, but I am sure I was the better for having my nose rubbed in the ninth edition of it. English political history at Oxford came to a full stop in 1885, no doubt because attempting to deal with more modern periods might have led to violent confrontations. (I was later to discover that American universities brought history down to the day before yesterday, if not the day after tomorrow.) In addition to the history of England, candidates were required to offer a period of general (that is, non-English) history, political science and economic history, and a special subject, chosen from a list of fourteen. Many Canadians chose British colonial policy, 1830-1858, but I took on military history and strategy, which suggests that I was already in danger of type-casting myself as a military historian.

This special subject involved a detailed study of the Peninsular War, on which C. T. Atkinson lectured, while the theory of war was the field of the Chichele Professor of Military History, Major-General Sir Ernest Swinton. Atkinson was famous for refusing to allow women students to attend his lectures; the idea perhaps was to allow him to make uninhibited use of what I once heard him refer to as "the picturesque language of the British soldier," though in fact his language was not very different from any other lecturer's. I think he liked to affect the rough military man, though his soldierly career had involved nothing very bloody. General Swinton, a distinguished retired Sapper officer whose contribution to developing the tank had been officially recognized, was not a historian in the usual sense but

* Officially, the Second Public Examination.

had a great fund of military knowledge. His lectures, I am sorry to say, were preternaturally dull; he would start the term with a following of twenty or thirty hearers, who would shortly dwindle to a hard core of three or four. I was part of the core, which had the advantage that one got to know the general. Oxford lecturers, like others, varied from the comparatively brilliant to the quite impossible. Mowat sent me to listen to one who lives in my memory chiefly for one remark. The Roman civilization in Britain, he said, was an exotic civilization; it struck no roots whatever in the soil of the island. "And if you ask me for evidence, I direct your attention to the fact that the Romans had central heating in their villas. They were the only people who ever lived in this country who felt the need for central heating." Suffering through the cold misery of an Oxford winter term, rendered the worse by the fact that we literally did not see the sun for eight long weeks, I reflected that so far as I was concerned the Romans were the only sensible people who had ever tried to live in the wretched country. It is only fair to add that in the summer term, given a little luck in the weather, Oxford can be something close to heavenly.

At the end of my first year at Oxford, Mowat left to take a university chair at Bristol. His successor at Corpus was a nice but inexperienced young Cornishman, Charles Henderson. He was more up-to-date than Mowat; I remember his difficulty in concealing his astonishment when I told him that Mowat had advised me to read Henry Hallam's *Constitutional History* (1827). I feel grateful to Henderson for sending me to be tutored in political science by the eminent R.B. McCallum of Pembroke College. I recall his asking me whether I was a reader of Emerson; I had to say no. MacCallum then surprised me by saying that my English style reminded him of Emerson. Since this was the first time anyone had ever suggested that I *had* an English style, I was pleased. Henderson might, I think, have had a distinguished career, but unfortunately he died young. R. B. Mowat, too, was cut off before his natural span; like my other teacher, Thornton Mustard, he was a civilian war casualty, killed in 1941 in the crash of a Ferry Command aircraft that was bringing him back from lecturing in American universities.[1]

Corpus was a tremendously "sporting" college. Small as it was, it exerted itself tremendously on the playing field. I do not absolutely guarantee the following statistics; but I seem to remember one summer afternoon when this college of some seventy-five undergraduates put two rowing eights on the river, two tennis sixes on the courts, and *three* cricket elevens on the pitch — plus, of course, a few coaches, etc. I was a very unsporting type myself, and what I didn't know about cricket in particular would have filled many large volumes, but I was in the third of those elevens. A Corpus "third eleven" really had to be seen to be believed; it consisted simply of the people around the college who were doing nothing else that afternoon; but we enjoyed ourselves, and I think people admired us for trying. This day we played Worcester College. Worcester was one of the few colleges that actually had a cricket field on the college grounds, and it took its cricket seriously. About all I knew about cricket was that the general idea was to use the bat to prevent the ball from knocking the bails off the top of the wicket. On this occasion I think I stood up to three balls. The first was to the off, and I let it go by. The second one hit me, I forget just where. The third took my wicket, and I retired. The sport I actually went in for most was fencing. I devoted quite a bit of time and (Oxford being what it was) money to it. I enjoyed it, but never got very good at it.

In the spring of 1929 Corpus scored four bumps in the inter-college boat races called Torpids (since the Thames or Isis at Oxford is so narrow, one achieves victory not by passing opposing boats, but by catching and bumping them). The win was celebrated by a Bump Supper, the first the college had had for years. It was a large occasion, and, for those interested in figures, eighty-six panes of glass were broken in the front quadrangle (a small quadrangle, too).* If the reader thinks this was childish, I agree. Late in the evening, however, there was an episode which led me to take a certain pride in the college's performance. The president and Mrs. Allen had invited the college to come for hot soup at eleven o'clock. The idea, I think, was that this prospective engagement might exercise a restraining influence in the matter of drink; if so, I fear it was a little simple-minded. But the Corpuscles came, in various stages of intoxication; and it was a remarkable experience to see them standing about in Helen Allen's dining-room presenting a determined appearance of sobriety. Only occasionally did some small incident betray the true situation. Notably, the college aesthete unfortunately felt moved to assist Mrs. Allen in dispensing the soup. He rushed up to her saying, "Boldness, Mrs. Allen, boldness is what we

---

* "Like many of the Upper Class / He liked the Sound of Broken Glass" (Hilaire Belloc, *About John Who Lost a Fortune by Throwing Stones*).

need," relived her of the ladle, and promptly decanted its contents on the carpet.

I think that bump supper was the first occasion when I ever tasted champagne; and the memory of it moves me to digress about my personal experience with alcohol. Our household in Toronto was dry; strange as it seems to me now, my family, not excluding myself, were believers in prohibition, and, of course, I grew up under a prohibition regime in Ontario. My father was, I think, as close to being a complete teetotaller as possible without actually being one. There was always a bottle of whisky somewhere in the house, but it was there for medicinal purposes and I suspect one bottle lasted for years. If my father had a patient faint on his hands, he certainly gave him a tot to revive him, a procedure which I am sure the medical profession has long abandoned. I don't think I ever took a drink until I got to Oxford. There the social atmosphere was quite different, and without any consciousness of sin I began to be a mild social drinker. At that bump supper I recall being aware of being very cold sober while pandemonium raged around me; and I also recall deciding that if I was going to enjoy myself at all I had better loosen up a bit. I solemnly recorded in my diary that I "came nearer to being tight than ever before, but never got quite out of control."

My military interests at Oxford were not exclusively academic. The university of course had a contingent of the Officers' Training Corps, complete with a signal section, and I got myself attached to it. The OTC's commanding officer was a regular, a guardsman, Lieutenant-Colonel M. B. Beckwith-Smith, who was very good to me.

In the summer of 1928 I went to camp for a fortnight with the OTC signallers, attached to the 3rd Divisional Signals of the regular army on Salisbury Plain, and in September went with them on the Southern Command manœuvres. We fought a war across southern England that had some overtones of the real war that was coming a little over a decade later. The British army had formed an Experimental Armoured Force which was being tried out in this "campaign." It was the main element of a "Westland" army coming up from the west country, to encounter a less mobile "Eastland" force consisting of the 3rd Division, which was covering Salisbury, where Eastland's army was supposed to be mobilizing. Westland also had a brigade of horsed cavalry. Once things got going we had a fairly exhausting experience. We made a night march forward from a bivouac under the beeches in Savernake Forest (near Marlborough) to the line of the Avon. After some contact with the "enemy" we found our flanks in danger and hastily made another night march in the reverse direction, taking up a strong position on the downs around Tidworth and daring the mail-clad foe to attack us. At that point the war was called off without a clash between the main forces. In the words of B. H. Liddell Hart, then military correspondent of the *Telegraph,* "the possibilities of the situation were far from exhausted. But the cavalry were."

Three personal impressions remain with me. One is the discovery that it is possible to walk while asleep — but only if the ground is completely level. The second is the further discovery that a drink of whisky is a very pleasant thing at the end of a long night march. The third is the disagreeable memory of riding a borrowed and skittish horse in the dark down a narrow road which grinding and groaning tanks are also travelling on in the opposite direction (Eastland too had a few tanks). But those few days of experience with real units of real troops, at full strength and with full equipment, operating under conditions at least approximating to those of active service, certainly taught me more about the business of soldiering than I would have learned in years of Friday-night "training."

One small thing struck me. Oxford had learned to talk about "the Dominions": but the army still spoke, simply and without derogatory intent, of "the Colonies" and "colonials." I was mildly astonished at finding myself called a colonial; but the word was so obviously used without any remotest idea of being rude or condescending that it would have been rather absurd to resent it, and I kept my amusement to myself. I don't believe I ever heard the word used about a Canadian during the war that began a decade or so later. Nevertheless, the fact that it was being used in 1928 suggests that the British army's political science was a little in arrears; and this may help to explain some of the difficulties Canadian commanders encountered in 1939-45.

During Oxford vacations, there tended to be a considerable migration of the Canadian community there in the direction of Paris. France was cheap in those days, and in Paris there was a ready-made base of operations for us: the then new Canadian House in the Cité Universitaire on the south edge of the city.

The situation in the Maison Canadienne was interesting and very disturbing. The majority of the residents were French Canadians, and the

French-Canadian intellectual in Paris has usually tended to be a violent *nationaliste*. There was also a minority of English-speaking Canadians, one of the chief of whom was my friend E. K. Brown, and these people reacted against the French-Canadian nationalism with very active hostility. It was Canadian dualism at its worst.

I remember arriving at the Maison Canadienne one July and being surprised to see a ragged pattern of Union Jacks hanging out of the scattered windows. The *concierge*, a Frenchman quite ignorant of Canada, explained politely that it was the *fête nationale du Canada*. It was actually the Twelfth of July — "Orange Day." The fact that Ed Brown and some of his friends were Roman Catholics had not affected the issue at all. I recall also that the English group had a sort of Bible — a dog-eared copy of Robert Sellar's *The Tragedy of Quebec: The Expulsion of its Protestant Farmers*.[2] This book's bitter denunciation of French-Canadian nationalism and clericalism fitted their mood, and perhaps they found in it material for baiting their French-Canadian housemates.

Looking back, I realize with something of a shock that I myself had little contact and no discussion with the French Canadians in the house; the Oxford contingent mingled only with the English-speaking group. The two-solitudes syndrome was only too clearly exemplified in that community. I cannot report at first hand just what the views of these young Quebeckers were. I feel sure, however, that the influence of the Abbé Lionel Groulx and his ideal of a Laurentian republic was strong among them. In an article published in 1929, E. K. Brown wrote of the cult of Groulx among French-Canadian students as "an ominous sign of the times." His feelings were quite different towards Henri Bourassa, for whose anti-colonial Canadianism he had much respect.[3]

In December 1928 I found the Anglo-Canadian colony in Paris in a state of angry disgust with Rodolphe Lemieux, speaker of the Canadian House of Commons and long a Liberal minister, who had been lecturing at the Sorbonne on, supposedly, "the political evolution of Canada." I heard the last of these lectures and also heard him on two other occasions, and this time at least I fully shared the views of the English-speaking group of militants. A Frenchman otherwise unacquainted with the facts would have gathered from Lemieux that Canada was to all intents and purposes a purely French country, and his general tone was thoroughly anti-British. I heard him sneer at the phrase "England, Mother of Parliaments"; the parliamentary idea, he said, was introduced into England by the Normans. He made a boastful reference to the signing of the Halibut Treaty of 1923 with the United States, and his highly dramatized account of the exclusion of the British Ambassador in Washington from the affair was loudly cheered by his French audience. It is a sobering thought that the Speaker of the Canadian Commons was more interested in Parisian applause than in giving his audience some understanding of the nature of the British Commonwealth or of the Canadian Confederation. The fact is that Rodolphe Lemieux was a pompous ass, and he would still have been a pompous ass if the Lord had made him English instead of French.

There was a slightly comic aftermath. Ed Brown was reading a paper to the students of the Maison Canadienne. I forget what the subject was, but he seized the opportunity to insert an antidote to Lemieux's interpretation of history. I provided him with some ammunition from the works of the learned Stubbs, which, of course, I had with me:

> It is seldom remembered in comparing Norman and Anglo-Saxon in point of civilisation, how very little the Norman brought in comparison with what he destroyed, and how very little he brought that was his own. His law was Frank or Lombard, his general cultivation that of Lanfranc and Anselm, far more Italian than native: in civilisation — taken in the truer sense of the word, — in the organisation of the social life, in the means of obtaining speedy and equal justice, in the whole domain of national jurisprudence, he was far behind those whom he despised with the insolence of a barbarian: he had forgotten his own language, he had no literature, his art was foreign and purchased....[4]

The succeeding passage, on the military and political virtues of the Norman, was of course disregarded. The whole thing, I fear, was an exercise in the reprehensible art of perverting history to serve particular purposes. But at least Stubbs' history was better than Lemieux's.

Before those days in Paris I had had very little contact with French Canadians or with the "French-Canadian question." Being suddenly confronted with the problem in such an extreme form shook me. Stephen Dale has recently reminded me that at the time I wrote him a letter expressing apprehension for the future of Canada, and that he took the view that I was unduly alarmed. It seems now that what I was witnessing was the preliminary tremors of an earthquake.

All the political bickering aside, the Maison Canadienne was a pleasant place to read for the Oxford Schools, and there were the Louvre and the Opéra and all the sights of Paris available. One day Jack Pickersgill and I visited the Donjon at Vincennes. Doris Shiell was studying in Paris, and she and I went to see the Yiddish play *Le Dibbouk*, which I found creepy. And from Paris one could undertake inexpensive sightseeing journeys to comparatively nearby places like Chartres or to more distant regions.

My last term at Oxford was very full: "I did a little cricket and tennis, and quite a bit of riding on Port Meadow, as well as a considerable quantity of reading, which continued right up to Schools." Those rides on hired horses on Port Meadow are a particularly pleasant memory. In due time I put on my silly white tie and "sub fusc" suit, to say nothing of my short commoner's gown, and presented myself at the Examination Schools. My verdict afterwards was that I hoped I had "a safe second." This turned out to be an accurate prognostication. It would have been nice to get a first, but I consoled myself with the thought that most Canadians doing history, including people like Donald Creighton who were considered quite bright, seemed to get seconds.

Just what did Oxford mean to me, and do to me? After nearly half a century, it's an interesting question to ask, but not so easy to answer. Intellectually, I am sure it did me good. I came away from it with a better-trained, sharper mind, and a better-stored mind, than I had had in 1927. In other respects I am not so certain. I don't believe I was ever fully at home there. I suspect I came to it with romantic notions that had little foundation in fact. I expected a warm family welcome and got what I now recognize as a normal cool English reception. I liked the place, and enjoyed my time there; but I don't think I ever felt I was a real insider. I made few close friends there. I have never been a professional Oxonian. I think I gave myself away when at the end of my first Oxford year I wrote in that diary of mine, with deplorable pomposity, "one never feels to Oxford *quite* as to 'one's own university'."

A quite different point occurs to me. I have been reading Charles Ritchie's diary of his Oxford days; he was there a couple of years before me. He writes, "A sort of mist of homosexuality does hang over Oxford like the mist of the Thames Valley and it would be hard to imagine the place without it." I can only say that that was not Oxford as I knew it. Today, of course, even in North America, we are persistently informed that homosexuality is a normal way of life. Things were different then. We talked about "pansies" and "fairies" but were not obsessed with them — not even in England. That, at least, is my recollection. But perhaps the fault lay with me. Perhaps I was in the wrong college. Or perhaps I was just simple-minded.

In the autumn of 1929 I sailed home to Canada — and on to Princeton. How did it happen that I was on my way to an American university? During 1928 I had begun to think inquiringly about jobs. I thought first of the University of Toronto History Department. In October, in a letter to G. M. Smith, who was now acting chairman of the department, I raised the question. His reply was to the effect that there was nothing available for next year, though he was "not unencouraging" about the future. "So now," I recorded in my diary at the end of the year, "I am searching for a lectureship or a fellowship somewhere." My future prospects were not improved by developments at Toronto. The university was not willing to confirm Smith as chairman, I think because he had written no books. Instead it imported from Manitoba Chester Martin, who had some scholarly writing to his credit. It had already brought in Frank Underhill from Saskatchewan, an appointment which the university administration certainly came to regret, for he proved a thorn in its side. He was a brilliant teacher, but really more polemicist than historian. He loved to shock the bourgeoisie, and his isolationist declarations during the years to come galled the Toronto establishment. I didn't know either Martin or Underhill; and Smith was so displeased by the university's treatment of him that he walked out and took a job as consultant in an investment house. This in 1929, with the stock market crash imminent! Shortly Smith was back in academic life, as chairman of history at the University of Alberta; that institution I think was very lucky to get him. Books or no books, I think the University of Toronto would have been wise to keep that splendid teacher.

I had formed in my own mind a plan, or at least a general idea, of operations. I had been consulting Ed Brown, who was more knowledgeable than I about the North American educational scene generally, and it occurred to me that if, in addition to my Toronto and Oxford experience, I acquired a Doctor of Philosophy degree in history from a good American graduate school my qualifications would be so impressive that job offers could not fail to flow in upon me. So I began writing off to institutions in the United States applying for fellowships. Princeton was kind enough to give me a small fellowship; and that changed my life. But when I arrived on October 1, 1929, I had no idea that I was going to stay there nearly a dozen years.

Chapter 4

A New Country

M y move to the American academic world was prompted, I think, by desire for new experience as well as by the idea that I was broadening my qualifications and thereby my status in the job market. But I went to Princeton with much ignorance, a good many mental reservations and no certainty. A good many Canadians of my generation regarded the United States with a somewhat dubious eye. We had been nurtured on memories of the War of 1812 and the Fenian Raids, and American neutrality in 1914-17 had left a mark that had not been wholly expunged by American intervention in 1917-18; the more so as it was popularly believed in Canada that Americans considered, and frequently said, that they had won the war, in spite of the fact that they had done comparatively little of the actual fighting. But when I went to England in 1927 I encountered anti-Americanism more virulent than any I had known in Canada. The same motives that operated in Canada were present in Britain, and in addition there was the very bitter question of the war debts and a sense that the newly rich Yankees were taking over the position in the world that properly belonged to the British.

I have a vivid recollection of one of my earliest weekends at Princeton. There was a "crew race" (it seemed to me then a curious phrase) on Lake Carnegie, the artificial body of water that the late wealthy Andrew had given to the university; and with some new acquaintances I walked down Alexander Street to watch. The scene is still clear before me, a tremendous display of "conspicuous consumption" such as I had never seen before. The road was congested with enormous and expensive cars, the canal with vast and opulent cruisers; and what struck me most was the fact that the sky was full of private aircraft. Over all was the chant of the newsboys: "Wall Street closing prices!" I never again saw such a scene at Princeton. A week or two later came Black Friday, and the Depression was on its way. What, I wonder, became of those aircraft? No doubt they were sold for junk. The slump that set in that fall would affect the lives of all of us for a decade to come.

I had been allotted a room in the Graduate College, a splendid Gothic pile standing on a hillock on the far edge of the town, beyond the golf course. I was to live there for years, always a little amused at the sham-Oxbridge atmosphere of the place, but happy and comfortable, and grateful. In the front quadrangle was a seated statue of the first dean of the Princeton Graduate School, Andrew Fleming West; the man himself, now retired, still lived in a modest house nearby, close to the handsome mansion he had provided for the incumbent dean, who was now Augustus Trowbridge. Gradually I learned the story of Dean West, and President Wilson, and the Graduate College.

Ignorant as I was of Princeton, as of so many things American, I doubt if I knew when I arrived there that Woodrow Wilson had been president of Princeton before he was president of the United States. He held the office for just eight years (1902-1910), and was almost certainly the university's greatest modern president, credited with transforming Princeton from "the best country club in America" into an institution of genuine intellectual distinction. He did this chiefly by introducing the "preceptorial system," which was simply the tutorial system familiar to me at Oxford, and before that at Toronto: teaching in small "preceptorial" groups to supplement lectures. To make this possible he enlarged the teaching staff by hiring some fifty distinguished scholar-teachers from across the country. and beyond it; the original "preceptors," of whom the contemporary students sang,

Here's to those preceptor guys,
Fifty stiffs to make us wise.

This was fine; but Wilson's ideas for other reforms got him into trouble. He attempted to lay hands on the undergraduate upper-class eating clubs, to one of which a student who was wealthy enough and popular enough might be elected at the end of his second year. The president's scheme was to substitute for these a "quadrangle plan" that would have produced something like the Oxford and Cambridge colleges. Many of the Princeton alumni disliked this intensely, and they rose in their might. Wilson was defeated; but the affair had attracted national attention, and Americans across the country had become aware of Woodrow Wilson as a supporter of democracy and an opponent of privilege.

Wilson lost another battle: the battle of the Graduate College. Dean West was determined that this structure ("the first building in this country to be devoted to graduate-student residence, until then neglected"), should be built in isolation on the site it now occupies; Wilson wanted it built on the main campus, with graduate and undergraduate students mingling together. Here again he was credited with being a practising democrat as well as an opponent of ivory towers. I cannot take this matter very seriously. Wherever the Graduate College was put, there was not going to be much liaison between graduates and undergraduates, for they were two different breeds of cat. Apart from all other considerations, the Princeton undergraduate in general was wealthy and the Princeton graduate student was poor. West got his way, for he controlled the money. Shortly Wilson received offers to go into politics; he resigned from Princeton in the autumn of 1910, and was immediately elected Governor of New Jersey. He went straight on to be president of the United States, and it is often said that the fights he lost at Princeton provided much of the foundation for his political career.

At Princeton, however, West remained master of the field. When I arrived in 1929 he sat in bronze, grimly facing the gate of his college, as if expecting his old antagonist to appear. It has been said that the memory of the Wilson-West contention "divided Princeton families forty years afterward."[1] That I cannot vouch for, but it was noteworthy in my time there that official Princeton, at least, hardly ever mentioned Wilson's name. As long as the flesh-and-blood West continued to inhabit the little house behind the Graduate College — and he lived till 1943 — the university treated the memory of the most famous, if not the greatest, man ever associated with Princeton almost as if he had never existed.

Princeton was an ideal place for a university: a small country town (it's considerably bigger now) roughly halfway between New York and Philadelphia. New York in particular, of course, was a magnet, and it was only an hour away by the Pennsylvania Railroad's fast trains. As a graduate student I didn't patronize the New York theatre much (I was too poor) but I did patronize the libraries, particularly Columbia University's and the New York Public Library. Also, my brother-in-law was teaching at Brooklyn College, and he and my sister could find a corner for me in their small but hospitable flat on 105th Street.

The community life at the Graduate College was agreeable. On the whole, perhaps, I fitted in a little better than I had at Oxford. This was just as well, as I lived in the college, as graduate student and instructor, for the greater part of a decade. It is a curious fact, however, that the people I saw most of tended to be the British and Canadian members of the group. Procter Fellowships (as in Procter and Gamble — soap money had done a lot for Dean West's college) and Commonwealth Fellowships brought a good many young Britons to Princeton. As a general rule, they were very able, and they made a large contribution to the place. Some I knew well, some not so well. Just recently, I came across a reference, in one of the books dealing with secret aspects of the Second World War, to Alan Turing as one of the great contributors to the now famous British code-breaking establishment at Bletchley; and I remembered knowing him, though certainly not intimately, at Princeton. Turing was a brilliant Cambridge mathematician who died young. One Englishman I did know very well was Robert Spence, a somewhat rough-hewn but very genuine and charming chemist from South Shields. Bob Spence was one of the many friends with whom, unfortunately, I lost touch; but he rose to be Director of the British Atomic Energy Research Establishment at Harwell and an F.R.S. One of the Canadians at Princeton then was Hugh Mac-Lennan, now a novelist of note. At this time, however, Hugh did not call himself a Canadian; he was a Nova Scotian, and his favourite villain was Sir John A. Macdonald, who, he said, had conned Nova Scotia into confederating with Canada.

The Princeton History Department as I knew it was not the "thrusting and innovative" body that I read about today. It had a good deal in common with the department I had studied in at Toronto. Notably, both were made up of very agreeable people, both were admirable teaching departments, and neither had a very distinguished record of publication. I suppose our historian of widest reputation at Princeton was Dana C. Munro, medievalist and expert on the Crusades. He was a charming old gentleman, but in the nature of things I didn't have a great deal to do with him. The occasion when I had closest contact with him was when he gave me my oral examination in French and German. It consisted of putting under my nose two rather abstruse passages of history in those languages and asking me to translate them. My French was moderately good, and I romped through the French paragraph with no great trouble. The German was harder (I had had no German since U.T.S.); the paragraph was complicated, and full of damnable abbreviations I had never seen before. But Professor Munro generously passed me. I have always felt that my French impressed him enough to carry me through the German.

The chairman of the department in 1929 was Thomas Jefferson Wertenbaker. I remember that his surname made me wonder if I was going to meet some rotund pipe-smoking German. Nothing of the sort; he was a spare, courtly Southern gentleman, a product of the University of Virginia, whose family had lived in that state for many generations. The department never called him anything but "the Colonel." In our long acquaintance, beginning with the day in 1929 when I first called on him in his office in Nassau Hall, I had nothing from him but kindness. His field was colonial American history, in which he had a considerable name.

The department had two Halls — Clifton Rumery Hall, known as "Beppo," and Walter Phelps Hall, known as "Buzzer." Beppo was a formidable scholar, though he had published nothing since his doctor's thesis, which was on President Andrew Johnson. His field was modern American history, and I had a good deal to do with him. Buzzer got his nickname from the fact that he was very deaf, and used a large old-fashioned hearing aid. He worked in British and modern European history. Though he published books, I think it must be said that he was no great scholar; but he was a delightful man and a very successful teacher, regularly voted by the students the university's "most popular lecturer." I cherish a story about him which I heard, I think, from Beppo. In 1917 Theodore Roosevelt proposed to raise and, he hoped, command a division for the U.S. army. Walter Hall, a great admirer of Roosevelt, was anxious to get into the division but knew that his deafness would prevent his getting any normal employment. He was proud of his cooking, and thought he might get a job in the division as a cook. He waylaid Roosevelt at the Harvard Club in New York. The ex-president appeared, as usual, rushing at high speed. Walter, overwhelmed by the sudden appearance of his hero, could only stammer out a word or two asking for a job as cook. Roosevelt was disgusted: "Cook! What are you wasting my time for?" He was dashing away, but Walter caught him by the arm: "Colonel, you don't understand. I'm deaf; they wouldn't have me as a soldier; but I thought perhaps you might take me on as a cook." Teddy melted instantly: "No, I didn't understand. Sure, you can be cook! I bet you're a darned good cook!" When the Roosevelt Division plan was vetoed by President Wilson, Walter found a civilian war job in the American Field Service.

When I came to Princeton I knew almost nothing about the history of the United States. This, I thought, was an opportunity to broaden myself. The department was strong in the American field, and I proceeded, with considerable effrontery, to offer American history as my "major field" in the preliminary examination for the Ph.D. However wise this may have been in one way, it was foolhardy in another; for I was competing against people who had, so to speak, imbibed American history with their mothers' milk, while I had no background in the subject at all and had to start from scratch. This might have involved me in disaster, and in fact when the time came Beppo Hall gave me a bad time on the examination; I suspect that he was teaching me a lesson. However, I got by.

Paradoxically enough, it was this American involvement that first gave me a serious interest in the history of Canada, which until then had had no special appeal for me. The two countries' experiences had been so much alike, and yet so different. Why had things developed in such diverse fashion north and south of the border? There were clearly many interesting problems to explore. So when the question of a thesis subject had to be faced, I turned towards Canada, and Canadian-American relations. First of all I was attracted by the Fenian movement, the Irish-American phenomenon of the 1860s that produced a series of raids across the border. One circumstance leading me in this direction was the fact that the Princeton Library had an exceptionally rich collection on the Civil War period (it had next to nothing on Canadian history as such). I put quite a bit of effort into research on the Fenian Brotherhood and its Canadian ramifications and repercussions. In September 1930 I made my first visit to the Public Archives of Canada in Ottawa, an establishment which I have been visiting regularly ever since. It was the first time I had been in Ottawa. Parliament was in session, the new prime minister, R. B. Bennett, having called it to raise the tariff; and I went to the gallery of the House of Commons and saw Bennett performing pompously and William Lyon Mackenzie King, now Leader of the Opposition, making it very clear that he was not enjoying that particular position.

I became a regular member of the community of summer visitors at the Ottawa Archives. As I look back now, I realize that the people who delved there in the thirties, night and day (you could work twenty-four hours a day if you had a pass), making endless laborious hand-written notes — for photocopying was yet unknown — were in fact laying the foundations of a new school of Canadian history. I remember especially A. L. Burt, of Alberta and Minnesota, who worked there summer after summer. The result, published in 1933, was *The Old Province of Quebec*, which unlike most of the books used in Canadian history courses when I was an undergraduate was an original recreation of the period it dealt with (1760-91); it was hewn out of the hard bedrock of the contemporary documents. In these years Donald Creighton, in the same spirit, was digging out of the Ottawa records the stuff of his first book, *The Commercial Empire of the St. Lawrence*, finally published in 1937. Even with the Depression constantly with us, it seems now a heady and exciting time. For me, it was the time when I discovered the fascination of reconstructing history from the records left by the men who made it, fitting it together like the pieces of a jigsaw puzzle: a fascination that has never left me.

In due course I was scared off the Fenian subject by the discovery that too many other people were working on it. I really need not have worried, for none of them produced a book, at any rate for a long time. But in the course of my researches I had come across the trail of another topic that seemed to me interesting: the question of the British military garrison in Canada after the concession of responsible government to the British North American colonies. The desire of the British government to reduce its military commitments in those parts was a long story, ending only with the withdrawal of the troops from central Canada in 1871, and complicated by a succession of embroilments with the United States, including that caused by the Fenians and the long crisis of the Civil War. I switched my thesis subject to this, but I tried to salvage something from my Fenian investigations, not only by utilizing some of the material for the new subject but also by writing some Fenian articles. In September 1931 the *Canadian Historical Review* published a long article called "Fenianism and the Rise of National Feeling in Canada at the Time of Confederation" in which I got off my chest some generalizations about the importance of the movement. My favourite Fenian article, however, is one which the CHR printed in 1934: "A Fenian Interlude: The Story of Michael Murphy." This was the story, a mixture of tragedy and comedy, of the Fenian leader in Toronto, who was arrested in April 1866, and had to be allowed to escape to the States because there wasn't enough evidence to convict him.

I have not yet mentioned my thesis supervisor. He was Robert G. Albion, a cheerful individual from Maine who was a prolific writer (and incidentally something of a military expert) and had a reputation for taking on lucrative odd jobs. He knew very little about Canada but was a helpful adviser generally. As a matter of fact, there is a great deal to be said for writing a thesis at a university where nobody knows anything about your field. I am sure nobody at Princeton was very certain whether my thesis was good or bad, but they knew it seemed to make sense, appeared to be based on a fair amount of research, and was written in passable English. Having got my A.M. in 1931 (the preliminary exam for the Ph.D. was qualification for this), I achieved the doctorate in 1933.

Over it all hung the dark cloud of the Depression. I was one of the lucky ones; I was comfortable and never hungry. But the future was always an unpleasant question mark, for there were no jobs. For my second year at Princeton the university kindly renewed my $900 fellowship. After that I was going to be on my own, and I had no resources. The immediate gap was filled by good luck, powerfully helped along by my brother-in-law, Harcourt Brown. He was conducting College Board examinations at Friends' Academy in Locust Valley, Long Island, and found they needed a temporary history teacher. I got the job and spent 1931-32 at Locust Valley, reputed to be the wealthiest township in the United States.

Friends' Academy was a modest Quaker co-educational boarding and day school with good standards. The students were in general a nice lot, though the place had its allotment of devils. I forget what my salary was; it was not munificent, but it kept me going and enabled me to put a very little aside. It was not an unpleasant year, but it made it clear to me that I didn't want to be a schoolmaster. A school teacher needs to be interested in children, a university professor needs to be interested in the subject he teaches, and that was my case. One of my chief recollections of Friends' Academy is that on "First Days" (Sundays) the boarders and the staff used to troop across the road to the log Quaker meeting-house built in the first half of the eighteenth century. The "service" consisted of the females sitting on one side, the males on the other, and nobody speaking unless moved by the Spirit. At first I was deeply impressed, and thought it the finest Christian observance I had ever known. Shortly, however, it became apparent that it was almost always the same people who were moved to speak, and they were almost always moved to say the same things. There was, nevertheless, one blessed day when nobody said a single word.

In June 1932, with the grand sum of $1,080.50 in the bank, I went back to Princeton to finish my thesis. But the next year had to be faced, and still there were no jobs. During all those Depression years when I was searching for employment, I heard of exactly one teaching appointment in history at a Canadian university. It was at the University of Western Ontario at London. I applied for it and didn't get it. Inquiries of various American universities bore no better fruit. I recall Professor Wertenbaker asking me why my own university, which had sent me to Princeton, didn't look after me. I replied that no one had sent me there; I had come under my own steam.

For me, as for the world at large, 1933 was the low point of the Depression. Luckily, my mother was in a position to help. I borrowed $400 from her in three lots beginning in March, and paid it back in small instalments from October 1934 to June 1937: evidence of the fundamental fact that it is easier to borrow than to repay. I remember also asking the university to allow me to postpone payment of what I owed it because the Canadian dollar, at that moment, was so very low, and my funds had to come from Canada; and the request was granted. Professor Wertenbaker threw me a lifeline. He had got from somewhere a grant for a research assistant. So I spent several months living at the Graduate College, and devilling for the Colonel; and very rewarding months they were.

The Colonel was working on what finally became his three-volume book *The Founding of American Civilization*, a study of the transit of European culture to the American colonies. The evidence he used was largely architectural, and my work for him consisted mainly of studying architectural material from Europe and America. I acquired an interest in architectural history which I have never lost. A by-product of this research was an article I wrote for the *Dictionary of American Biography* on Robert Smith, the Philadelphia architect who designed Princeton's venerable and famous Nassau Hall (1756). I came to the conclusion that Smith got his basic design from James Gibbs's *A Book of Architecture*, a book well known in the colonies. Gibbs's building at King's College, Cambridge, was almost the only academic building illustrated in the books of design available to colonials, and I have no doubt that this design, with the expensive ornamentation stripped off and a small cupola added, was the source for Nassau Hall.

Finally, in the spring of 1934, there was evidence that for me the worst of the Depression was over. Princeton University then appointed me instructor in history for one year at a salary of $1,800; and very well pleased I was. For five years thereafter I was annually reappointed at gradually increasing stipends; by the spring of 1938 I was up to $2,500, which in those days would buy a good deal. The university had a rule that after five years' service an instructor had to be either promoted or dismissed. I don't know how serious the discussion was in the department about my case, but the fact remains that they took the plunge, and on April 20, 1939, promoted me to assistant professor for three years, at a salary of $3,000. I began to sniff, in a small way, the sweet smell of success.

Teaching at Princeton was a congenial occupation. The students, though no more eager for learning than the average undergraduate, were in general pleasant and intelligent. They were mostly Easterners, and from the upper crust of American society. The story was told of an undergraduate who regularly referred to Americans living west of the Alleghenies as "the peasantry." I have a record book for the years 1935-38; the names are predominantly Anglo-Saxon. They mean little to me now; forty years on, I cannot fit faces to them. How many of these boys, I wonder, died in the Pacific, or North Africa, or Normandy? From what I saw of them, I am sure most of them would have tried to be in the forefront of the battle.

As a junior member of the department, I taught freshmen and sophomores — the sophomores in Wilsonian "precepts" of five to eight students, and the freshmen in sections of up to twenty-five. As we all tended to be generalists in those days, particularly the juniors, I taught mainly British and European history. In due course Bob Albion, who as a New Englander had the sea in his blood, started an upper-class course in maritime history which I got involved in; this was another case of beginning an interest which I have never lost. I gave only the odd lecture until my last couple of years, when I was given the job of doing the second-term lecturing in our big freshman course in British history. Going in to give those lectures to two hundred or so freshmen in McCosh Hall was something of an adventure, a little like going into the big cage; there were times when I thought I really should have carried a kitchen chair and a revolver loaded with blanks. But it was a challenge and I enjoyed it. These students had had no background whatever in British history. This was a bit of a problem, though I think they found the subject interesting. Here I can report a fact that struck me at the time: when they grew restless, in the latter part of the course, I could always bring them back to the subject by reading a passage from Winston Churchill. Winston riding in the charge at Omdurman; Winston describing the signing of the Irish Treaty of 1921 — these things would reduce them to rapt attention, such is the power of a strong piece of English prose. I remember explaining to them that Churchill would never be prime minister: the English thought him too brilliant and too erratic to be trusted.

Naturally, there was no Canadian history to be taught; Princeton would have thought the idea too grotesque for consideration then, although they now have an Institute of Canadian Studies. But I sneaked some Canadian contraband in under the British history label. For instance, in my final lecture in May 1939 I quoted Lord Baldwin's recent speech in Toronto:

> And now we know that, should the challenge come, we shall be there.
> In Luther's words, "We can no other." We were there when the
> Spanish galleons made for Plymouth: we were on those bloody fields of
> the Netherlands when Louis XIV aimed at the domination of Europe:
> we were on duty when Napoleon bestrode the world like a demi-god,
> and we answered the roll call, as you did, in August, 1914. We can
> no other: so help us, God.[2]

I went on to mention the debate that had been going on in Canada over what Canada would do if war came; and I took it on myself to tell the students that if anyone told them Canada would stand aside they were not to believe him. After the lecture a student came up and told me that a relative of his was chargé d'affaires at the American legation in Ottawa, and that he had reported to the State Department that in case of war Canada would be neutral. He asked for my comments. I'm afraid I was rather rude to the youngster. I said: "I have two comments. First, your relative clearly isn't fit for his job. Secondly, I know where he got his misinformation: he got it from the Canadian Department of External Affairs." Even then people had an idea of the extent of isolationism in the East Block in Ottawa.

"Publish or perish." Nobody ever said, or even hinted, anything like that to me at Princeton, but then it was pretty clear that I didn't really need encouragement to publish. Once my thesis was finished and it had got me my degree I looked for a way of getting it into print. A hopeful possibility seemed to be the Imperial Studies series, published by what was then called the Royal Empire Society of London (moving with the times, it is now the Royal Commonwealth Society). I submitted it and in March 1934 they accepted it.

Memory is a feeble instrument (a point the proponents of "oral history" often forget). I had convinced myself that the thesis was published almost exactly as it was submitted to the university. I no longer have a copy of the thesis in its original form; but my file of correspondence with the RES proves that my memory was wrong. Arthur Percival Newton, Rhodes Professor of Imperial History in the University of London and "Organiser" of the Imperial Studies Committee, wrote to say that they thought the first chapter "rather thin and unconvincing" and that elsewhere some evidence might be eliminated in the interest of economy. I rewrote Chapter I completely, and made excisions in the other chapters.

There were distinct limits to the RES's generosity, since obviously there were limits to its resources. The publishers, Longmans, Green & Co., estimated the cost of producing the revised manuscript at £177 11s. 3d. The Society was ready to pay £100; finding the other £77.11.3 was up to me. For me in 1935 this was no small sum; and I managed it only with the assistance of the Carnegie Endowment for International Peace, as I shall explain in a moment. However, *Canada and the British Army, 1846-1871: A Study in the Practice of Responsible Government*, was published by Longmans in London on 6 April, 1936. I busied myself with suggesting places to which review copies might be sent, and sent some myself to individuals who I thought might be interested. One of these was the Governor General of Canada, Lord Tweedsmuir. I admired him, and had met him at Hart House, when he was plain John Buchan, under the auspices of Burgon Bickersteth. I remember talking to him about his novels, and he remarked, "As a man of letters, I'm a farce." Now my little offering was acknowledged by an ADC, who thanked me for my book *Canada and the British Empire*. One wasted book. There were several quite favourable reviews, including one by J. L. Morison, another person I admired, in the *Canadian Historical Review*. I had never met him, but liked his books; and when George Brown, the *Review* editor, asked me for a suggestion for a reviewer I mentioned him. He was so kind that I really don't dare to quote him.

The thesis led me into a larger project to which I was to devote a vast amount of work which in the end came to absolutely nothing. At the beginning of 1934 Professor James T. Shotwell, Director of the Division of Economics and History of the Carnegie Endowment for International Peace, was developing his ambitious project *The Relations of Canada and the United States* which was to result in a shelf of impressive volumes. It was probably Bartlet Brebner who put me in touch with him; they both read the thesis and I found myself commissioned to contribute to the series a study bearing some title like *Armament and Disarmament in North America* which would be a study of the military relations between the United States and Canada and a realistic examination of the history of the celebrated undefended border. I was paid an honorarium (ultimately $750) which it was understood would enable me to pay that £77 to Messrs. Longmans. That was useful. The Carnegie Endowment also distributed some copies of *Canada and the British Army.*

I set to work. The job turned out to be a big one. Unlike some of the other volumes in the series (Donald Creighton's *Commercial Empire of the St. Lawrence* is an example) mine was not a study already in existence which was pushed into it; it had to be written from the ground up, and involved a great deal of research in original sources. I worked in the Ottawa Archives. I worked in Washington (the National Archives did not yet exist, and the records of the Adjutant-General's Office were in an old garage with a flat tarred roof, the atmosphere of which on a hot summer day had to be experienced to be appreciated). In due course I began writing. My department very kindly relieved me of teaching for the first term of

1938-39 so I could get on with it. I still have the chapters: two of them deal with the War of 1812, "The Eagle Tries His Claws" and "War on the Inland Seas." I think it is a pretty fair manuscript, if I do say it myself. By the outbreak of war the manuscript was complete to roughly 1871, and 1940 saw me in the army.

Going off to a very uncertain future, I decided to deposit the unfinished manuscript with the Carnegie Endowment and authorize them, if they saw fit, to put it in the hands of an editor and publish it as it stood. On May 27, 1941, Bart Brebner wrote to me in London:

> Dr. Shotwell and Arthur MacFarlane* have been reading your manuscript and both of them are much impressed by it. I myself have not had time to have a look at it, but I talked with them both yesterday and they have become confirmed in their earlier impression that it would be better to set the manuscript aside for completion after the War. I do not think that I am breaking any confidence when I say that one serious consideration in this decision is their feeling that it would probably be undesirable to publish a study which concludes with the last really bad period of Canadian-American relations at a time when those relations are unprecedentedly close and trusting. . . . On the whole, it seems to me that irrespective of these considerations, you would never be happy about having a book of yours prepared for publication by someone else, and having done such a substantial job up to 1871, you would want to finish the thing off yourself.

That is all right, but it reminds me of something about Shotwell. He had never, I suspect, fully recovered from his experiences at the Peace Conference in 1919, when he was a member of the American "Inquiry." He thought he was being an international statesman when he was in fact merely organizing a respectable scholarly project which few except scholars would be interested in and which certainly would have little influence on international events.

Having already done some violence to chronology, I may as well do a little more and finish the sad little story here. When I came back in 1946 I wrote Brebner. On April 1 he replied:

---

* An editor, an expatriate and I think embittered Canadian, who on the basis of his marks on the manuscript disliked it intensely. He, I think, thought it anti-American.

... The important thing for you to know, I guess, is that he [Shotwell] has no more money for the Series and has been unsuccessful in trying to get more from the Carnegie Corporation. He has sunk everything he controls in atomic studies. One result of this is that we are not getting new printings of the ten or a dozen volumes of the Series whose first printings are exhausted...

Shotwell wrote:

I am terribly sorry about the volume in manuscript which you have left with me. The Endowment has embarked upon a new policy with reference to research, and I am unable to carry out the original plan. It is a splendid piece of work, and will be a great contribution to history. ...

In June 1946 I collected the manuscript at Shotwell's office; so far as I can recall he was not there.

And so five years of research went down the drain. People have told me I ought to have sued, but that would not have occurred to me at the time. Anyway, I was disgusted, and never went back to the manuscript. My colleague Mac Hitman covered much of the same ground in his *Safeguarding Canada, 1763-1871*, published in 1968, but included comparatively little material from the American side. Fortunately, I was able to salvage a little from the wreck. In the *American Historical Review* for October 1950, I published an article called "The Myth of the Unguarded Frontier, 1815-1871," which contained a good bit of the pith of my research; and in January 1941 the same journal had printed an article of mine entitled "An American Plan for a Canadian Campaign," based on a fascinating document I had discovered in that torrid garage in Washington. But my connection with the Carnegie Endowment is not an episode that I look back on with pleasure.

Chapter 5

Consequences of Hitler

I was in Princeton as the Second World War approached, and indeed during its first year, when the United States was neutral. It was not a pleasant period of history for anybody, and certainly not for me.

Hitler came to power in Germany the year before I began to teach at Princeton, and needless to say "the situation" was the almost invariable topic of discussion in classes and elsewhere. On the whole there was remarkably little difference of opinion. The American people were against Hitler, and as the reports of repression and violence and pogroms came in, and the Nazi Revolution showed signs of extending itself into other countries, their hostility became only more marked. A decent and democratic nation had no intention of condoning this sort of thing. Whether a decent and democratic nation, three thousand happy miles away, had any intention of *doing* anything about it was however quite another matter.

We were an international community in Princeton, and particularly at the Graduate College where I continued to live until my marriage. In addition to the large British and Canadian group there were also a few Germans. We had, for instance, Percy Schramm, who I think was there before the situation reached its worst. He was a medievalist who was the greatest living authority on the history of the English coronation. (Later he kept Hitler's headquarters war diary.) We also had Dr. Malsch, a post-doctoral fellow in chemistry. Malsch was there when the situation was nearing its worst. Poor fellow, he had a bad time. The New York and Philadelphia press was crammed with the atrocities of the Nazis, and Malsch didn't believe a word of it. I suspect he was not a Nazi, but he was a patriotic German, and his soul was seared morning and evening when the papers came in. I think he practically gave up research and devoted himself entirely to reading what Dr. Goebbels would have called "the fabrications of the Jew-controlled press" (I imagine that is what Malsch called them within himself). I have often wondered what became of him. I hope he found out about Hitler, and survived the war.

As for the British and Canadians, we read, and shivered. Britain was not three thousand miles from the Continent, but only twenty-one. Canada had her three thousand miles, but she also had her ties with Britain, and most of us could not conceive of Britain fighting for her life and Canada standing by. I don't think we said a great deal, except by way of rude remarks about Hitler, until the Americans began to call the British cowards for not standing up to Adolf. This became a fairly common form of activity, particularly after the advent of Neville Chamberlain in 1937; and it must be said that it did draw an occasional mild rejoinder, usually along the lines that the British might possibly be a bit bolder if they could see an ally or two who were willing to put their fists where their mouths were. But the abuse continued, and many Americans seemed quite unable to see anything inconsistent about urging the British to be big and fierce while themselves expressing an unalterably fixed determination to be neutral.

I spent my summers chiefly in Canada, partly researching in Ottawa, partly writing and seeing my friends in Toronto. So I saw something at first hand of the debate that was going on as to what Canada should do in case of war. Looking back now, I think it was more of a sham fight than some people realized at the time. A small group of academic isolationists, notably Frank Underhill at Toronto and Frank Scott at McGill, were making a very loud noise, and perhaps there were times when they really believed that they were leading public opinion; but I suspect that the Canadian public essentially didn't know they existed. What was really happening, I think, was that the great mass of people, in English-speaking Canada at least, watching Hitler's performance, were gradually and painfully coming to the conclusion that he would ultimately have to be stopped by force, and that Canada could not avoid taking part. The final turning point, it seems to me, was the Munich crisis of September 1938, when war seemed possible at any moment and trenches were being dug in the London parks. I was in Toronto that week, about to return to Princeton, and I have the most vivid recollection of walking down Bay Street and seeing the crisis reflected in the grim faces of the passers-by. No one had any doubt after that experience, I think, that if war came Canada would be in it. The isolationists realized after Munich that their battle was lost.

One theatre of the Canadian debate was a series of conferences on Canadian-American Affairs which the Carnegie Endowment financed as an offshoot of its Canadian-American study. There were three of these, in 1935, 1937 and 1939, held alternately at St. Lawrence University, Canton, N.Y., and Queen's University at Kingston. These meetings became increasingly concerned with the situation abroad, and the last one talked about little else. I didn't play much part in the beginning. For one thing, I was comparatively young, and in those days the young tended to restrain themselves in the presence of their elders; moreover, as a Canadian living in a foreign land, I felt disposed to keep a brake on my tongue. Also, I believe that those of us who thought that in case of Britain again becoming involved in a great war Canada would inevitably be involved too felt less need than the isolationists to argue about it; we felt we were members of a silent majority whose influence would be decisive if the worst came to the worst. However, in the third conference, held in June 1939, I was invited to make a fairly major contribution, sharing a session on "Defence and External Obligations" with Senator Elbert D. Thomas of Utah. Munich was behind us, and I remarked, quite incidentally, "if a war involving Britain comes again in Europe, Canada certainly, and the United States quite probably, will find themselves parties to it."

Anything even remotely resembling a "military expert" was rare in the Canadian community in those days, and suddenly I found myself in some demand. I wrote for the Canadian Institute of International Affairs a paper called "New Trends in Canadian Defence Policy" in connection with a British Commonwealth Relations Conference held in 1938. The result was an invitation to write for the Institute a little book covering much the same ground. I wrote to Shotwell in March 1939 a bit apologetically that this was an easy and comparatively minor job and that I was devoting an occasional evening to it "in the intervals of working on the bigger book." The little book was in fact completed just in time for the outbreak of war, and since it had been planned as a contribution to discussion in a perilous but not a war situation the project came to a full stop. After consideration the Institute decided to proceed with it, cutting out the final chapter in which I made suggestions for the further development of the defence program, for which I substituted a short one on the early stages of the war. *The Military Problems of Canada* finally appeared late in 1940, after I was in uniform.

Meanwhile important things were happening in my personal life. With that assistant professorship, and that $3,000 salary, I was for the first time able to think of marriage. A little red notebook shows that on 16 July 1939 I actually had $1,918.34 in the world. That may not seem much to marry on, but it was a fair sum of money in those days. The reader has met Doris Shiell, an associate in the Players' Guild at University College — she was always devoted to the theatre — and again in Paris. She came back from studies in France to work in the University Library at Toronto. She and I were married in Toronto on 26 August 1939.

Take note of the date. We might have had the Second World War for a wedding present, but Hitler put it off for a week, not out of consideration for us, but in the hope that perhaps British intervention might be prevented. I remember sitting on the sofa with Doris at her family house on the evening of the 25th and hearing the cheerful news that Ottawa had called out the first 10,000 men. I remarked that if the Canadian government had actually reached the point of *paying* 10,000 men to do military duty the situation was probably past saving.

The goal of our honeymoon was Quebec City (that was as much as we could afford); but we stayed over in Kingston. Here I had a new acquaintance, who in the future would turn out to be an important connection. Brigadier H.D.G. Crerar had been reading the draft of *The Military Problems of Canada* for the Canadian Institute of International Affairs, and this had brought us into contact. (I rather think he had also read *Canada and the British Army.*) He was commandant of the Royal Military College, and when he and Mrs. Crerar heard we were in Kingston they very kindly invited us to lunch. Doris was properly impressed by the commandant's house and the white-coated batman who waited on table; she felt, I think, that there might be something to be said for the military life.

Going on to Quebec, we did the sights there; but the thing that I remember has nothing to do with the ancient battlefields or the fortifications. One evening as darkness was falling we were walking on Dufferin Terrace looking out on the St. Lawrence with the other tourists. Suddenly we were aware of a large dark shape sliding rapidly and silently down the river past the city. It was a blacked-out liner, probably one of the Canadian Pacific's *Duchess* ships, stealing out to sea. It seemed more of a portent than anything else we had seen, more than the cheerful airmen on the trains, moving to their war stations. We remembered it a few days later when we heard what had happened to the *Athenia*.

On our way back to Toronto, we paused in Montreal, at the La Salle Hotel. It was there, for us, that the thing began. Sunday, 3 September, and Hitler's failure to reply to the British ultimatum demanding that he suspend his invasion of Poland. Sitting at lunch in the hotel dining-room, at one o'clock we heard the King broadcast: Britain was taking up arms against "the mere primitive doctrine that Might is Right": "It is to this high purpose that I now call my people at home and my peoples across the Seas, who will make our cause their own." Nobody sang "God Save the King" or engaged in any public display of emotion; but there was, I imagine, considerable private setting of teeth. Canada was not yet officially at war — that was to await the meeting of Parliament on 7 September — but no one thought of this as more than a formality. In the circumstances, as may be imagined, I was not desperately anxious to rush off to the ends of the earth; but that afternoon I telegraphed the District Officer Commanding Military District No. 2, "Services available if required."

My old militia unit was not itself being mobilized, and there were more than enough active officers available for the signal units that were being formed. The reply to the letter with which I followed up my telegram thanked me and told me that the letter had been filed "for ready reference in case of necessity." I also sought advice of Brigadier Crerar, who replied that in his view "I am inclined to believe that the soundest thing to do would be to return to Princeton, for the time being, anyway. I don't see any large scale movement of "Land Forces" from Canada to the other side for the best part of six months, anyway...." So this is what I did. Doris and I went to Princeton and moved into the university apartment at 112 Alexander Street that had been reserved for us, bought enough furniture to furnish it, and settled down for a year in the neutral United States.

One thing sticks in my memory. Passing through New York City, we had an hour to kill between trains, and we went to a newsreel theatre. Films were beginning to come in from the countries at war. There was one shot, inconceivably dull, of troops mobilizing in Canada — I rather think, of Lord Tweedsmuir reviewing local units in Ottawa. To my utter amazement, the New York audience broke into loud applause. It was the only time in my life I have ever known an American audience to show any interest in Canada. A few days afterwards in Princeton we saw the famous newsreel shot of Hermann Goering rubbing his fat hands in glee at the news of the bombing of Warsaw. I remember the deep spontaneous growl of anger that it drew from the Americans who saw it.

We found that year in Princeton embarrassing. We were guests in the country, and it was obviously not a good idea to get involved in American domestic controversies. Among the Americans themselves there was a great variety of opinion. There were I think almost no Americans who wanted Germany to win, and those who did were mostly Germans or kooks. At the other end of the scale there were rather more — but not many — who favoured immediate active intervention on the side of the Allies. In between were the people who supported the Committee to Defend America by Aiding the Allies, and the people who believed in keeping out of war at any cost, and various permutations and combinations. Disputation was constant, and it was hard for British subjects to keep out of it. I made myself rather too audible once at an early stage. The veteran leftist editor Oswald Garrison Villard was prominent among the more extreme isolationists, and he came to Princeton to speak. Winston Churchill had just announced (18 December 1939) the arrival in Britain of the 1st Canadian Division, "strongly escorted, and covered by our main battle fleet." Villard, adopting the rather peculiar argument that the Allies were so weak that they were a poor risk to support, remarked in his speech that if it took the whole British fleet to get a Canadian division across the Atlantic the British must be in a bad way. Of course, he had misunderstood the difference between "escort" and "cover." I interrupted him and told him so. I am sure people thought it was very rude of me; and in any case my interruption was ineffective because he was too deaf to understand me. But no doubt a few people in the audience reflected that the war was coming to quiet Princeton.

Sometimes American attitudes verged on the comic. On the dark day in April 1940 when the Germans broke into Norway my American friends were going about wagging their heads sadly and saying, "Too bad; too bad; but thank heaven it's no affair of ours." The next day, at a party, when there had been a misleading gleam of victory and it appeared that the Royal Navy might be cutting the German communications with Norway, the same people were saying brightly, "Isn't it fine? Our side's winning." This is the literal truth. Then came the Allied disaster in France and the Dunkirk evacuation; and unalloyed gloom descended. The chairman of the History Department now was Raymond J. Sontag, a man whom I liked and respected, but who was perhaps the strongest isolationist in the department. I had always credited him with having an intellectual basis for his views; but now it appeared that he was merely frightened. He came up to me at a department meeting and said, "Charlie, surely the British will surrender now? They will have more sense than to try to go on fighting. One should look at these things in the long light of history, in the light not merely of today but of the situation fifty years from now." I replied, "Well, Ray, I had never thought before that we might be defeated. Now I have to say I see that as a possibility; but it has never occurred to me that the British might think of surrendering. And I don't see the point of submitting to injustice and misery for fifty years when perhaps you can save the situation by standing and fighting for five." Ray went away discouraged. It was painfully clear that what he was afraid of was that if the British were so perverse as to insist on going on fighting the United States would inevitably be drawn in in the end.

The only activity that could by any stretch of the imagination be called war work that came my way during this grim year was purely literary. The *University of Toronto Quarterly* (not yet the exclusive preserve of literary critics and philosophers) invited me to write a regular article on the progress of the war; and I contributed four such articles ("As the Storm Broke," "The First Four Months," "Blockade and Counter-Blockade" and "The Desperate Grapple") before I was called to other things. I imagine both the editors and readers of the *Quarterly* were relieved when I put on khaki and the series ended.

My other war effort of a literary type, apart from revising *The Military Problems of Canada*, consisted of producing at the request of the Canadian branch of the Oxford University Press a pamphlet called *Canada and the Second World War* for a Canadian sub-series of the *Oxford Pamphlets on World Affairs* series. I was in good company in this Canadian group, other authors including Stephen Leacock, B. K. Sandwell and André Siegfried, translated by George M. Wrong. So far as I can recall, nobody mentioned the horrid word "money" in connection with this project; for me it was just a very modest contribution to winning the war, and I hope the same was true of the Oxford Press.

Through the momentous summer of 1940, with Hitler in control of the European coasts facing the British Isles, and Britain bracing for invasion, I remained a civilian, writing at intervals to Military District No. 2 and receiving assurances that they would "keep me in mind for the future." I should perhaps mention that regulations prevented individuals with officer qualifications enlisting in the ranks, something which, quite frankly, I had no great desire to do anyway. However, in the background things were happening that would decide my fate. Brigadier Crerar had gone to London early in the war to set up Canadian Military Headquarters there. On 22 July 1940, a major-general now, he came back to Canada as Chief of the General Staff. On 24 August, in reply to a letter from me mentioning my unemployed state, he indicated that "since the outbreak of the war I have had hopes of seeing you employed in a service capacity for which you are so particularly suited." He inquired whether, if a service appointment were offered, I would be in a position to accept it. I assured him I would. He cautioned me not to resign my position for the moment. Finally, on 11 October, Crerar wrote to inform me that the Minister of National Defence, Colonel J. L. Ralston, had authorized my appointment as Historical Officer, General Staff, at Canadian Military Headquarters, London, with the rank of major. I wrote at once accepting. At Princeton the university, having already been warned that some such thing might happen, was most co-operative. I left poor Doris to deal with the domestic chores of moving and storing our household goods, and pushed off to report myself in Ottawa.

One special thing I had to do. The Great Fear that fell on the United States after the fall of France had resulted in the enactment of a draft law, and it came into effect so rapidly that I had registered for the American draft before I managed to get into my own country's army. Now it was a pleasure to write the Selective Service Board in Princeton and tell them that I was no longer available for their purposes.

Although today it seems a little hard to believe, the whole thing came to me as a complete surprise. It had never occurred to me that I might be an official army historian. I had thought of myself as probably a brigade signal officer, and rather an inefficient one. Mental adjustment to the new development took some time.

When I presented myself at the Woods Building, which housed the central ganglion of the Department of National Defence in Ottawa, I think I expected to find some slight display of military pomp and some evidence of regard for security. What I found in the lobby was two elderly soldiers (or, at any rate, individuals in battle-dress) deep in a game of checkers. I interrupted them long enough to ask where I should find General Crerar's office. The reply was, "Who's he?" I explained that he was the Chief of the General Staff. They then told me where to find him and returned to their game. When I penetrated into the CGS's sanctum I found him apparently planning the defence of the Maritime provinces with the aid of an Esso road map. He received me kindly and explained that before going to London I would be spending some time with the Historical Section of the General Staff. He passed me on to the Director of Personal Services, Colonel Hennessy, who arranged the formalities of taking me into the army. Pat Hennessy was a fatherly gentleman whom one scarcely associated with blood and battles; it was a shock a little over a year later to hear that he had been killed at Hong Kong. I went through my medical examination, in which I had the experience of having some young civilian (not a doctor) find something slightly wrong (sugar in the urine?) and ask me, "Do you *want* to join the army?" I was slightly taken aback but said yes. (I was in the army for nineteen years after that, was medically examined every year, and nobody ever found anything wrong.) So I was in, got a suit of battle-dress out of stores, ordered a suit of service dress (khaki with brass buttons) from a tailor on Sparks Street (and a very bad suit it was), and set about my historical duties.

Here I must introduce the reader to Colonel Archer Fortescue Duguid, D.S.O., director of the Historical Section of the General Staff. First, however, a little background. During the First World War it was very properly considered that a history of the exploits of the Canadian forces in that war should be written. Early in 1917 Brigadier-General Ernest A. Cruikshank was given the task of collecting material and records for this purpose, with particular reference to events in Canada. Cruikshank had been a militia officer and an amateur but prolific military historian who had written a great deal on the War of 1812. He had been taken into the Permanent Force in 1909 and had commanded a military district in Canada before and during the war. A few days after the Armistice in November 1918 he was appointed director of the Historical Section. By 1920 he had actually produced, and had had printed, a history of the Canadian operations through the Second Battle of Ypres (April 1915). This curious little book consisted of a narrative text of less than 30 pages, followed by over 300 pages of miscellaneous documents. It is scarcely surprising that it did not meet with approval. Senior officers who read it, including Sir Arthur Currie, were unanimous that it should not be issued. General Cruikshank was retired to pension and subsequently found a job as chairman of the Historic Sites and Monuments Board of Canada, in which appointment he spent the rest of his working life erecting plaques bearing historical inscriptions of varying degrees of accuracy.[1]

Who was to take Cruikshank's place? There was in existence, alongside the Historical Section but not part of it, something called the War Narrative Section. This had been formed overseas and had drafted the interim report by Sir Arthur Currie on Canadian Corps operations in 1918 which was published in the *Report of the Ministry, Overseas Military Forces of Canada*, for that year. In 1919 several officers in the section were "returned to Canada for special purposes, such as the completion of the Historical Account of the Canadian Expeditionary Force."[2] The senior officer left in the service at the beginning of 1921 was Major A. Fortescue Duguid. He was an artillery officer with a good war record and a McGill degree in civil engineering. The War Narrative Section was now merged into the Historical Section and Duguid was taken into the Permanent Force, seconded for duty as director with the temporary rank of colonel. The date of his appointment was 14 May 1921. He still held this appointment and temporary rank at the outbreak of the next war.

Under Duguid the section went to the other extreme from Cruikshank. He later wrote that the 1921 terms of reference merely gave him the task of collecting and sorting material for the history, which would be written by some later appointee; he himself was appointed historian only in 1932.

Thus he met mounting criticism of his failure to produce a history. No doubt with the passage of time he came to believe in the truth of this interpretation of his duties. Actually, however, the Order-in-Council of 1921 not only gave the Historical Section headed by Duguid the duty of collecting and classifying historical material, but also assigned to it the task of compiling and publishing complete historical accounts of the Canadian forces at home and abroad.* He planned a general history of eight volumes; and the first one, the only one ever produced, was published in 1938, twenty years after the Armistice.[3] This was regarded as a minor national scandal; and General Crerar in conversation with me, while never saying a word against Duguid, made no secret of the fact that in hiring me he was trying to provide against another such fiasco in connection with the second war. I think he had grasped the fact that history is better written by historians than by civil engineers.

The name Duguid is Scottish, the first syllable being stressed when pronounced, and Duguid's intimates called him "Scotty." At some point during the war Doris heard the CBC call him "Colonel A. Fortesk Du-Gwee," and I'm afraid that is what we called him thereafter in the privacy of the home. My personal relations with him were never really disagreeable; he was a gentleman, though a very pompous one, and we never had an actual altercation. I am sure he regarded my appearance on the scene with displeasure, though I didn't fully realize this in the beginning. Left to himself, I feel certain he would never have brought a professional historian into his organization. His staff consisted of people from the Permanent Force and the civil service, and among them he was lucky to have a couple of natural researchers — Ed Pye, a civilian, and Lieutenant-Colonel J. F. Cummins of the Corps of Military Staff Clerks. Cummins, from the ranks of the old British regular army, was self-educated; I was told that he had done it by reading every volume of Everyman's Library, as good an education as anyone could prescribe.

I think I had met Duguid before October 1940; we had certainly corresponded, probably in connection with my work on *The Military*

---

* Duguid's later version may have been influenced by the fact that in 1928, apparently because of the failure to make progress, a committee was appointed to consider the matter. It recommended that a historian should be appointed and that Duguid should be limited to the preparation of material. But no action was taken and the original terms of reference in fact remained in effect.

Problems of Canada. And I had reviewed that one volume of history he produced in 1938. I said of it, with what now seems to me exaggerated praise, "The book is... a quite astonishingly complete, competent and admirable job." I also however remarked in passing, "Its worst literary fault is a tendency to conscript the humble comma for duties for which it was never intended."[4] (Duguid had a habit of using a comma where a semi-colon or a full stop would have been in order.) Writing me a letter on another matter, he added a postscript about this: "Your point about the comma is quite inadmissible. I had advice from high authorities, including Sir Andrew Macphail, and they all agreed with my usage." My recollection is that he said nothing else about the review. Frank Cummins told me that Duguid's whole staff lined up and begged him not to write that postscript; it would, they told him, unnecessarily convert a friend into an enemy — which it didn't, though it left a strange impression on me. Frank also said that Sir Andrew Macphail had made exactly the same criticism as I had!

Duguid's real interest in life was heraldry. When I arrived in Ottawa I was amazed to be told by his staff that he was devoting most of his time at the moment — and the services of Captain Neal, his cartographer — to designing the George Cross. This decoration had recently been instituted to honour acts of gallantry not performed in the actual presence of the enemy, such as defusing unexploded bombs. Nobody had asked Duguid to design the George Cross; it was entirely his own idea. When, after weeks of work, he sent his design off to Buckingham Palace, he inevitably received a polite letter of thanks informing him that a design for the Cross had already been drawn and approved by the King. Somewhat earlier he had designed what he called the battle flag of the Canadian Active Service Force. It was a white flag with the Union Jack in the hoist and three red maple leaves "conjoined on one stem" in the fly. To make it quite complete, in the upper right corner there was a blue stovelid bearing a *fleur-de-lys* in gold. General McNaughton gave the flag some countenance and it flew from the masthead of the *Aquitania* which carried his headquarters to Britain in 1939. Ultimately, however, the Duguid flag was simply forgotten, and the flag that flew at Canadian Army headquarters in the field was the Canadian Red Ensign.

In the intervals of his heraldic activity, Duguid drafted instructions for my guidance overseas, and took me around to meet various people in

Ottawa who might have something to contribute to my endeavours. Thus I met such individuals as John Grierson, the head of the National Film Board, and L. W. Brockington, the silver-tongued orator who enjoyed, briefly, the title "Recorder of Canada's War Effort." As for my instructions, another member of Duguid's staff, Bill Boss, sagely told me privately that when I got overseas I would be on my own, responsible to the chiefs of the overseas army, and would not have to worry about Duguid. He turned out to be right.

Doris joined me in Ottawa, we found lodgings and had a few weeks together there before I left for London. By that stage of the war the government had forbidden Canadian women to go overseas except on official duty, so we had to look forward to indefinite separation. The prospect was rendered more interesting, if hardly cheerier, by the fact that London was under fire. The German air blitz on the city had begun in September, and everyone thought of me as going into the front line.

When it was considered that I had learned all I could from Duguid and his staff, arrangements were made for my passage to London. I was to travel in Troop Convoy 8 (that is, the eighth large "flight" of Canadian troops to go overseas), sailing from Halifax with the prospect of Christmas at sea. I went to Halifax by train, leaving Ottawa early in the morning of 13 December 1940. Doris went with me as far as Montreal. I kissed her goodbye at Bonaventure Station, and watched her walk away down the platform (she was not one of those who stand about and wave). That was the last I saw of her for four years. Then the Maritime Express carried me eastward on my way to the war.

Chapter 6

Cockspur Street

Halifax (universally known by a national joke as "an Eastern Canadian Port") was new to me. We drew in there on the evening of 14 December. I wrote to Doris, "Three other lads and I got a taxi and cruised about the city seeing what we could in the dark." I didn't tell her that our group, maintaining tight-lipped military security about our voyage, were told by the taxi-driver, "That battleship in the harbour is the *Revenge*. She'll be taking you out." (She did.) Subsequently we embarked in the motor vessel *Capetown Castle* which was to carry us to England. She was a fine modern ship of the Union Castle Line, still with all her peacetime fittings. Unfortunately, built for the South Atlantic run, she was a little cool for the North Atlantic in December. On the morning of 16 December our convoy began to move out to sea, watched and waved at by a large crowd on the roof of the Nova Scotian Hotel. So much for security.

It was only by the special grace of God that the voyage of Troop Convoy 8 didn't turn out to be a national disaster. True, we started out well protected. As ocean escort, to protect us against surface raiders, we had the *Revenge*, an old tub, it is true, but carrying eight 15-inch guns. And we had two Canadian destroyers and overhead a flying boat. Soon these turned back and we were left with the battleship, a comforting motherly object. (Shortly, however, our attitude towards her was somewhat modified when the transports formed up around her in a tight circle; it appeared that instead of her protecting us, we were protecting her from torpedoes.) We were four transports: *Capetown Castle, Pasteur, Pennland* and *Columbia*, carrying between them about 7,000 Canadian soldiers.

Thus for some time we voyaged over the grey and very turbulent winter sea. Then, towards evening on the 21st, *Revenge* began to drop astern and parted company from us. She had, apparently, been called away to pursue a reported raider. The transports were alone on a wide, wide sea. It was understood that an escort of six destroyers was coming out from the United Kingdom to take us through the submarine zone. However, they wholly failed to appear. It must have been on the 23rd that in my capacity as ship's orderly officer I visited the bridge and found the captain marking a point on the chart with a pencil and circling it. I made bold to ask him what this meant. That, he said, was where we were supposed to rendez-vous with the destroyers. And where, I asked, were we now? He silently indicated the same point. I looked around the empty horizon and inquired what might have happened; and the ancient mariner replied laconically, "Navy never could navigate." That afternoon our most distinguished passenger, Air Vice-Marshal L. S. Breadner, Chief of the Canadian Air Staff, moved his ample frame out on deck, likewise looked round the still empty horizon and inquired, "Where are those slugs?" The fact is that those 7,000 Canadian troops and the air vice-marshal, who would presumably have been missed in the circles he moved in, went through the whole danger zone without a smitch of escort by either air or sea. (Presumably the dirty weather that prevented the escort from finding us performed the same office for the Germans.) Had we been less lucky there would certainly have been questions in various Houses, and mourning in a good many others.

At dusk on the 23rd the convoy separated, presumably making for different ports. The *Capetown Castle* increased her speed. All the transports, including the slow 13-knot *Pennland*, got in safely. On the morning of the 24th we were in sight of land and that afternoon in fair weather the *Capetown Castle* was sailing up the Firth of Clyde. We anchored at Gourock for the night, Christmas Eve being celebrated "fairly uproariously" on board. On Christmas Day we moved up to Glasgow, our troops constantly exchanging shouted greetings with people on shore and passing vessels, and being fascinated by the amount of naval shipbuilding in progress.

There we landed. In Glasgow we met a rating from the Canadian destroyer *St. Laurent* who told us that his ship and five other destroyers had searched fruitlessly for our convoy for three days. With other officers travelling independently I caught the night train for London. Here my ignorance served me well; I really ought to have gone to be processed at the Canadian base units in the Aldershot area, but this experience I escaped. On the afternoon of 26 December I reported at Canadian Military Headquarters in the Sun Life Building, 2 Cockspur Street, S.W.1, next door to Canada House and just out of Trafalgar Square.

The brick blast walls outside the doors of the Sun Life Building reminded us that there was a war on. People called the place "Fort Montague," but not in the hearing of the senior officer, Major-General Percival John Montague, C.M.G., D.S.O., M.C., V.D., (always called "Price"), a fighting soldier in the first war, a judge of the Court of King's Bench in Manitoba in civil life, and now Harry Crerar's successor as head of our static headquarters in London. He was famous for calling everybody "boy" or "lad." (When the Canadian Women's Army Corps came on the scene, he had to add "young lady" to the repertoire.) He received me affably, though (I told Doris) "he said he had expected somebody with long white whiskers." I always got on extremely well with him. My immediate boss, however, was the Brigadier-General Staff, Brigadier Maurice Pope, M.C. Maurice Pope was a Permanent Force sapper, an officer and a gentleman. The service of Canada was ingrained in him. His father was Sir Joseph Pope, secretary and biographer of Sir John A. Macdonald, and Canada's first Under-Secretary of State for External Affairs. He also had in him the blood of the other founding race: his mother was a Taschereau. He was a man of reading and cultivation. Back in 1930, Major M. A. Pope had shared something called the Canadian Defence Quarterly Essay Prize with "an obscure and very junior" militia subaltern named Stacey; his account in his memoirs of this affair and our later association is written with a delicacy and courtesy that still threaten to bring tears to my eyes.[1] He had a distinguished subsequent career, in the war and afterwards, in the areas where military affairs and diplomacy mingle. His amiability and breeding made him a natural diplomat; but both British and American negotiators, and I am sure others too, could testify also to the presence in him of a vein of iron.

I had become friendly with a fellow passenger in the *Capetown Castle*, Lieutenant-Colonel G.A. McCarter, known as "Nick," a regular gunner. After a night or two at the Cumberland Hotel we both found ourselves service flats (one room each) in a house at 44 Queen's Gardens, off the Bayswater Road, near Kensington Gardens. The Germans left us largely alone during our first couple of nights in London, but it was *reculer pour mieux sauter*. On Sunday, 29 December, Nick and I recreated ourselves by going out to Richmond by bus. We were close to home on the return trip when the sirens went and a noisy raid developed. As we stood near the Kingsway tube station watching a great glare in the sky to the east, and listening to bombs and gunfire, a citizen came hurrying past. Nick, in the best ignorant colonial manner, asked him "Is this a *big* raid?" He looked at Nick in some astonishment, then said politely, "Yes, this is a big raid,"and rushed off towards home. It was indeed a big raid; it was the fire-raid that very largely burned down the City of London and forced the authorities to introduce "fire-watching" — obliging a proportion of the employees of offices and other commercial and industrial establishments to stay on the premises at night to deal with incendiary bombs. One of the casualties, incidentally, was Longmans, Green, & Co.; so the entire existing stock of my poor little book *Canada and the British Army* went up in smoke.

Even before this, London had, of course, been sadly scarred. The Sun Life Building was still being repaired from the effects of a heavy bomb that had landed just at its back door in Pall Mall East on 11 October. Yet on the whole the thing that impressed the newcomer most was the extent to which the city was obstinately insisting on going about its business in spite of the Germans. Its business, and also its own peculiar little customs. I wrote to Doris,

> Speaking of the humours of the present situation reminds me that one of the queerest things I have seen lately concerns the statue of King Charles I in Trafalgar Square. As you know, it is regarded as one of the few good statues in London, and therefore was completely covered early in the war (I presume) by some sort of protection with an outer shell of corrugated iron.* As you know also, the local adherents of the House of Stuart have an annual habit of decorating the statue on the

---

* This and other statues were subsequently evacuated from the capital altogether.

anniversary of the chopping which took place nearby. The anniversary
came round recently and it is clear that the Jacobites refused to be
discouraged by circumstances; for when I passed the spot yesterday I
noticed three wreaths of white roses hanging solemnly on the front of
the King's corrugated iron casing. There's loyalty for you!

The London theatre, which had been almost entirely killed by the autumn
blitz, was showing signs of revival when I arrived. The greatest horror of
war in London — and when I say "horror" I mean just that — was the
blackout. It was a source of constant misery and constant danger. I wrote
on 25 January:

> There is one good thing: thanks to the days getting longer, "blackout
> time" is getting later and later in the evening — it is well past six
> o'clock now — and it will soon be back to eight in the morning. This
> makes London a pleasanter place. All the shops close up tight when
> dusk comes on, and the city is very gloomy. . . . You will have noted
> from the advertisements in the *Observers* I sent you . . . that matinees
> now happen at 11 a.m., the main performance being at 2:30. There are
> no evening theatres at all, of course, and so far as I know no movie goes
> on past 9 p.m. But life in the daytime is pretty normal.

Colonel Ralston, the Defence Minister, and General Crerar turned up
in London about the same time I did, having I assume flown the Atlantic.
Early in January 1941 the minister gave a cocktail party at the Dorchester
Hotel to which I, along with all the other field officers at CMHQ, was
invited. The High Commissioner, Vincent Massey, was there, as was my
old preceptor Mike Pearson, now official secretary at Canada House. I
heard golden opinions of Mike on every side; he was, people said, a tremendous asset to Canada in London. He could get on with anybody: with
the military and the civilians, with the British and the Canadians. Another
person I met at that party was Pierre Dupuy. He was just back from his
first famous trip to make contact with Marshal Pétain's government at
Vichy, and he was getting a great deal of mileage out of it. Few greater
diplomatic adventures, one gathered, had ever taken place; his car being
forced off the road by the Gestapo was merely one of the dramatic incidents he had to relate.

Over a month passed after I reached England before I met the man who dominated the Canadian Army Overseas, and indeed the whole Canadian community in Britain — for Lieutenant-General Andrew George Latta McNaughton, General Officer Commanding the Canadian Corps, was Canada's most striking personality of the war period, bar none. His headquarters was near Leatherhead in Surrey. Brigadier Pope intended to take me there and introduce me to the Corps Commander, but the brigadier was taken ill and thereafter was convalescing for some time. So the task of helping me "make my number" with the Corps Commander fell to Lieutenant-Colonel H. A. Young, who was second in command of "G" Branch at CMHQ. Hugh Young was a Permanent Force Signals officer, a graduate of the Northwest Territories and Yukon Radio System, who in later days would be an infantry brigade commander in Normandy, Quartermaster General in Ottawa and, in the end, Deputy Minister of Public Works, and always a good friend of mine. Going to see the Corps Commander — already a legendary figure — was a somewhat alarming prospect at best; but Hugh confided to me, to make things a bit worse, that somebody on the Corps staff had conceived a very curious idea about my functions. This person, whoever he was, clearly could not believe that the authorities in Ottawa would actually send somebody overseas merely to concern himself with history. (*History!*) So he had decided that I had been dispatched to spy on the Corps Commander on behalf of the government. This I pondered cheerfully as the staff car bore Hugh and me towards Leatherhead on the morning of 29 January. How little I need have worried!

As it turned out, I didn't meet Andy McNaughton; I collided with him. His headquarters was in Headley Court, a large Edwardian mansion belonging to the Cunliffe-Lister family. His office was halfway up the main staircase. As Hugh and I approached the door it opened and Andy emerged — characteristically, as I was to discover — as if shot from a gun. When we had, so to speak, sorted ourselves out, Hugh introduced me. The general seized my hand. I have never forgotten his words (their dramatic quality, I was also to discover, was likewise characteristic): "You find us in the midst of a grave constitutional crisis. I'm glad you're here. I need your advice." And, still holding my hand, he drew me into his office and called to his *aide de camp*, "Bring me the Brooke file."

The Corps Commander prefaced the conversation that followed by saying, "Nothing I say to you must go beyond this room." He then showed us a "secret and personal" letter to himself from Major-General G. R. Pearkes, V.C., commanding the 1st Canadian Division, concerning a command and signals exercise, called "Victor," lately concluded. In this, large portions of Pearkes' division had been taken from under his command, over his protests, and placed under British formations; in the end his division was divided between four if not five different commanders. McNaughton clearly intended to make an issue of the matter. It raised, he said, a fundamental constitutional point, involving his own responsibility to the government and people of Canada for the proper handling of the troops entrusted to his command. He asked us whether we thought he was right to do so. I need hardly say we both assented. A lieutenant-colonel and a major were hardly likely to disagree with a lieutenant-general, least of all with Lieutenant-General McNaughton; but forty years later I still think he was right.

Subsequently McNaughton took the matter up with Sir Alan Brooke, then Commander-in-Chief Home Forces, personally and later in writing; and from him he obtained what he considered satisfactory assurances against the Canadian Corps being broken up, or Canadian divisions being subdivided without their commanders' consent. Nevertheless McNaughton recognized that special operational circumstances might sometimes require such action; and he instructed his Canadian divisional commanders that in cases where they might be detached from the Corps and it was desirable that a portion of their divisions might be placed under the command of another formation, their action should be guided "by one principle, namely, that the resources at your disposal are used to obtain the maximum possible effect on the enemy." Brooke went along with Andy in this affair, doubtless feeling he had to; but I think it is clear that he did not like it, and he certainly did not forget it. He threw it up to Andy in 1943, when he was using his influence to remove him from command of the First Canadian Army.[2]

During our conversation the general showed Hugh and me his paper *The Principles of Imperial Defence: A Canadian Aspect*, written while he was at the Imperial Defence College in 1926-27. In this, which I was later able to read at leisure, he suggested that in any future war the position of a Canadian commander with respect to the British command would approximate to that of Sir Douglas Haig *vis-à-vis* Marshal Foch in 1918, which left Haig still accountable to the British government for the safety of his troops.

Even tactically, the paper suggested, the Canadian, while probably under the orders of a British commander-in-chief, would not be "free from responsibility to the Canadian government" in this respect. This paper doubtless shook some of McNaughton's British hearers when it was presented at the IDC, and its ideas were certainly still unacceptable to many British soldiers in 1939-45.

Such was my introduction to Andy McNaughton, Canadian; and I learned more about him a little later on that 29 January when I sat beside him at lunch in his mess. (My old friend Burgon Bickersteth was a little way down the table.) The general mentioned the recent Ogdensburg agreement with the United States and said, with I think some exaggeration, that Canadian soldiers had long been working towards such an arrangement as an expression of the "practicalities" of the North American situation; he mentioned a visit he himself had made to Washington.[3] He also said that the real prime movers towards the constitutional development that led to the Statute of Westminster were soldiers, convinced of the need for it by the experience of the last war. The autonomy of Canada was worked out on the battlefield; and he said that while the last war was still in progress a group of Canadian officers (the only one he mentioned by name was Talbot Papineau) discussed the matter repeatedly and arrived at the conclusion that a wider autonomy was needed. And the general made another remark which I noted and remembered: the "acid test of sovereignty" was the control of the armed forces.[4]

McNaughton at this time was at the height of his personal powers, and the impact of his personality was extraordinary. Meeting him was like shaking hands with a dynamo. He seemed to radiate energy. This sense, combined with the bright eyes, the shaggy hair and eyebrows, the "rather melancholy" expression which I remember an English newspaperman noting, left an indelible feeling of contact with a most remarkable and unusual human being. It was not surprising that the British press should sometimes speculate about McNaughton as a possible Supreme Commander for the future Allied invading forces, though such speculation was highly naïve, disregarding as it did the basic fact that the great powers were certain to reserve that appointment for one of their own.

I should add that McNaughton gave me the strongest assurances of support in the task I was undertaking. I would have, he said, access to all the records of Corps Headquarters, except those concerning future operations. He also told me that if I ever encountered difficulty or opposition I was to come straight to him. Here I may quote something I wrote long afterwards: "I never needed to; though I think I did mention once or twice that the general had made that remark, and the mention was a considerable solvent of difficulties."[5]

One particular little affair brought me into further contact with the Corps Commander at this time. He was a vice-president of the (now Royal) Canadian Geographical Society; and the editor of the *Canadian Geographical Journal* had asked him for an article on the Canadian Army Overseas. The general, having heard that a historian was on the way, suggested that I should write it. During that first visit to Corps Headquarters I submitted an outline; and thereafter I went seriously to work, reading the war diaries and other available sources and putting together the best brief account I could of the rather extraordinary Canadian events in Britain during the past year, including the abortive expedition to France just as that country was collapsing and the part subsequently played by the Canadians in the plans for defending the United Kingdom against the anticipated invasion. On 19 February I gave the draft to the Corps Commander's ADC, Lord Duncannon, to take to him. A few days later I got it back. On the front was a hand-written note which pleased me very much:

Dear Major Stacey

Herewith your draft of article for Cdn Geo. Journal: Brig [Guy] Turner and I have made a few notes in various places which may be of help to you.

My only comment is that I would like to have the number of times my own name is mentioned, considerably reduced, and I would be obliged if you would so arrange.

Both Brig Turner and I consider that you have put together a very remarkable account of our doings in 1 Cdn Div Cdn Force 7 Corps and Cdn Corps and on this I offer my very best congratulations.

Sincerely yours

A McNaughton

24 $\frac{2}{41}$

I was amused to find how little idea McNaughton, a man of remarkable ability, had of how history is written. He said he was astonished that a person not present at the time could produce so adequate an account of events. I replied, quite truly, that he and his staff had kept such complete records that the task was easy. He then remarked that in the desperate circumstances of 1940 he had felt it vital to keep full records of events — if only because they might, in case of disaster, become a subject of inquiry. The appearance of the article was somewhat delayed by the fact that the Germans sank the ship carrying it to Canada. A duplicate was sent and it was published in July 1941.[6]

The article that was published, however, was not quite the article I had written. The text that General McNaughton had approved with so little trouble had to be approved again in Ottawa; and changes were made. Frank Cummins wrote me privately describing the process, and it would be a pity not to let the reader in on it:

> The Minister [Ralston] . . . after praising the article highly, issued a number of instructions, comments and suggestions, some of which wouldn't do at all. . . . In one respect the Director [Duguid] gave way — about Canadian tunnellers at Gibraltar . . .
>
> Your reference to statesmen in Canada not foreseeing the possibility of Canadian troops going overseas in another war, had to go — absolutely. . . .
>
> I hope you will not have ground to quarrel seriously with the editorial changes. I worked with the Director throughout and can assure you that almost every one of them was made at the behest of the Minister. The sentence which you will find has been added at the very end of the article is an exceedingly pale reflection of the purple patch that had been called for. . . .
>
> In the course of passing back and forth between Historical Section, C.G.S. [Chief of the General Staff], Minister and Prime Minister (oh yes, the P.M. had to O.K.) your two letters to Dallyn [the editor] were removed from the file and efforts to recover them have failed. Fortunately, we had taken the precaution to have copies made before the file started out on its journeyings so no harm was done, but otherwise it would have been disastrous. . . .
>
> The pictures — which we had placed in two large envelopes in strict sequence — also got mixed up and came back bearing evidence of much handling: one had disappeared entirely. . . .

Colonel Ralston had even done me the kindness of correcting my grammar, changing "was" to "were" in circumstances in which, Cummins suggested, the change was at least open to argument.

The most extraordinary feature of this transaction is the fact that the wretched article had actually gone up to Mackenzie King. This, combined with the remarkable attention to detail displayed by the Minister of National Defence (which I gather was quite typical of him) leaves one marvelling that the leading members of the Canadian government had nothing better to occupy them in the year of grace 1941. But the article was evidently regarded as affecting the image of the government, and its image was something which that government regarded as very important indeed.

The reader will not be surprised when I say that I had become devoted to General McNaughton. That devotion never left me, and now that he is gone I still remember him with deep respect and affection. I know that his judgment was not the equal of his intellect, and he made serious mistakes, the worst being when he went into politics. But with all his faults he was a great man, and the most compelling personality it has ever been my fortune to encounter.

I have so far said little or nothing about my official job and how I went about it. General Crerar's original letter of October 1940 had defined the task as "the collection and preparation of material for the future use of the official historian and the placing on record of historical material not otherwise recorded or available." That is to say, I was in much the position which Duguid represented himself as having been in at an earlier stage. Nobody knew who the official historian would be or what sort of history he might write. Obviously it was impossible to plan a history in detail in 1940, when it was not even certain we would win the war. Duguid prepared some long-winded draft instructions which were sent overseas in advance of my own departure. When I reached London I found that they had produced an adverse reaction from General McNaughton's staff. As I look at them now, I am not surprised, for they talked of my attending conferences and implied that I should be kept informed of plans for future operations. I suspect that this was the origin of the "spy" idea of which I have spoken. The draft was amended to everybody's satisfaction and in fact the instructions were then largely forgotten and I worked by rule of thumb. (In due course, when people had grown accustomed to my face, I was to be found at conferences and even, sometimes, heard about future operations.) I was required to maintain a monthly diary to be forwarded to Duguid, and my writings were to be sent to him by secure means.[7]

In practice I functioned by producing a series of numbered "reports" on miscellaneous subjects great and small. No. 1 (sent off on 31 December 1940) dealt with the passage of Troop Convoy 8. No. 2 (dispatched on 7 January following) was concerned with the public relations organization at Canadian Military Headquarters. This was a matter of importance to me, for the PR people could do a great deal for me; often I travelled with them, and the correspondents they shepherded, to events that seemed worthy of historical note. The chief public relations officer at CMHQ was Captain (later Colonel) W. G. Abel, a Canadian who had been in advertising, I believe, in London; the brains of the section, I think it is fair to say, were chiefly provided by Lieutenant (later Lieutenant-Colonel) Eric Gibbs. When suitable opportunities arose to visit Canadian units or establishments outside of London I seized them, and used the visits as bases for reports. One trip of unusual length was in May 1941, when I went with a press party to visit companies of the Canadian Forestry Corps working in Scotland. That provided Report No. 29. Field exercises gave me a lot of business; thus at the end of September 1941 I spent several days based in Hertford College, Oxford, as a guest of the War Office, observing Exercise "Bumper," the biggest manoeuvres ever held in England, in which a dozen divisions, including those of the Canadian Corps, fought across the country north and west of London. (Read all about it in Report No. 49.) I also attended the conference on "Bumper" at the Staff College, Camberley, and heard the Chief Umpire, a comparatively unknown general named Montgomery, distribute praise and blame. And all the time I was learning; learning about the Canadian Army Overseas — its organization, its armament, the peculiar and multifarious terms and abbreviations it used in documents. (It was, I remember, Tuzo Wilson, a Princeton friend now an officer in the Engineers, who explained to me, with only slight condescension, that a G.1098 was a unit equipment table.) And not the least important thing I was doing was widening my acquaintance; getting to know people who would be helpful to me in the future.

CMHQ was not at all a bad place to be from this point of view. People from field units were always visiting there; people came and went on postings. One often met the visitors over lunch in the Canadian Officers' Club, which was within a step of the Sun Life Building. It was run by Mrs. Massey, and was sometimes irreverently referred to as "Mother Massey's Hash House." I had heard some fairly disparaging things said about Alice Massey in Canada, but I heard few in London; there she was at her best. Usually she presided over the hot dish herself, and since English rations had a tendency to produce a rather liquid menu she frequently cautioned the customer to "take a spoon." Another gathering place for Canadian officers was the hospitable East India and Sports Club in St. James's Square, which took many Canadians in for the duration; I ate numerous lunches and dinners there.

Life in wartime London, the reader may be thinking, sounds not too unpleasant; nor was it, at least in daytime. At night, before June 1941, it was rather different.

I missed the blitz of September-November 1940; but I was in on London's biggest single raids, beginning with the famous fire raid of 29 December. Life in London under the bombs was a lottery. I was there almost continuously from Christmas 1940 until the end of the war, through the bombing and the V-1s and the V-2s; in all that time I was never in a building that was hit while I was in it, I was never really close to an exploding bomb, and I never saw a dead body. Yet there were people who arrived at our headquarters from Canada and were bombed out the first night. (I should add that I heard a good deal of noise, and I was certainly rather badly frightened on a number of occasions.)

As with everything else in this life, you got used to it. I remember a fairly normal evening: coming out of the Sun Life Building as dusk was falling and crossing Cockspur Street to wait for a bus opposite the statue of George III (not yet evacuated). The siren went, then the guns began; and tiny pieces of metal (bits of anti-aircraft shell) began to tinkle down on the pavement. I put on my tin hat. In a few minutes the big red bus came along, I climbed aboard and paid my pennies to the clippie (the girl conductor) and it bore me off towards Queen's Gardens through the ruckus as if nothing out of the way was happening; and indeed nothing was.

The "big nights," luckily, were not very frequent.[8] On the night of Saturday, 8 March 1941, bombs fell near CMHQ for the first time since my arrival there. I was in the office that night; so, I remember, was the senior Protestant chaplain, Canon C. G. Hepburn of Ottawa, and we exchanged encouraging noises across the floor we were on as the noise outside developed. About nine p.m. we heard the whistle of bombs and explosions shook our building. We found later that those bombs had come down two or three hundred yards away and had demolished a tailor's shop in the Haymarket and Garlands Hotel. Another bomb we certainly heard was the one that smashed into the Café de Paris in Coventry Street and killed a large number of merrymakers, including four Canadian soldiers. April brought the two big raids which we Londoners always spoke of as "the Wednesday and the Saturday" (the 16th and the 19th). About the Wednesday I wrote to Doris, "Its most unpleasant feature was the fact that it made sleep quite impossible, as the sound of engines, A.A. guns and (every so often) bombs kept up continuously from dark until close to dawn; this is the first time this has happened since I have been here." The Saturday I reported, accurately I think, as not in the same class: "My landlord, and a naval commander and his wife, and I had an impromptu party in the basement; I contributed the cake you sent me, which was much appreciated. I was glad I had saved it up. They all remarked that fruit cake like that is impossible to come by in these parts now."

The last of the big raids — the one that killed more people than any other and destroyed the chamber of the House of Commons — came on 10 May. I cabled Doris next day to tell her I was all right, and followed the cable up with a letter:

> Last night's raid was another nasty one, but perhaps not quite as heavy as that of the night of 16 April. This raid was definitely less unpleasant than that one in at least one respect: the B.B.C. reported at one o'clock to-day that 33 German planes had been shot down, and that ought to trouble them. I was just going to bed when the siren went, and as soon as I came to the conclusion that it was going to be a large occasion I got up and put on battle-dress and my helmet and went out to see what things looked like. I spent some time with our local A.R.P. [Air Raid Precautions] wardens. These civil defence workers are really amazingly calm and composed about the whole thing, and are interesting to talk to. They come from all classes and their accents are correspondingly mixed. Several times we heard machine-gun fire overhead (a very pleasant sound in such circumstances) and once I saw an actual air fight, with tracer bullets flying in both directions. At the end of the exchange, I believe I saw the plane that was being chased catch fire, though I

could not be certain. Of course, you never see the planes (so far I have not laid eyes on a German machine, though I have *heard* plenty of them); but the fiery tracer and the sound of guns tells you when a fight is on. After a bit I found myself getting cold, and I went indoors and spent the rest of the night until things began to slacken off with my landlord and his wife in the lower part of the house. The raid was less violent towards the end, though there were still noisy spasms of gunfire.

I remember the landlord relieving his feelings, as we sat on the floor in the lower hall, by saying, "Devils! Devils!"

That phase of London's ordeal was almost over; for the Germans were turning east. On 22 June, unbelievably, Hitler attacked Russia. I remember two things about that development. One is reading the War Office intelligence summaries before that date, which quite accurately forecast what was about to happen, and reflecting that the poor old War House was obviously one hundred per cent wrong again. The other is dining with Hugh Young at the Mount Royal Hotel a day or two after the attack. He had spent a good part of the day going around the War Office collecting opinions of the Russian outlook for the information of Ottawa. The consensus he got was that Russia would be finished off in three weeks. That time the War House really was one hundred per cent wrong.

For all the danger and discomfort, most of us who were there felt that there was no better place to be than London in those days of 1940-41. The North American academic world which I had for the moment put behind me seemed distant and unreal. Occasionally I received bulletins from it. Friends in the Princeton History Department reported a great disruption in the department; different friends gave different versions, but it was clear that there had been much unpleasantness. One wrote, "We have had histrionics, heroics, and (what really caused most of the trouble) the feeling that a small clique of favorites was running the department." In the midst of the turmoil Ray Sontag resigned as chairman and took off for a new post in California. I wonder whether the strain of the war was telling even in that remote neutral backwater. I was not sorry to be out of it. The most encouraging manifestation was a letter from Ray which seemed to indicate that that redoubtable isolationist had totally changed his views of a year before.

Doris had gone back temporarily to her old job in the University of Toronto library, where she was in contact with the Canadian academic scene, in which it was evident the old isolationism was not yet entirely dead. I was moved in the spring of 1941 to write her a letter in which I let myself go a bit on the subject of the war and mentioned Donald Creighton:

> I have thought of Don a number of times lately, recalling his apparent personal resentment against the war (though it is hard to see what it has done to *him*) and his disgust with people who give way to "nationalism" under the stress of these times. Just why a scholar, of all people, should fail to appreciate the nature of the issues that are being fought out in this war with the Nazis is beyond me; I don't like this war either, but the more I think about it the more I come to the conclusion that there is no slightest chance of a reversion to decent normal ways of living without Hitler & Gang being thoroughly smashed. And I think that that is more and more the light in which people in this country, which is suffering so heavily, are seeing the question; they are thinking simply of getting back to decent living, with the lights on again and a chance to enjoy their old pleasures and nobody to make them afraid — and they know that there is only one way to get back. Leslie Howard made a movie short lately in which he defined the British war aims as "Life, liberty and the pursuit of happiness," and while this was doubtless partly intended as propaganda directed towards the States I found myself wondering whether the phrase wasn't more truly applicable today than in the rather unimportant little crisis which led Thomas Jefferson to coin it.

I rarely inflicted such homespun philosophy upon my wife, and I ended up by writing, "But forgive my talking like a newspaper writer."

Chapter 7

Aftermath of a Dress Rehearsal

A fter the German attack on Russia the threat of an invasion of Britain, which had given the Canadians there the feeling that they were doing a useful job, rapidly receded. But they remained in England, still training, and looking forward now to a share in some great offensive movement against German-occupied Europe. Such an enterprise began to look more practicable after December 1941, when Pearl Harbor blew the United States into the war.

The Canadian force in Britain had continued to grow, and in April 1942 the headquarters of the First Canadian Army was set up there, with General McNaughton as Army Commander. My friend General Crerar gave up the post of Chief of the General Staff to come overseas and take command of the Canadian Corps (now to be the 1st Canadian Corps) in succession to McNaughton. Late in 1941 this corps moved into Sussex and came under the operational command of the General Officer Commanding-in-Chief the British South-Eastern Command. Lieutenant-General B. L. Montgomery, soon to be famous, shortly took over this appointment.

On my humble level I watched and recorded these events. My domestic arrangements altered. Nick McCarter having long since departed to command anti-aircraft units at Colchester, I was alone at Queen's Gardens;

and at the beginning of August 1941 I set up housekeeping with two "technical liaison" officers, Fraser Fulton and Tuzo Wilson, in Epsom, with a batman to "do" for us. But we found the long journeys by way of blacked-out trains and stations rather tiresome. Moreover, the house lacked central heating, and we Canadians, like the Romans, insisted on this; so when our lease ran out at the end of three months we moved to the other side of London, settling at 36 Meadway, Hampstead Garden Suburb, a corner of the capital with a charm all its own. The household now consisted of Fulton, myself and Arnold Peck, another technical type, a Permanent Force Signals officer who rose deservedly to brigadier and is still a good friend of mine. We travelled to and from work by the Northern Line of the London Underground, walking from Golders Green station across the corner of the Hampstead Heath Extension. One of the attractions of Meadway was the neighbours. The Coleman family consisted of Reg, a lawyer who had served in the Artists' Rifles in the old war, his wife Meda who had distinguished herself by writing to the War Office asking for a supply of hand grenades so she could drop them from an upper window on the heads of invading Germans coming down Meadway, a son in the navy, and three charming daughters. Around the corner were David and Gladys Patey; David was a surgeon at Middlesex Hospital. Nicer people it would have been impossible to imagine. Nearly forty years later, I still exchange Christmas greetings with those of the group who are still around.

In September 1942 we lost our Meadway house, and I moved back to Queen's Gardens, lucky to get in. But we missed the pleasant suburb and our friends there; and when, in May 1943, 38 Meadway became available, Fraser Fulton and I hastened to rent it. There I stayed, with a succession of different officer housemates and batmen, until after the end of the war. Hampstead had not suffered greatly from the attentions of the enemy; and when the flying bombs began coming to London in 1944 it turned out to be a better 'ole than most, for these things tended to fall short. The southeast got more than its share of them; in the northwest we got the "overs," which were not terribly numerous.

Meanwhile, those early months passed in peaceful succession, and all I had to chronicle was such things as a detachment's bloodless expedition to Spitsbergen in the summer of 1941 or Exercise "Tiger," Monty's great endurance test carried out in May 1942. And then suddenly there was a very bloody Canadian battle, and I wasn't there.

I had acquired the habit of using my periods of "privilege leave" to visit parts of Britain that I didn't know, or wanted to know better. Companionship being hard to arrange, these trips had to be solitary, but I was fairly used to solitude. Walking or biking, I got a few days' exercise such as seldom came the way of a Whitehall warrior when on the job (though we did sometimes play softball in Hyde Park). Thus in July 1941 I spent a leave at the Bull at Burford, west of Oxford. One of my trips from there was down to the Vale of White Horse, which I had never seen. I looked forward to seeing the ancient White Horse itself, on its famous hill; but when I cycled into the village of Uffington, from which it should have been visible, no Horse was in sight. A young woman (she might have been the schoolmistress) came along wheeling a bicycle. I inquired politely about the Horse. She looked uncomfortable and hurried off without replying. This was so un-English that I was bothered. I tried another villager and to my astonishment got the same result. Then along came the Oldest Inhabitant, and I tried again. The Oldest Inhabitant looked at me keenly and said (this is absolutely and literally true), "Ye beant a German, be ye?" I said, no, I was merely a wandering Canadian. He then told me, what I had of course begun to suspect, that the Horse had been blacked out to prevent its being used by the Luftwaffe as an aid to navigation. This was clearly Uffington's own great War Secret, and somebody had drilled the villagers carefully in the importance of keeping it. I never have seen the White Horse of the White Horse Vale.

And then in August 1942 I went to Scotland. I had acquired an affection for Blair Atholl and the Atholl Arms Hotel when visiting the Forestry Corps, and now I went back there. After a night in Edinburgh I reached the Atholl Arms in time for lunch on Wednesday, 19 August; and there I heard the news. The Canadians had raided Dieppe that morning.

I telephoned CMHQ and asked if I should come back. They didn't seem to think there was much point in it. I spent two days walking in the glorious Highland scenery; but I was troubled. I wanted to get back and hear what had really happened, and to start work on what was clearly going to be a big job.

That I had known nothing at all about the planned raid was the result, in part at least, of being stationed at CMHQ. Nobody there, not even General Montague, had been let into the secret, even though CMHQ controlled the hospitals that would have to deal with the casualties. In these circumstances, it would have been hard to tell *me*. It is true that both my formal instructions and General McNaughton informally had made it clear that I could not be informed about future operations. Even so, I think it is possible that General McNaughton or General Crerar might have let me in on Dieppe if they had thought of me. Nobody on a lower level would have ventured. At any rate, I wasn't in on the raid, and I have always been sorry. Of course, if I had been there I mightn't have survived to write about it.

A note I wrote for my family the day I got back to London serves as a record of first impressions:

> ... I made my way down to the office to hear the talk about the raid. As the newspapers have said, our casualties were quite heavy; I shall not go into details at the moment, but a lot of good fellows whom I had got to know are either dead or missing. It is our first real casualty list of the war (after nearly three years!) and it is not easy to get used to the idea of so many friends and acquaintances being suddenly snuffed out. But it seems to be agreed that our fellows did well; the show went off to schedule; the damage to the Hun must have been very considerable (especially to his nerves); and one keeps on hearing of individual deeds of gallantry. ... There will be repercussions of Dieppe in our newspapers for some time to come; and I am quite sure that it will be months before my own job in connection with it will be finished.

That last remark at least was an understatement. I may introduce the story of what followed by quoting my next letter to Doris; the date is 14 September 1942:

> I have gone more than a fortnight without writing to you. This is unprecedented and very disgraceful; but it has an explanation, which is the fact that during the said fortnight I have spent more time out of London than in any similar period since I came to this country, and have worked harder (I almost think) than ever before in my life. ...
>
> The cause of my journeyings and my hard work is, of course, the Dieppe affair. I have been given, not one, but several special jobs in connection with it, none of them really within my normal sphere. First I was given a job connected with recommendations for honours and awards for gallantry arising out of the raid; and before that job was

more than begun I was called in to work on an account of the operation for release in Canada. The latter job was interesting, but as always in such cases it entailed a long struggle with the security experts as to what it was and was not safe to publish for fear of helping the Hun, and the finish of the argument left me exhausted and generally the worse for wear. Inevitably also the result was that I had little time for the honours job and had to leave it to two helpers who had been given me; this had the further result that I have just spent two days more in the country working all day and a considerable part of the night to set right the things that they did wrongly or inadequately...

The honours job needs little more description. It had its origin in the simple fact that General Crerar was displeased with the form in which the recommendations were presented to him, and I was called in to put them into better English. This work I did at Headquarters 2nd Division, which was in a country house near Horsham, Sussex. It brought me into contact with Major-General J. H. Roberts, the divisional commander, whom I think I had not met before. I remember his manner as subdued, and I suspect he was still in something like a state of shock as a result of having had a great part of his division shot to pieces in a single morning.

The other task cannot be so briefly dealt with. It began with a cable which General McNaughton received from Ottawa on 27 August. It began, "There is a feeling here that the public ought to have some authoritative statement in the form of a white paper or some similar document prepared by Canadian Army or CMHQ in which the participation of the Canadians at Dieppe is dealt with in a factual way as a military operation from the time they left England until they returned with some indication of the preparation necessary...." On the 31st I was called from Horsham to CMHQ and told that I was to write this "white paper." I cannot help recalling at this point that my famous instructions of 1940, as finally approved, provided that I would not be called upon "to produce a contemporary history or, as a general rule, to write press releases or current commentary relating to the Canadian forces for present publication." No one thought of these now, and I should not have dreamed of recalling them. I seemed to be functioning as a sort of writer-in-ordinary to the Canadian Army Overseas, and I found life very interesting if a bit strenuous.

At CMHQ on 31 August I met Brigadier M.H.S. Penhale, General McNaughton's Brigadier General Staff, and Brigadier Churchill Mann.

Brigadier Mann had been the senior Canadian staff officer involved with Dieppe, as General Roberts' G.S.O. 1 at the 2nd Division. When the raid was revived after being cancelled, he had been promoted to the job of Brigadier General Staff at H.Q. 1st Canadian Corps , but he was lent back to General Roberts and was present on 19 August as the senior army officer in the duplicate headquarters ship provided in case Roberts' ship should meet with an accident. He was a bright, very articulate young man with a reputation as a wit. He had lately visited the Canadian divisions and lectured to officers on the raid. Unfortunately I didn't hear his lecture, but people who did told me that he kept his audiences in stitches with his comic account of the affair. I remember thinking how very different the military and the civilian attitudes were towards bloodshed, and how shocked people at home would have been had they heard about this. It's possible that after the full grim facts had had time to sink in, the military attitude, including Mann's, might have been rather more chastened.

After the request from Ottawa had been explained to me, the two brigadiers, with me tagging along, went across to Combined Operations Headquarters, which was in a modern building in Richmond Terrace off Whitehall. We saw the Vice Chief of Combined Operations, Lord Louis Mountbatten's second-in-command, Major-General J.C. Haydon. Penhale explained the situation and said that as it was now known that the enemy had captured a copy of our operation order it was considered that security was less important and a statement based on General Roberts' preliminary report might now be issued. Haydon saw no objection but said he would consult the Chief of Combined Operations. I went back to 2nd Division and the job on honours.

On 2 September I heard from Penhale that the CCO had given approval in principle to the issuance of a statement; I was told to draft it. I at once proceeded to do so. Next day I completed it and in the afternoon drove over to Headley Court where General McNaughton and Brigadier Penhale read it and indicated some desired changes. I revised it that evening, had it typed and next morning started off to London, in accordance with General McNaughton's instructions, to get it cleared at Combined Operations Headquarters.

That 4th of September was one of the worst days I remember. At CMHQ I reported to Hugh Young, now Brigadier General Staff and my boss. He spoke to General Haydon, who said I was to show the draft to one Colonel Neville. At five to two I telephoned Colonel Neville, who was at lunch, and left my number. At ten to three I called again and was told that Neville was at a meeting. I explained that the matter was urgent and said that General Haydon knew what it was about. At ten to four, to my surprise, Haydon phoned me and asked what the trouble was. I told him I was awaiting a call from Neville. He switched me over to Neville; I briefly explained the situation (he seemed to know nothing about it) and he told me to come over at once. I did so, but when I reached COHQ I was not able to see Neville. I was shown into the waiting-room and after some delay a Squadron-Leader Gillman of the COHQ Public Relations Section arrived and introduced himself. He did not invite me into his office, but read the draft in the waiting-room, said that he believed some points would have to be excised, and added that it would be difficult to deal with the matter that evening. I left the draft with him and said I would communicate with my superiors and phone later.

After consulting Hugh Young I phoned COHQ and left a message for Gillman telling him that Ottawa was pressing, and that it was greatly desired to have the matter settled that evening. About ten to seven Neville telephoned me. He said strongly that the draft was objectionable: "The CCO will not give this his blessing; we definitely don't like it." I told him I would report to my superiors. I reported by telephone to Hugh and on his instructions phoned Army Headquarters and left a message describing the situation for Brigadier Penhale. Leaving a copy of my draft for Hugh, I went back to 2nd Division Headquarters and my honours and awards job.

The next day was, if anything, rather worse. At lunchtime Hugh Young telephoned me at Horsham and told me to come back to CMHQ at once to work with the Combined Operations public relations people on revising the release. I apologized to General Roberts, left a copy of the draft release with him, and drove to London, getting there about four o'clock. At CMHQ Hugh told me that he had seen Lord Louis Mountbatten that morning. The Chief of Combined Operations had shown some disgust over the Canadians' loss of the operation order (I remember Hugh reporting him as remarking that even Boy Scouts knew better than that) and had ruled that nothing was to be published that would in any way tend to *admit* the loss.* He said that publication of my draft would be worth £500,000 to the Germans. The COHQ public relations types were now at work revising it.

At COHQ I received a very considerable surprise. I found that the task of rewriting my draft had been confided to a United States officer, a Major Lawrence. I did not know then, but learned much later from Quentin Reynolds' book *Dress Rehearsal*, that Jock Lawrence was a product of Hollywood, who a few months before had been working for Metro-Goldwyn-Mayer. (In retrospect, it seems perhaps not altogether unsuitable that a man who had done publicity for Sam Goldwyn should now be doing publicity for Dickie Mountbatten.) There were already a good many U.S. officers on the Combined Operations staff. There were no Canadians. Putting an American on this job was, to say the least, extraordinarily tactless. At the time, I fear I suspected it of being a calculated insult. Now, I am inclined to think it was just an exceptional piece of stupidity. What Lawrence had done was predictable. In the words of my notes made at the time, "He had cut out many facts and substituted adjectives; his draft (which he pointed out was merely a basis for discussion, 'for me to blue-pencil') was in terms which could not be issued by the Cdn Govt. I discussed it fairly amicably with him and S/L Gillman and then carried it back to CMHQ where I discussed it with Brig. Young. He instructed me to revise it the next day, putting it back, as far as possible, into the *form* of my original." I'm afraid I have rarely been angrier than I was when I left Mountbatten's establishment that day. Hugh Young recalled afterwards that I came into his office white-faced; he had never seen me that way before.

To end a long story briefly, I revised the white paper again over the weekend. Brigadier Young approved it, and Gillman and Lawrence thought it acceptable with some very minor changes. General McNaughton likewise approved, the CCO finally gave his blessing, the Ministry of Information gave formal censorship approval, and on 9 September I handed it to my brigadier for dispatch to Ottawa by bomber. The Minister of National

---

* Nobody presumably pointed out to the CCO that the origin of the trouble was the fact that the order itself (which he had approved) authorized each brigade headquarters to take two copies ashore.

Defence released it on the 18th. To our astonishment, it got rather extraordinary play in the London press. The *Daily Telegraph* printed it verbatim (all 4,000 words of it); *The Times* printed a long summary. I wrote to Doris, "This is good in one respect at least: the first reports were unfortunate in that they tended to conceal the fact that the scrap was mainly a Canadian show. That, I think, has now been set right." In Canada the impact was probably less; for three days earlier the Department of National Defence had released the full Dieppe casualty list. That dreadful roster filled half a dozen newspaper pages. After that my narrative (rendered more anodyne by COHQ's cuts) must have seemed like a somewhat lame apologia. The anti-government Toronto *Globe and Mail* printed it on page three. The *New York Times*, however, put it on the front page and called it "a plain-spoken résumé"; which perhaps was more than it deserved.

What were the cuts COHQ made, to prevent the Germans getting information worth £500,000? There were a lot of them; I shall mention only the major ones. I had quoted the local objectives of the raid from the operation order. This was cut. Details about the decision to withdraw were deleted. A statement that many of the objectives were not attained went by the board. The account of the pre-raid training was almost entirely removed. We had given the names of the commanders of the Canadian units involved; these were allowed to stand, but those of the British commanders were cut. Finally, it amuses me now to note a change that was made in the paragraph concerning command. I had written, "The whole operation was under the general supervision, and the plans were subject to the approval, of Vice-Admiral Lord Louis Mountbatten, G.C.V.O., D.S.O., Chief of Combined Operations. Canadian plans were concerted with the latter by Lieutenant-General H.D.G. Crerar, D.S.O., General Officer Commanding a Canadian Corps." As published, this became, "Canadian plans were concerted with the Chief of Combined Operations (Vice-Admiral Lord Louis Mountbatten, G.C.V.O., D.S.O.) by Lieutenant-General H.D.G. Crerar, D.S.O., General Officer Commanding a Canadian Corps." The Canadian reader was thus denied any real understanding of the important part played by Lord Louis and his headquarters in the affair.[1]

Written prematurely and hurriedly, to meet an immediate official need, as history the white paper left much to be desired, quite apart from the laming effect of the censorship. It contained one serious factual error, the statement that a radar station was captured. This was included in the original COHQ communiqué, and the capture was in fact reported and logged during the operation; but it didn't happen. And General Crerar (who ought to have seen the draft before publication, but did not) pointed out to me that the phrase used to describe the fate of the Royal Regiment of Canada on Blue Beach ("only a temporary lodgement was obtained") was unsuitable; the lodgement was only too permanent. But Colonel Ralston must have felt that the paper met his needs, for he incorporated almost the whole of it in his speech introducing his next estimates in Parliament. I suspect it bored the House of Commons stiff.

One final post-Dieppe anecdote. Hugh Young (who always seemed to pick up the best and most authentic London gossip) told me that on the day after the raid Mountbatten appeared at the American headquarters in Grosvenor Square with "a bushel basket of decorations" for the small detachment of American Rangers who had accompanied the Commandos in the raid. (He didn't come to CMHQ.) I, in my simplicity, asked why Lord Louis should be so much interested in sucking up to the Yanks? Hugh's reply was, "He wants to be a Supreme Commander." And Lord Louis became exactly that the following year.

The repercussions of Dieppe have continued to the present day. An early one happened in March 1943 with the publication of Quentin Reynolds' book *Dress Rehearsal: The Story of Dieppe*. Reynolds was an American correspondent who had acquired much popularity in Britain with his books *The Wounded Don't Cry* (1940), *London Diary* (1941) and *Only the Stars Are Neutral* (1942). Mountbatten gave him an interview and greatly impressed him. Mountbatten's staff, notably my friend Major Lawrence, arranged for him to be present at Dieppe in the headquarters ship *Calpe*. (People who were in *Calpe* told me that he was never on deck the whole time the ship was off Dieppe. General Roberts' batman warned the people in the wardroom at the end that the destroyer was pulling out and that they had better go on deck if they wanted to see anything. Reynolds, I was assured, reluctantly laid down his glass and moved towards the ladder; at that moment, however, there was a particularly loud bang "upstairs" and Reynolds returned to his seat.) He had, of course, no knowledge of the planning; but in his book he asserted that General McNaughton had insisted that his troops should be used in the raid. He very strongly implied that Mountbatten had made a good plan, based on attacking from the flanks, but that the Canadians had changed it, inserting the frontal attack on the town. And he said that General Roberts handled the attack differently from "Mountbatten's way," bringing reserves "from the flanks" to reinforce the faltering frontal attack. The third of these charges has some substance, in that Ham Roberts did continue to reinforce the main beaches (though not "from the flanks") when in the light of hindsight it would have been better to abandon the operation. Roberts' defence must be that the information he had about conditions on the beaches was both limited and inaccurate.[2] The first charge is quite untrue; Andy McNaughton would never have pressed for putting his forces into action merely for the sake of action, as I know from hearing him talk on various occasions. It is the case, however, that General Crerar, who held quite different views on this matter, took advantage of being in command in McNaughton's absence in Canada in February and March 1942 to urge Montgomery, Sir Alan Brooke and Mountbatten to give the Canadians opportunities in raids. Perhaps Reynolds' statement is a garbled version of this.

As for the second and most important charge, concerning the origins of the frontal attack, it is entirely unfounded. The frontal attack was part of the Outline Plan for the operation, which was complete before any Canadian had anything to do with the planning. There are no really contemporary records of the making of the Outline Plan (at least, no one has ever found any), but a somewhat later account in the COHQ records says that the naval officers were opposed to a frontal attack but indicates that it was insisted upon by officers from GHQ Home Forces; so some anonymous officer of the British Army seems to get the discredit. It was certainly not any Canadian; nor, apparently, was it Mountbatten, though he accepted and approved the orders. Incidentally, Reynolds says, rather curiously, of the chapter in which he makes these allegations, "This chapter was, I am sure, read by the Office of Combined Operations."

On 13 March I was summoned to Army Headquarters. National Defence Headquarters had requested General McNaughton's comments on the remarks in the Reynolds book for incorporation in "a corrective statement" by the minister. Supposedly the Army Commander wanted my advice. Andy really needed no advice from me; but I stood beside him as he stood at his tall desk and drafted a reply. Perhaps I had better quote my notes, including his remarks about the Chief of Combined Operations:

The General said his problem was to deal with the matter without starting a feud in this country. He believes that the half-truths contained in the Reynolds book as quoted by NDHQ (the clear implication of which is that a good plan made by Lord Louis Mountbatten was subsequently altered for the worse and that the matter was badly handled by General Roberts on the spot) had their origin in the C.C.O. or one of his staff [this, indeed, is pretty obvious from the book]. General McNaughton said that he considered the C.C.O. "a public menace," but we could not engage in public controversy on the matter. He drafted Tel. No. G.S. 554 suggesting a statement by the Minister in general terms; I brought the draft back to C.M.H.Q. where it was shown to Brig [Elliot] Rodger [now Brigadier General Staff] and despatched. . . .

General McNaughton remarked today that he felt it most undesirable that the Germans should have any knowledge of his constitutional position as an independent commander; if they knew that he was in fact responsible only to the Cdn Govt, they wd certainly attempt to exploit this knowledge, both in propaganda and in operations in the field. . . .

The General said that he considered the statement in GS 554 a baldly true account; the planning of Dieppe had been most careful, and there were no reflections to be made on the manner in which the operation had been conducted. If an investigation of the affair (similar to that on the Hong Kong affair) was to be made, General McNaughton wd resign and let the investigation proceed; but it was impossible for a General to carry the burden of an investigation while also retaining a command in the field.

McNaughton's cable declined to contribute to such a statement as was proposed on the ground that it would prejudice Canadian relations with the British authorities, particularly the Chief of Combined Operations, would "be interpreted as seeking to shift responsibility from us to them," and would give useful information to the enemy. Of this I wrote later, "It was a sound and patriotic decision, but one which in the end probably did General McNaughton himself considerable harm." The Reynolds allegations went unrefuted, and McNaughton's image, and I think that of Canadian generalship at large, was somewhat tarnished in Canada. Mountbatten's image, on the other hand, did not suffer at all from the spectacular failure of the biggest operation his headquarters ever sponsored. The Reynolds book, with its almost comically inflated description of the C.C.O. ("hard, cold, shrewd — the perfect war leader") was a triumph of public relations. Looking at it all these years afterwards, I find myself wondering whether perhaps it may have had just a little to do with Mountbatten's appointment a few months after it was published as Supreme Commander, South-East Asia.

The libellous story that the Canadians were responsible for the frontal attack has gone marching on through the decades. Lord Mountbatten himself, who in his later years tended to talk about Dieppe "without book," helped to keep it going. In September 1973, in a speech in Toronto, he told the story of Home Forces' responsibility for the frontal attack but insisted on dragging the Canadians in too, saying, "this was what the army and air force authorities — the Canadians in particular — insisted on." I thought of taking up the matter in the local press but didn't; but when the speech was published in the *Journal of the Royal United Services Institute for Defence Studies* (London) I wrote a letter to the editor politely pointing out this and other errors, including a wholly inaccurate account of the shackling of prisoners after the raid. The editor sent my letter to Lord Mountbatten, who wrote a reply. The editor insisted on improving both letters before publishing them; we both accepted his emendations, and the admiral and I exchanged amicable personal letters.[3] He agreed he should withdraw the words "the Canadians in particular," and the whole reference to shackling; but I think he still did not appreciate the point that it was when the Outline Plan was being made that the frontal attack was put in, and that the Canadians had not appeared on the scene at that stage.

Beyond the immediate tasks with which the Dieppe raid saddled me in the weeks after it took place lay a much larger and longer one. Dieppe provided me with the heaviest job of historical research that fell to me during the war. It was going to be of great importance to the future official historian; it was obviously going to continue to be a centre of controversy; and it was an extremely complicated operation, fought in five different areas on land as well as in the air and on the sea. Putting together documented narratives of it took up all the time I could spare from other tasks for the better part of two years.

I began with a "preliminary report" (No. 83) which was simply the draft of our white paper before it was emasculated by COHQ with some appended notes. I sent it off to Ottawa on 22 September 1942, and then went seriously to work. The documentation was large. There was the enormous operation order (people laugh at it, but its size was mainly the result of the loading tables; there had to be a detailed table showing the men, vehicles and equipment that had to go on every craft, and there were 237 craft). Corps Headquarters had arranged for every man who returned from the raid to write a personal narrative of his experiences, and while some men undoubtedly avoided doing this many did it, and the result was a fascinating mass of evidence. I supplemented this by numerous interviews, of which I wrote memoranda. There were corps and division files, and a great number of miscellaneous documents, including message logs.

In the beginning there were great gaps in our knowledge, for many of the men who could have given us information were dead or in German prison camps. (Of the seven Canadian unit commanding officers who landed, only one came back; two were killed, the rest were prisoners.) With the passage of time, the gaps were gradually filled. Escaped prisoners turned up in London, each with something to add to the picture, some with a great deal. Captain G. A. Browne, a highly intelligent artillery officer who had landed with the Royal Regiment of Canada, appeared in January 1943 and added to what we knew about that tragic episode. In October 1943 something very important happened, when our first batch of prisoners exchanged on medical grounds arrived from Germany. Among them was Major C. E. Page of the Calgary Tank Regiment. We had known next to nothing about the action of the tanks ashore, for almost nobody — and no officer — who had been in a tank on shore had come back. But Major Page had held conferences in the camp where he and most of the other officers of his unit were confined, and was able to tell us where nearly every tank had gone and what it had done. For the first time the tank story was clear to me. In the spring of 1944 Lieutenant L. C. Counsell of the Royal Hamilton Light Infantry was repatriated from Germany, bringing with him, in addition to much information in his head, a narrative by his commanding officer, Lieutenant-Colonel R. R. Labatt, secreted in a false bottom of his water-bottle. About the same time we got our first information from the other side. Allied forces somewhere captured documents which included a German account of Dieppe. For the complete German picture, and the chance to talk to the main body of the Canadian prisoners, we had of course to wait until the end of the war.

Dieppe added to my burdens in another way. I found myself "liaising" with various British authorities who wanted information about the raid. A month after the operation Hilary St. George Saunders turned up in my office. In normal times librarian of the House of Commons, he had acquired fame as the author of the Ministry of Information's vivid and highly successful booklet *The Battle of Britain*, published in the spring of 1941. (It was published anonymously, but it soon became known that Saunders was the writer.) I presume that this led Lord Louis Mountbatten to enlist him as "Combined Operations Recorder." Now Mountbatten had told him to produce with all speed a detailed report on the raid for confidential circulation. He had been to Generals McNaughton, Crerar and Roberts, and according to him they had all promised full co-operation but told him I was the person to see. As it happened, before the raid there had already been an arrangement made for exchange of information between our offices. In the weeks that followed I was kept busy feeding him documents. When his report (which I had read and commented on in draft) appeared in the form of a naval "confidential book" it was very useful to me, not so much for the narrative as for the British documents that were appended to it. In due course General Robert Laycock, Mountbatten's successor at Combined Operations Headquarters, gave me full access to all the COHQ records; and after the shooting was over I spent a night in the battleship *Ramillies* at Portsmouth, interviewing Rear-Admiral John Hughes-Hallett, who as a captain had been Naval Force Commander at Dieppe, and reading the papers about the raid that he had preserved.

Early in 1943 we discovered that Saunders had been writing for publication another Ministry of Information booklet entitled *Combined Operations*, containing a long account of Dieppe. We did not see this until it was in proof, when it was sent to Canada House by the Ministry of Information. Apart from various minor errors, there was a glaring omission: no mention was made of the Canadian casualties. Saunders' explanation was lame, and on our insistence the casualty figures were put in. The new Canadian Chief of the General Staff, Lieutenant-General Ken Stuart, was in London, and in conversation with me he was very firm on this point. The person I dealt with at the Ministry of Information was a Mr. C. Day Lewis, who was very accommodating.

The long series of reports on Dieppe that I produced (some of them running to many pages) were not intended for publication; they were for the use of the unknown person who would write the future history. They were in narrative form, but they quoted all the important pieces of evidence *in extenso*. The idea was that the historian could write straight from them, and would not need to go again to the original documents. This was perhaps a little too much to hope. In the end, as it turned out, I was the historian myself, and I certainly found those reports valuable, though new information continued to come to hand to the moment of publication, and after. In writing the Dieppe story, at least, I could be grateful for having been so fully immersed in the facts during the months and years following 19 August 1942.

Forty years after, Dieppe continues to excite controversy. About a dozen books have been written about the raid. The media go on worrying the subject. The Canadian Broadcasting Corporation rediscovers Dieppe every few years and produces another elaborate television program about it. It keeps turning up in the press. In these circumstances, I cannot resist the temptation to make a few comments myself.

Many people at the time were convinced that the Germans had had advance warning of the raid and were waiting for us. This was particularly true of our men who became prisoners; various Germans told them so. The explanation of this is evident: there was a general alert in effect all along the coast, simply because moon and tide were right for raiding on 19 August. People still assert that the Germans were warned. But it is quite clear that the Germans at Dieppe had no foreknowledge of the raid. Evidence at the time indicated this — the fact that a German convoy was wandering down the coast towards Dieppe at the moment of our attack, the fact that the German air force took hours to get into action after the raid began. Still more conclusive, however, is the evidence of the German documents. The battle is extraordinarily fully documented on the German side. I read a tremendous stack of German war diaries, from the regimental level up to the Commander-in-Chief West; they all told the same story — no warning whatever previous to the moment of the collision with the convoy. There are some matters about Dieppe, and many about other aspects of the history of the war, about which I am not prepared to express a confident opinion; but this is not one of them. It has been suggested that a warning reached Hitler's headquarters; if it did, and I have seen no real evidence that it did, it was not passed to the garrison at Dieppe.

Seen in the clear light of hindsight, the Dieppe plan of attack does not appear as a good plan. The people at Combined Operations Headquarters made a doubtful decision when they chose as a "target" a town on a coast mainly composed of unscalable cliffs, with the largest opening, at the town itself, commanded by high headlands on either side. The further decision, to attack frontally at Dieppe instead of relying on flank landings, likewise seems to have been a fundamental mistake, though arguments of some apparent weight were adduced in favour of it at the time; as we have seen, the responsibility appears to rest with anonymous British army officers. The Canadian error was in accepting the Outline Plan based on this idea. It would be easy to make game of Colonel Mann writing in the beginning that the plan seems to offer "almost a fantastic conception" of the place to land tanks, and then going on to convince himself, and advise General Roberts, that it is acceptable.[4] In May 1942, I think, however, almost any Canadian staff officer would have done the same. Canadians had been in England since 1939, and had seen no action. To turn down the Dieppe plan, and let some British division take on the operation, would have been virtually inconceivable. If Dieppe had been done without Canadians taking part, there would have been a howl of rage from every Canadian formation in the United Kingdom.

Of the ultimate value of the raid to the Allied cause I have no doubt, though some of the dividends were not at all what the Dieppe planners had expected. A good many tactical and organizational ideas were suggested, or given new emphasis, by the Dieppe experience; and some specific items of assault equipment were developed as a result of it, and used with effect on the Normandy D Day. But above all, there was a fundamental effect on Allied thinking at high levels about the problems of a major assault on the coast of Europe. General Crerar pointed out just after D Day that until Dieppe people believed that such an assault could be carried out "on the basis of securing tactical surprise, and without dependence on overwhelming fire support." The Allied plans for major assault operations in existence at the time of Dieppe (I took some trouble to get hold of them) are simply the Dieppe plan writ larger. These plans were quietly abandoned from that moment, and instead of an attack supported by nothing heavier than small destroyers and Boston bombers we begin to hear of tremendous fire support — battleships, cruisers, heavy bombers, army artillery firing from the sea: the picture of D Day. Lord Mountbatten's contention that "the battle of Normandy was won on the beaches of

Dieppe"[5] may have been a bit exaggerated, but it makes a great deal of sense all the same.

Some authors, and some writers for the media, have grossly sensationalized Dieppe. The casualty list makes it easy meat for people with a tendency this way. Bad mistakes were made, and there was also some remarkably bad luck; there was a very skilful and determined enemy. As a result great numbers of lives were lost. This sort of thing happens in war. But this has not been enough for the writers I mention. Not content with describing the honest mistakes that were made, they have also felt it necessary to suggest that people involved in planning and executing the raid were moved by disreputable motives. The late Terence Robertson was one of the leading sensationalizers, and the title of his 1962 book, *Dieppe: The Shame and the Glory*, well exemplifies what I mean. Glory there was at Dieppe and, as I have said, mistakes; but shame? Robertson never explains what the word is intended to connote; but the imputation seems clear. A more recent team of writers, in a book based on the CBC's latest presentation on Dieppe, imputes blame to "those who wanted it in the first place, for their inability to resist playing the military and political game of war."[6] Again there are no facts, no specific accusation against anyone; but again there is the imputation, this time apparently of frivolous motives.

One wonders whether it is at Mountbatten that these people are pointing. Mountbatten's ambition and egotism were notorious; but I don't believe that the Dieppe operation can fairly be said to have been the result of personal motivation. Mountbatten did not sacrifice men's lives for his own aggrandizement or for fun. It is well established that when Winston Churchill expressed doubts about the Dieppe project the Chief of the Imperial General Staff, Sir Alan Brooke, the British government's senior military adviser, told him that such an operation was a vital preliminary to any invasion of North-West Europe.[7] The motives of the senior Canadian officers cannot be impugned. General McNaughton had nothing to do with originating the raid, though he accepted and approved it. General Crerar pressed for opportunities for the Canadians to take part in raiding operations, but he was clearly moved by concern for the army's morale, and the vast majority of the officers and men of the army would have cheered him on. Whoever it may be directed against, to me the imputation seems baseless and improper. I was delighted to find in a recent book on the operation[8] a quotation from Lieutenant-Colonel Cecil Merritt of the South Saskatchewan Regiment, who won the Victoria Cross on Green Beach: "We were very glad to go, we were delighted. We were up against a very difficult situation and we didn't win; but to hell with this business of saying the generals done us dirt."

Chapter 8

Getting on with It

When I arrived in London at the end of 1940 I had no staff at all. I did my own typing, just as I had been accustomed to do in civilian life. After a few weeks I acquired a clerk and began to operate in a manner a little more becoming the dignity of a staff officer. But apart from this I was entirely on my own for nearly three years.

In the spring of 1942 I began to be aware of the desirability of getting some help. Under the static conditions of the day I had managed to keep fairly well abreast of Canadian events in Britain since my arrival; the reports I had written covered them in essentials. But it was evident that when the active operations we were looking forward to began I should at once be swamped. Moreover, I had managed to do next to nothing about the interesting happenings of 1939-40, before I took up my post, and I was painfully aware of the importance of compiling a narrative of those events. I was backward about asking for manpower to be allotted to a job that many would consider non-essential; nevertheless, I had to think of asking for an assistant.

Early in March 1942 I wrote a "submission" along these lines; and General McNaughton's comment was, "I am very much in favour of this so that the comprehensive narrative of our operations and developments in 1940 may be prepared at an early date for otherwise there is a danger that we may lose the full story of this phase, because much of the intimate history of the more important parts remains in the minds of individuals and has never been committed to paper." In these circumstances it is not surprising that the War Establishment Committee accepted the project "without my having to give evidence." We had the "vacancy" now: who was to fill it? The first person mentioned was Gerald S. Graham of Queen's University; but he turned out to have joined the navy. Minds turned to Major George F. G. Stanley, a historian at Mount Allison University in civil life, with some military writing to his credit and now reported to be serving at a training centre in New Brunswick. We asked for him. The reply from Ottawa was that he was not available. I assumed that his commanding officer was, in the normal way, unwilling to give up a valuable officer. General Stuart was in London and I had a chance to discuss the matter with him. He agreed to send a personal cable, and George Stanley reported in London on 14 October 1942.

George, it turned out, had not had the faintest idea what the job entailed; nobody had bothered to tell him. But he was the ideal person for it: an excellent scholar, a practised writer, an experienced soldier, and with energy to burn. He set to work with zest on the 1939-40 narrative, and before long we were sending out draft chapters for comment by participants. He had arrived at just the right moment; as I have explained, I was up to the neck in Dieppe, devoting to it every moment I could spare from miscellaneous tasks of liaison and administration. These tasks, unfortunately, continued to increase in number and complexity.

Here is a fairly representative day's entry from my diary; the date is 3 December 1942:

> Wrote Mr. [G. Elmslie] Owen [in charge of War Artist activities at British Ministry of Information] enclosing two copies of *Canadian Geographical Journal* for October . . . [this contained another article by me, "The Canadian Army Overseas, 1941-1942", illustrated in part by Canadian War Artists' pictures].
> Dictated further section of DIEPPE report.
> Discussed with Major Stanley his plans for first two chapters of narrative of Canadian Overseas Events, 1939-40. His scheme of organization seems very sound.
> Interviewed Major A. T. Law, Camerons of C., re his experiences at DIEPPE, and dictated part of a memorandum of this interview

[Major Law commanded the unit after the commanding officer was killed].

Showed three portraits by Lieut. [Lawren] Harris [Jr.] to the Rt. Hon. Mr. Massey, who thinks very highly of them.

After discussion with Brigadier Rodger, B.G.S., despatched to N.D.H.Q. [National Defence Headquarters] telegram G.S. 4028 requesting copies of [our] Reports Nos. 1-18 [we wanted these back to have them available for consultation in case of need].

This extract lets out of the bag a cat previously concealed: we were now involved in a war artist program, which was taking a great deal of my time. I must go back a bit and tell this story.

It is well known that in 1914-18 Lord Beaverbrook organized a considerable scheme for an artistic record of the Canadian effort. People remembered this and from the beginning of the new war there was agitation for a similar program. I found in Ottawa in 1940 that Colonel Duguid had corralled a painter whom he had heard of in the army, Private E.J. Hughes, and had put him to work painting to his direction. Duguid's ideas on art seemed to be largely photographic; I remember him pointing out to Hughes that the screw-heads on the Bren gun were not quite accurately placed. Subsequently Duguid also got hold of Hughes' partner in civil life, Orville Fisher. A more influential and knowledgeable critic was at work in London in the person of Vincent Massey, the High Commissioner. Massey made the initiation of a war art program one of his chief personal interests, but even so it was a long time before he contrived to sell his ideas to the Canadian government. In the meantime a good deal was accomplished unofficially overseas.

In October 1941 Massey discovered that an artist of high reputation and ability, W. A. Ogilvie, in civil life an instructor at the Art Association of Montreal, was serving overseas as a trooper in the 17th Duke of York's Royal Canadian Hussars. He arranged with General Montague for Ogilvie to be attached for three months to CMHQ to work as an artist. The idea apparently was that he should work under Public Relations. It seemed to me that if there were to be army artists they belonged in the business of historical recording rather than in that of publicity. I took it up through normal channels and was duly told that they should be my responsibility. I had never met Will Ogilvie, but an interview on 14 October was the beginning of a long military association and a lifelong friendship. The same day General Montague and I went to see the High Commissioner and the senior officer agreed that Ogilvie should be made a sergeant, acting, unpaid (this, the general said, was as far as his authority would stretch), and should be attached for a fortnight to the Canadian base units in the Aldershot area to sketch. Equipment could be paid for out of the SO's contingent fund. I wrote letters of identification for Will and sent him off. When he came back, with an excellent group of sketches, I arranged temporary working accommodation for him in the Sun Life Building. A new project was launched.

About the same time I found myself making administrative arrangements for a British artist to paint Canadian troops. This, too, undoubtedly was the result of an initiative by the High Commissioner. All I knew about Captain Henry Lamb was that he was an eminent painter who sported the unusual combination of letters, MC, ARA. I did not realize, as I do now, that he had been a noted member of the Bloomsbury Group, nor did I connect him with the famous curvilinear portrait of Lytton Strachey. As the MC indicated, he was one Bloomsberry who had not been a conscientious objector in the first war. He enjoyed working with soldiers and, he said, Canadian soldiers in particular; and I for my part enjoyed making arrangements for him, for he was an agreeable man. In March 1942 I spent a day driving him down to the Thames estuary, where he was to paint with the 2nd Canadian Heavy Anti-Aircraft Regiment, which was manning big 4.5-inch guns in that area. We had as a companion Ed Hughes, who had arrived from Canada a few days before.

Will Ogilvie's situation as an unpaid sergeant living in sergeants' messes on a trooper's pay was quite impossible, and late in 1941 General Montague decided that his authority extended to making him a staff-sergeant with pay. But all concerned were sure that an artist in our army could not do his work adequately without the status of an officer. In January General Montague sent Ottawa a cable, drafted by me, mentioning Hughes and Fisher as well as Ogilvie; and with rather surprising celerity (actually, in less than a month!) a reply was received promoting all three to the dignity of second lieutenant. It was as an officer, therefore, that Ed Hughes came to England.

This raised another question. In the Canadian army a second lieutenant with one pip on his shoulder was an unqualified officer, a virtually unknown animal in the Canadian Army Overseas. How were we to qualify Ogilvie and Hughes for that second pip, so that they would not attract stares in all Canadian military gatherings? The books contained no procedure for qualifying war artists for rank; but our training authorities were equal to the emergency. They had what they called a "D.D. and P." course, designed for imparting a modicum of military knowledge to doctors, dentists and padres; this, it was felt, was just the thing for artists. Will and Ed were accordingly sent off to attend one of these courses, after which they were duly declared to be lieutenants, put up their second pips, and ceased to be stared at.

Meanwhile, in the remote distance, Ottawa was discussing the question of whether there should or should not be war artists at all. Mr. Massey was certainly exerting influence, and so was Colonel Duguid, for what that might be worth, and so was H. O. McCurry, director of the National Gallery of Canada. A setback was indicated at the beginning of April 1942, when we were told that Fisher, whose imminent dispatch had been announced, would not be coming; no more artists would be sent, and the appointment of Mrs. Lilias Newton, whom Massey had asked for as a portrait artist, was rejected. However, we went on with our slightly illegal program overseas, and in October 1942 Lieutenant Lawren Harris, Jr., who had become rather fed up with being intelligence officer of the Governor-General's Horse Guards, joined our stable of painters (he was primarily a portrait painter, so Ottawa's recalcitrance in the matter of Mrs. Newton was frustrated). That same month I had a chance to show some of our finished products to the Minister of National Defence, Colonel Ralston, who was in London. He said their quality was higher than he had expected, and in general was friendly. Nevertheless, I found his attitude rather lukewarm. When I mentioned this to Colonel Clyde Scott, his military secretary, Scott replied, "Well, you know, he's colour-blind; I have to tell him what tie to put on every morning."

Perhaps it was this little exhibition that did it; at any rate, soon after the New Year of 1943 I recorded, "Communication received from Canada House on policy re War Artists: Prime Minister has accepted recommendation that six artists be appointed for Army, to have rank of Lieut. Portraits discouraged." A committee was set up in Ottawa to watch over the matter, and in July a parallel committee began to function overseas, with Mr. Massey as chairman and the senior officers of the three armed services in London as members. With the thing on an official basis it got larger, and took even more of my time. In the army we took the view that it was desirable that the artists appointed should have some military experience if possible. Mr. Massey was tacitly accepted as the final authority on overseas appointments. A good many people came forward looking for employment. Most were turned down, but Sergeant T. R. MacDonald and Sapper Bruno Bobak passed the Massey scrutiny and were commissioned.

Charles Comfort, an eminent artistic figure by any standard, arrived from Canada in April 1943. George Pepper and (at last) Orville Fisher came in the autumn, and Campbell Tinning a few weeks later. In May 1944 Alex Colville blew in. After he had worked for a month I wrote, "He seems to me a talented but very inexperienced painter." Jack Shadbolt was never officially appointed as a war artist, but he worked as an administrator while Eric Heathcote was absent in Canada, and I was able to give him opportunities for painting. Molly Lamb (who later changed her name to Bobak) arrived after the fighting was over and painted the activities of the Canadian Women's Army Corps in the final days of the army overseas. In talent and in energy our artists were, like the rest of mankind, uneven. Some were tremendous producers, who made the most of the opportunities given them; some took things rather easier.

I may as well say that I considered it my job only to provide opportunities to artists. I had no intention of telling them how to paint, and only to a very small extent did I tell them what to paint, though I did make occasional suggestions. I didn't count the screws on the Bren guns in their pictures; and when in May 1943 I received a letter from Duguid "remarking that pictures so far executed by War Artists Overseas are unsatisfactory, and that he is awaiting report on this matter from Lieut. Comfort," I regret to say I did not change my procedure. In general, the pictures that were produced impressed Massey as good art and me as good history.

The enlarged program meant that we had to have somebody to make administering the artists a full-time job, for I had other things to do. By good luck the man was to hand: Captain (shortly Major) Eric Heathcote, MM, in civil life art director for the T. Eaton Co. and no mean painter himself. He could be relied on to be sympathetic to the artistic point of view, and at the same time to keep his feet firmly on the ground. He arranged studio accommodation for the artists, saw to obtaining the materials they needed (not altogether simple in wartime England), saw that their work was properly recorded, and looked after their travels and attachments.

The artist program brought me into pretty frequent contact with the High Commissioner. The young aristocrats of External Affairs in Canada House must have become comparatively inured to the spectacle of Major Stacey trooping into Mr. Massey's office to exhibit the latest crop of pictures or to discuss artistic problems. The High Commissioner's office, I may mention, overlooked Trafalgar Square and was roughly half the size of a football field; Massey sat at the far end from the door, his desk across the corner of the room. The comparison with Mussolini was inevitable and irresistible. However, I got used to it, and Massey was very good to me. In fact, he and Mrs. Massey occasionally asked me to dinner at their flat. The first such occasion was at the end of 1941, and I described it to Doris:

> On the second-last night of the year I was invited to dine with the
> Masseys at their suite in the Dorchester, and it was a very interesting
> evening. I wished you had been here to enjoy it, as there was quite a bit
> of theatrical talk, about *Raymond* and *Noel* and some actor-friends of
> Mr. Massey's who are thinking of putting on *King Henry V* in
> battle-dress. Brockington was there, and a couple of other people.
> Before dinner we listened to Churchill's speech from Ottawa ["Some
> chicken! Some neck!"] (which came through here at eight in the
> evening, and was very clearly heard). . . . I was quite late getting home
> to Hampstead Garden Suburb. It is an hour's trip from the West End when
> you have to reckon with changing tubes and doing a bit of waiting.

A rather triumphant occasion for Massey, I think, was the service held in Westminster Abbey on 1 July 1942, the seventy-fifth anniversary of Canadian Confederation. All the Abbey pageantry was "laid on" (as the phrase was) for this occasion; and Colonel Hepburn, who sat beside me, remarked that he hoped that the local clergy didn't have to give up coupons for the vestments they were wearing. We were in the nave, and behind a large pillar at that; and as all the best people were in the choir, and everything happened there, we *saw* little of the actual service, though thanks to the loud speaker system we *heard* very well. And we saw the King and Queen at very close range, as they came in through a side door only a few yards from our places. The King looked harassed (as well he might, in view of the news of the fall of Tobruk); but the Queen was as cheerful and radiant as ever.

Massey read the lesson ("Let us now praise famous men..."), and the Archbishop of Canterbury preached; I'm sorry to say that I was not greatly impressed by his discourse. There was something a little bit unreal about the affair in general which I found it difficult to explain to myself at the time; a day or two later, I realized that no Canadian clergy took part in the service. It was rather peculiar to hear the Westminster clergy giving thanks for the prosperity of Canada. The Right Reverend the little old Dean of Westminster had to read through "An Act of Remembrance and Thanksgiving" — pretty clearly written for him, I should say, by Mr. Massey — full of the names of Canadian national heroes. He did his best, fumbling only a little over the wholly unfamiliar words, until the very end, when, seeing daylight and release ahead, he finished in a blaze of glory with the names "Charles Tupper, Wilfred — Wilfrid — Laurier and *Herbert* Borden"! People winced visibly, and no doubt the radio carried the word to Canada, where still more people would wince.

I don't think it occurred to me at the time that, Canada not being blessed with a state church, it would have been very hard indeed to select Canadian clergymen to take part in such an occasion. One feels sure that Mackenzie King was not enthusiastic about this service in Westminster Abbey — any more than Sir Wilfrid Laurier was for the famous memorial service for Queen Victoria that Lord Minto arranged in the Anglican cathedral in Ottawa.

Incidentally, I had arranged for Ed Hughes to be admitted to the Abbey's organ loft so he could sketch the occasion. The resulting picture, unfortunately, was not a success.

I continued to be stuck with jobs that were not really my pidgin. I went on grinding out articles for the *Canadian Geographical Journal* including one on the Spitsbergen affair and one on Dieppe. The arrival of George Stanley allowed me to transfer part of this burden to him, and relieved the *Journal*'s readers of seeing my name quite so often.

In the autumn of 1943 I was given what was really a public relations job. Charles Murphy, an editor of *Fortune* magazine, was writing an article on the Canadian Army Overseas which was to be illustrated with some of our pictures. This was considered important, and General Montague told me to give him, in effect, the red-carpet treatment and help him all I could. He took me to lunch at the Dorchester a couple of times and I provided him with a lot of historical information. I was astonished when he told me that General Crerar was shortly going out to the Mediterranean in command of the 1st Canadian Corps. This, at that time, was extremely secret information and I wouldn't have dared give it to him on any terms. Who told him I don't know, but it must have been someone very high up, possibly Crerar himself. Murphy was unusual in that he was interested in Harry Crerar; most correspondents found Andy McNaughton, a more charismatic character, far more worthy of attention. In the course of one of our lunches he shook me severely by asking me for a characterization of Harry. I explained that I was a half-colonel (this, in fact, had just happened) and that I didn't make a practice of issuing statements to the press on the qualifications of lieutenant-generals. He calmed my fears by swearing he wouldn't quote me, and persisted. After reflecting for a moment or two I stuck my neck out and said, "General Crerar seems to me the sort of man who would never make a bad mistake." Murphy said, if I remember rightly, "That's very interesting," and there the matter ended.

Time, Life and *Fortune* were, of course, under the same umbrella, marked Luce. In those days I didn't see *Time* regularly. But many months after that day in the Dorchester I picked up an old copy in a British officers' club in, of all places, Algiers. On the cover there was a rather poor portrait of Harry Crerar, wearing the badges of a full general, to which at that time he was not entitled. And under the portrait was the caption, "Canada's Crerar: For Him, No Bad Mistakes." I felt that I had really made a mark in history.

As a matter of fact, looking back, I don't think my off-the-cuff opinion of Crerar was far wrong. He was not brilliant, as McNaughton was, but his judgment was far better than McNaughton's. I think it can be said, in retrospect, that Harry really never did make a bad mistake, whereas Andy made a great many. And men who don't make bad mistakes are very useful in war.

With active operations obviously approaching, and our work ramifying in every direction, I was pressed not only by circumstances, but by my superiors, to ask for a larger staff of writers. Here is my record of a conversation with the Chief of the General Staff (General Stuart) at CMHQ on 12 February 1943:

> Showed C.G.S. pictures by Ogilvie, Hughes and Harris and handed him Major Stanley's draft copy of first chapter of narrative.
>
> C.G.S. outlined his views on the preparation of a Canadian Official History. He is very anxious for every possible measure to be taken with a view to publication soon after the conclusion of hostilities. Also emphasized the need of ensuring proper co-ordination of the written word, photographs and paintings.
>
> C.G.S. also pointed out the necessity of the history recording the moral, mental and spiritual factors, not appearing to the casual observer, which go to the making of an army and which have made it possible for us to keep an inactive army in England for three years without loss of morale or serious difficulty with the men. The C.G.S. also spoke of the need of increasing the staff of the Historical Section here and suggested that Staff-Course-trained officers passing through the section and working here for several months at a time, might be very useful.

After consideration by the War Establishment Committee what emerged by the end of October 1943 was an authorized historical staff at CMHQ of twelve officers, headed by a lieutenant-colonel (me) and including four artists. One of these officers was attached to Headquarters 1st Canadian Corps in the Mediterranean theatre, and over and above there was an historical "increment" to the headquarters of the 1st Division in that theatre, amounting to four officers, two of whom were artists. It was, in fact, quite a little empire. Needless to say, I liked the promotion, but nevertheless I felt a bit embarrassed.

After the promotion appeared in orders I received a succession of telegrams The culprit was not identified for some time, but George Stanley finally owned up. The telegrams ran as follows:

> WE OFFER OUR CONGRATULATIONS   WINSTON
> PRINCETON AND I ARE DEEPLY GRATIFIED AT YOUR
>   SUCCESS   FRANKLIN
> CONGRATULATIONS   ANDY
> SMASHING SHOW   EISENHOWER

WELL DESERVED PROMOTION   MONTY
GOOD WORK LAD   PRICE [MONTAGUE]
GOOD WORK WISH YOU WERE HERE   GUY [SIMONDS]
PHOOEY   ADOLPH
USSR WAS NOT CONSULTED   JOE.*

Finding the people to fill the vacancies was not altogether easy; historians don't grow on trees, and there were many people who considered themselves qualified who on trial turned out not to have what it took. On the whole, however, I was extraordinarily lucky. In the summer of 1943 Sam Hughes joined the ship: a grandson of the celebrated Minister of Militia of the first war, with all the brilliance (and only a little of the eccentricity) of his famous family; he was in due course to abandon what would have been a fine career in history to be an ornament of the Ontario Supreme Court. General Stuart had recommended Gerald Graham to us; he also recommended another Queen's professor whom I was delighted to get. Eric Harrison, who arrived in September, would lend lustre to our little galaxy. Shortly afterwards a Queen's graduate student, Mac Hitsman, an officer in the Ordnance Corps, came to us. He stayed, plagued by ill health but making a great contribution, until he died. Jack Martin, a McMaster man with a Princeton graduate degree, joined us in November 1943, on a lucky day for me. Early in 1944 we got Jim Conacher, also a Queen's product and an historian of the very first order, who would in due course be a leading figure at the University of Toronto. Still another Queen's man, Joe Engler, fated to give his life in the service, and John Spurr, a librarian by profession, appeared about the same time, and a little later came two British Columbians, L. A. (Joe) Wrinch and Murray Hunter; the latter would have a long and useful career in army historical work and end up as a professor at Carleton University. Others came subsequently, but this was the group with which we faced the advent of the Canadian army's full-scale shooting war.

Contacts with other countries' historians helped fill my days. The British army scorned the idea of having historians in the field; British

---

* I finally got back at George in December 1981, when he was appointed Lieutenant-Governor of New Brunswick. I took it on myself to deputize for the Muse of History, telegraphing, "Delighted that one of my most distinguished servants has finally received suitable recognition. Clio." George didn't twig. He had forgotten 1943.

historical work went on at a much higher level, in the Historical Section of the Cabinet Office. My contact here was with Colonel H. B. Latham, who kept me posted on developments. The British were not above making preparations for writing history while the war continued; a high-level advisory committee of eminent historians was set up, and narrators were put to work on narratives of campaigns. Very intelligently, the British decided that their official history should cover civil as well as military aspects of the war, and the civil side was placed under an eminent Australian scholar, W. K. (later Sir Keith) Hancock, with whom I had some dealings. I, of course, was responsible for the Canadian Army Overseas and nothing else. The Canadian approach to the history of the war was fragmentary and haphazard by comparison with the British; there was nothing like a national historical policy. Nobody in Ottawa on a high level interested himself in the matter, and the historical profession attempted no initiative.

The Americans' approach was more like our own. The U.S. army took an interest in our organization, and may even have been influenced by it. My first opposite number was Colonel W. A. Ganoe, the author of a one-volume history of the army. He was elderly but active and enthusiastic, and we had pleasant relations with him. He was fond of citing German precedents, and after his first visit I found that my officers had put a sign on our door, *Historische Abteilung*. He was succeeded as historian of the European theatre by Colonel (later Brigadier-General) S.L.A. Marshall, a lively newspaperman with whom I had many stimulating conversations at intervals as the war went on. I remember him boasting that of the seven Americans who were the first to meet the Russians on the Elbe in April 1945, three were historians! I was never able to top that one.

The summer of 1943 brought us the excitement of the secret preparations for the Sicilian invasion, which for the first time introduced our troops into a protracted campaign. This I reserve for the next chapter. But while the 1st Canadian Division was involved in this enterprise the rest of the Canadian force in England continued to prepare for the greater adventure to come — the assault on North-West Europe.

The exercises went on. In March 1943 the celebrated Exercise "Spartan" took place, in which General McNaughton commanded six divisions in a mimic campaign against the forces of Eastern Command.[1] On the first of the month I was suddenly sent for to help run the Visitors' (or Information) Room at Headquarters Second Army (the designation for this exercise of McNaughton's army headquarters). Our location was first at Witley Common and later at Wallingford. Until "cease fire," which happened on 12 March, I was kept busy with other people keeping the map up to date and explaining the "war" to various important visitors who turned up. "Spartan" really did not go especially well. In particular, the advance of the 2nd Canadian Corps (including the Guards and 5th Canadian Armoured Divisions) was disappointingly slow. This formation never brought enemy armour really to battle, and in addition was weak in passing information to headquarters. The 1st Canadian Corps bore the brunt, and did considerable damage to enemy armour.

The most serious error General McNaughton made in connection with this exercise was in committing to it at all the green 2nd Canadian Corps headquarters (under Lieutenant-General E. W. Sansom) and its incompletely trained and equipped signals organization. Andy, I think, was looking at the affair from the point of view of its training value; a very secure person, I doubt whether he ever considered the possibility that a poor performance by the army might reflect on himself. But it certainly did. The good performance of the 1st Corps, on the other hand, doubtless enhanced the reputation of its commander, Harry Crerar. One person who suffered was poor Ham Roberts, who lost the command of the 2nd Division not because of Dieppe, as has been alleged, but because of Crerar's poor view of his handling of the division in "Spartan" seven months later.

Chapter 9

Battles in Italy, Intrigues in England

The landing of the 1st Canadian Division in Sicily on 10 July 1943 inaugurated for our little band of historians and artists the first attempt at recording the history of a Canadian campaign as it proceeded. In Sicily we tried out the organization which we later used in the bigger affairs on the Italian mainland and in North-West Europe.

On the actual Sicily D Day I was on leave in Dorset, and this is the entry I made in my diary:

> On Saturday, 10 Jul, in Weymouth, I learned of the landings made in Sicily that morning by Allied Forces, including a Canadian component. I had known for some time that a Canadian Force, basically composed of 1 Cdn Inf Div and 1 Cdn Army Tank Bde, was moving to the Mediterranean to participate in operations, and had known that the operations would begin this week-end; but I had not had definite information of the objective [and, I may add, had carefully avoided making any effort to find out].
>
> Arrangements have been made for historical "coverage" of these operations. Capt. A. T. Sesia is at HQ 1 Cdn Div as Historical Officer, and Lieut. W. A. Ogilvie, War Artist, is also with the Division, having been attached to it prior to its final training in Scotland. A directive governing the employment of both these

officers was drafted by me on instructions of Brigadier General Staff, and issued to HQ 1 Cdn Div by General Montague on 24 May 43. It is to be hoped that the arrangements made will produce good results.

The story of how these arrangements came to be made may best begin on a high level, with some facts about command. There were a good many changes during 1942, chiefly as a result of a survey of the situation in the Canadian Corps made by General Montgomery with the consent of General Crerar.[1] One of these changes saw Major-General H.L.N. Salmon succeeding General Pearkes in the command of the 1st Canadian Division. Salmon was in command of the division when, as the result of pressure from Ottawa, it was substituted for a British division in the plan for the Sicilian assault. But he was not fated to command it in Sicily. Here the story touched me in a curious and painful way. On 28 April 1943, having lunch in Mrs. Massey's club, I ran into Lieutenant-Colonel C.F.J. Finlay of the Canadian Planning Staff (an organization whose very name suggested that things were brewing); we often met there and sat at the same table. I asked him whether he could read a report I had written about some combined training that had been going forward. He said apologetically that he was so busy at the moment that he couldn't take this on. The following day we heard that General Salmon had been killed in an air crash in Devon, and Chuck Finlay with him. They had in fact been flying out to Cairo for planning consultations connected with the coming operation. This disaster was not allowed to delay the planning. On the same day General McNaughton appointed in Harry Salmon's place Major-General G. G. Simonds, who had only lately been appointed to the 2nd Division in succession to Ham Roberts. Guy Simonds, young, handsome, able and ambitious, thus unexpectedly got his big chance.

By mid-May I was discussing with Brigadier Rodger the people to be used for historical work in an unspecified future operation abroad. The first idea was to use as historical officer Sam Hughes (who had not yet actually joined us, but was on the strength of the intelligence section of CMHQ) with Will Ogilvie as artist. A few days later, however, the senior General Staff officer at 1st Division, George Kitching, suggested using instead of Hughes one Captain A. T. Sesia, who was then a junior General Staff officer on the divisional headquarters. I was an old enough soldier by now to suspect that there were motives here other than regard for the best interests of history; but it was clearly desirable to keep the divisional staff sweet, and on interviewing Sesia I thought he was probably equal to the job. So we gave him a crash course in historical work, and Gus Sesia and Will Ogilvie were our team for the invasion of Sicily.

The 1st Canadian Division did well in Sicily, and the historical arrangements we had made produced useful results. Gus Sesia in a letter to me written at the end of July, when the Canadian fighting was nearly over, told me his troubles. There had been a tendency to use Gus as a headquarters dogsbody instead of letting him get out to interview knowledgeable people and advise units and formations on how to keep their records, which was what he was there for. The one great historical "lesson learned" in Sicily was the need for independent transport; the historian and the artist had to have their own vehicles or they simply could not get to the places where they needed to be.

The historical triumph in Sicily was Will Ogilvie's. In October officers returning from there delivered 35 magnificent watercolours, which he had painted under most difficult conditions, carrying his equipment on his back and hitching rides as he could. I recorded my delight at the time:

> The whole group of 35 pictures constitutes a really amazing record of the Canadian operations in Sicily, and appears fully to justify the employment of War Artists from the historical point of view. This series of pictures includes the exercises in Scotland, the voyage out (e.g., a Seaforth subaltern briefing his platoon on "Circassia"), scenes on the Pachino Peninsula at the time of the landing, some excellent battle scenes (including artillery in action against Leonforte, and General Simonds and his staff set up in Assoro and directing this attack) and activities after the withdrawal of the Division from the line (men swimming in the Mediterranean, etc.) These pictures will be, what I had hoped for, a record of genuine national importance.

Nearly forty years later, I still feel the same. I know of no other pictorial record of a campaign anywhere to match the one Ogilvie made in Sicily. And it seems extraordinary to me that the custodians of these pictures in Canada — the National Gallery and more recently the Canadian War Museum — have never given the public an opportunity of seeing them all together in one place. When the War Museum in 1980 put on an exhibition of Will's war pictures, and kindly invited me to open it, only a few of the Sicilian watercolours were included. The best impression of them — and that an inadequate one — is given by the reproductions in our booklet *From Pachino to Ortona*, published in 1945 and long out of print. There the reader may appreciate something of the impact I felt in October 1943 when I first looked at these remarkably vigorous and pungent pictures, bringing into a drab London room the colour and excitement of Canadian battles fought under the hot Sicilian sun.

Andy McNaughton had hoped, optimistically, that after Sicily the 1st Division would return to England, bringing with it battle experience to assist the First Canadian Army in the great cross-Channel operation that lay ahead. Little he knew the people in Ottawa. They (primarily Ralston and Stuart) immediately began to pull strings to build the Canadian division up to a corps, committed to the long campaign in Italy that now loomed ahead, with the Canadian army in England cut down to a single corps. It was clear by the end of August 1943 that, whatever happened, Canadian activity in the Mediterranean was going to continue, and I got authority to send out Sam Hughes and Charles Comfort "to work with Capt. Sesia and Lieut. Ogilvie in the next phase and ultimately to relieve them."

During the autumn of 1943 things were going on backstage of which ordinary members of the Canadian community in London heard only vague and disturbing rumours. Early in November Ralston and Stuart arrived from Ottawa. I showed them Ogilvie's Sicily pictures, which greatly impressed them. What they were there for, however, was a show-down with General McNaughton. The Army Commander was at odds with them over their desire to send more troops to the Mediterranean, thereby breaking up the national army that McNaughton had created. The British War Office, and particularly Alan Brooke, taking advantage of this Canadian domestic quarrel, was trying to unseat McNaughton, arguing that he was unsuited to command an army in the field. This crisis resulted on 13 November in the resignation of General McNaughton.[2]

The Minister of National Defence now left for the Mediterranean to visit the Canadian troops there. His return in December involved me in an incident worth chronicling. At 11:05 on the morning of the 13th Ralston's military secretary, Colonel Sandy Dyde, sent for me and told me, with some obvious embarrassment and to my astonishment, that the minister was giving a press conference at the Ministry of Information at *noon* (!) and required for the occasion a set of notes on the Sicilian and Italian campaigns. I rushed back to my office, where my staff received the news with dropped jaws (we were accustomed to dealing with generals, whose demands were usually comparatively reasonable, and had had little experience with politicians). Luckily Gus Sesia had now rejoined us, and with his help I put something on paper. By that time Ralston had left for the Ministry of Information. There was no time to get a staff car. I hailed a taxi and pursued him to Malet Street. I put the piece of paper into his hand as he walked down the corridor to the conference room. He did not thank me — presumably he thought I had been too slow — and he made no use of the notes during the conference.

That press conference was a Canadian public relations disaster. I had lately seen on the newsreels films of conferences held in that same room by the Australian Menzies and the American Willkie, both of whom scored triumphs. Nobody brought a newsreel camera for Ralston; presumably the cameramen had private information. But the London press corps was there in force, and the minister had a great opportunity, which he totally muffed. He had no idea how to deal with the press. In particular he did not know that the first principle is to convince them that you are taking them into your confidence, and then to take them into your confidence in good earnest as far as is practicable. (How often I had seen McNaughton applying that principle!) Everything published about that conference was going to be censored anyway; but on the platform there was a wretched little British brigadier (one who had failed at every other job, one speculated) whose job it was to rule on matters of security. Whenever Ralston was asked a question, he always asked the little man whether he could answer it; and the little man, needless to say, always said no. To make matters worse, the minister was getting deaf, and he often had to ask the questioner to repeat the question. Finally, Eric Gibbs later confided to me that he had particularly begged the minister to make a reference to the Eighth Army and how pleased Canadians were that their troops were serving in it. ("The English," Eric truly remarked, "love the Eighth Army." Ralston forgot to mention it.

I think I reflected then, and I certainly have often reflected since, how characteristic that conference was of the Mackenzie King government, and how it summed up that government's difficulty in selling itself to the Canadian public and particularly the Canadian forces. Here was an admirable, sincere and industrious minister who had been selflessly devoting himself to the nation's service for years; and he was utterly incapable of communicating effectively with an audience which was eager to hear him and would have reported him across a large part of the world if he had said anything worthwhile. Had Canada had a war minister (or any other cabinet minister) capable of speaking with some degree of passion and eloquence, the whole atmosphere of the Canadian war effort would have been different, and many of the government's difficulties would have been alleviated.

After the conference Canadian correspondents gathered round. Ross Munro asked Ralston about rumours of the retirement of General McNaughton. The minister would say nothing for publication, but said, "I am gravely concerned about General McNaughton's health. Any statement that may be made will be through normal official channels" — or words to that effect. On 27 December it was announced that General McNaughton was retiring for medical reasons. I wrote to Doris:

> You will have read in the papers that we have lost General
> McNaughton. You can imagine how many people were saddened by
> the news. It is very hard indeed that after four years during which he
> has built up this army from more or less nothing into what it now is, he
> should have to drop out just on the eve of the big show. The papers are
> suggesting that our friend Crerar will become Army Commander in his
> place [in due course, this happened]. I suspect that he would be just as
> competent a field commander as Andy; but I don't believe that anyone
> can ever occupy quite the place in the heart and mind of the Canadian
> Army Overseas that "The General" did. The man's versatility was
> astonishing, and the burden he bore was tremendous. As being the
> senior military representative of Canada in this country for so long, he
> had special responsibilities that don't fall to an ordinary Army
> Commander, and his own interests were astonishingly wide; he seemed
> able to talk to anybody about anything, and to very good purpose too.
> And with it all, as I have told you, he remained a most warm, human,
> friendly, unassuming person, a compelling personality if ever there was
> one, and yet wholly without conceit.

After the New Year I was asked to go to Headley Court to discuss the disposal of the general's files with his faithful personal assistant, Doug Cunnington. We then went on to his house nearby to get his instructions.

He had been ill for some time but was now well enough to be up. "He looks very worn," I recorded, "but is as dynamic as ever." I was proud that he did me the honour of entrusting his most secret papers to my keeping. He spoke of the disposal of his personal war diary, and directed that of the three copies one would come to my section, for perusal by me, and use by the officers of the section when the controversial aspects had subsided. A second would go to Records under seal; the third he requested me to despatch to NDHQ (Director Historical Section) with instructions that it was to be held to his order and delivered to him when required, in the meantime not to be opened. He said he would require these in his discussions with the government. He was returning to Canada shortly.

I noted that he said that the "recent crisis" had great constitutional importance (a phrase that recalled our first conversation back in 1941); and he also remarked that he was going back to discover whether what had happened was the result of the action of the government of Canada or "the work of two men." He didn't specify who the two men were; but I knew, and he certainly knew that I knew, that they were Ralston and Stuart.

I felt deeply moved. I was at a loss what to say; but I could not take leave of this man whom I so greatly admired without some word. I said something like, "Sir, I hope that some day I shall serve under your command again." And he said, "Well, Stacey, perhaps you will." I have often wondered what was in his thoughts. Did he have in the back of his mind the idea that some day he would sit in Ralston's seat? Such a thing had not occurred to me.

The remembrance of Mrs. McNaughton sitting quietly by during this conversation prompts me to set down some things which could never have been included in an official history. Andy and his wife are both gone now, and things can be written which it would have been quite improper to write at an earlier time.

General McNaughton was extraordinarily dependent upon his wife. John Swettenham, his biographer, has described how in the first war, when he was serving in France, she went to England and remained there; and Andy never failed to write her a daily letter. In December 1939, when duty took their husbands overseas again, Mabel McNaughton and Verse Crerar both followed them to England. Mrs. Crerar later returned to

Canada, as her husband did, but Mrs. McNaughton stayed on. When General McNaughton set up his headquarters at Headley Court, he rented a house close by called "Largiebeg," and there he and Mrs. McNaughton lived until he lost the command of the army. Early in 1942, as I have mentioned, he returned briefly to Canada for official consultations. I remember the sense of shock with which I read, in the CMHQ cable docket, the exchange of messages with the Minister of National Defence in which the general asked the government, as a special case, to permit Mrs. McNaughton to accompany him and (more important) to return to England afterwards. Andy was asking a privilege for himself which was denied to his officers and men. It didn't seem like him. I have no doubt that he was under pressure from Mabel as well as from his own feelings. It is not surprising that Ralston's messages betrayed a certain reluctance (which I am sure did not help his subsequent relations with the McNaughtons); but the general got what he wanted. One cannot help thinking that it should have been possible for Mrs. McNaughton to have stayed alone in England for a mere couple of months; but apparently even a temporary separation was not acceptable.[3]

After the war General Charles Foulkes, who had been McNaughton's last Brigadier General Staff as Army Commander, told me that he had been conscious of the fact that as the general's official adviser he had unofficial rivals. There were occasions, he said, when he would obtain what he considered a sound decision from McNaughton in the afternoon, only to have it reversed the following morning. "I knew then," he said, "that the kitchen cabinet had met." Personal advisers got at the general through Mrs. McNaughton. One of the general's close friends, whom Charles Foulkes recalled, was Major-General R. M. Luton, the senior medical officer overseas, who occupied a house close to "Largiebeg."[4] Undoubtedly McNaughton got much advice also from Brigadier (later Major-General) Guy Turner, his inseparable *fidus Achates* since the days of the unemployment relief camps in 1932. Turner was certainly a most faithful friend, but as to whether he was a person of very high capacity or good judgment I would be less sure. These were presumably the core of the kitchen cabinet.

Later, when I was writing the painful and tragic story of his removal from his command, I had to print the rather extraordinary cable he sent to Mackenzie King on 10 November 1943 in which he wrote, "I have lost all confidence in Ralston and I must say that I can no longer remain in comd of First Cdn Army responsible to any government of which he is a member." I wrote, "One would like to know who, if anyone, was advising McNaughton at this stage." To that question, of course, there can be no final answer; these things were not set down on paper, and the participants are dead. But I have no doubt at all, in my own mind, that the kitchen cabinet had met. Doubtless also the optimism that was such an obvious trait in the general himself had played its part. The assumption that his position was so secure that he could in effect call with confidence on the Prime Minister to dismiss his Minister of Defence is remarkable. It is not surprising that General Sir Bernard Paget called the telegram unbalanced. King, forced reluctantly to choose between the general and the minister, inevitably supported Ralston; but by a masterpiece of personal diplomacy he avoided giving any offence to McNaughton, and kept the general available as an alternative Defence Minister when his own break with Ralston came.[5]

Early in February 1944 I had a long conversation with General Stuart (who was now Chief of Staff at CMHQ and acting Army Commander pending General Crerar's return from Italy), during which he gave me his version of the recent controversies. He said that the initiative in the removal of General McNaughton had come from the British — from Generals Brooke and Paget — "who felt that he was neither physically nor temperamentally fitted to command an Army" (here I am quoting my notes of the conversation).

> General Stuart said that on the basis of the opinions he had formed he had felt it was his responsibility as military adviser to the Government to recommend that General McNaughton should not continue in command; he felt he owed it to the fathers and mothers of Canada and to the 200,000 young Canadians who make up First Cdn Army. General McNaughton had "burned himself out"; he had worked so hard for four years that he was no longer capable of bearing the burden of command. He had been urged repeatedly to concentrate upon the command of his Army and leave other matters to C.M.H.Q., but he would not do so and insisted upon "having a finger in every pie," although commanding an Army was quite enough work for any one man, however able.

Stuart warned me against McNaughton's memoranda, "frequently written some days after the events described and, he suggested, not giving a true picture of them." He said that General McNaughton had suffered from what he called "obsessions": two of these were a long-standing dislike of Ralston, and an exaggerated regard for Canadian autonomy, on which he was, General Stuart said, "hipped." McNaughton had lately been unjust to General Crerar, denying him his confidence, Stuart thought, because Ralston had consulted Crerar without reference to McNaughton, his superior. Crerar, Stuart said, was "the finest soldier Canada had ever produced"; though he added, I recall, that he did not possess McNaughton's magnetism: "Men loved Andy McNaughton," but they didn't love Crerar.[6]

In all this there is clearly a good deal of sense as well as a certain amount of exaggeration. I have little doubt that Stuart was right about McNaughton's prejudice against Ralston, and I have always thought that Andy probably undervalued Ralston's support for his policies during his years in command. As for McNaughton's fitness or otherwise to command in the field, one could argue indefinitely. McNaughton himself said he was a victim of a grudge that Brooke had held against him ever since Vimy Ridge. I set down years ago the opinion that Crerar was probably on balance a more suitable man for the field command, and I see no reason to change it.

Stuart remarked during our conversation that he had once been one of McNaughton's best friends, but that Andy had now "struck him off his visiting list." Less than a year later, when Ralston went out and McNaughton succeeded him as minister, Stuart was dismissed on the instant.

I am sure Stuart was right when he said that Crerar could not command men's love as McNaughton did. This was particularly true about the other ranks. I believe that McNaughton was in fact the only Canadian senior general who managed to establish a warm relationship with the rank and file. Crerar, Simonds, Foulkes and Burns were all cold fish. So, from all I hear, was Currie in the earlier war. They all had great qualities in their various ways, but they could not endear themselves to the Canadian soldier. Nor did they do too well even with the officers, who sometimes compared their dour ways unfavourably with the cheery demeanour of their British counterparts. Readers of Brigadier J. A. Roberts' memoirs will remember how enchanted he was when Sir Brian Horrocks, after half an hour's acquaintance, called him "Jim." The unsmiling Canadian generals had never managed anything warmer than "Roberts."

In these days I was grappling with little problems of my own. As early as the last week in August 1943, reading the memoranda of interviews and other papers received from Gus Sesia in Sicily, it seemed to me obvious that here we had material of great potential training value. Here was information, hot off the griddle, about how the war was being fought by those in contact with the enemy, the problems they were encountering and the expedients they were using to overcome them. Should this material merely be filed away for the "future use of the Official Historian"? This seemed to me to make no sense, and my superiors agreed with me. There were obvious and not entirely frivolous military objections to circulating unofficial opinions on how to fight the war, which might be quite at variance with official doctrine. But official doctrine could only be sound if founded on actual experience, and this was one way to get the record of actual experience into the hands of people who could turn it to advantage. So in September we began sending out our "Extracts from War Diaries and Memoranda," with cautious covering letters signed by the Brigadier General Staff, CMHQ, explaining that these were "for information only" and not to be considered expressions of official views. Almost immediately we began to receive requests from recipients for additional copies, and from other headquarters to be added to the distribution list. The people in charge of tactical investigation at the War Office found these things valuable, and in time the distribution list looked like a sort of military *Who's Who.* A by-product of this activity was my taking over from Records (which was part of the Adjutant-General's Branch) the responsibility for custody and administration of war diaries. The officer in charge of this, Major C. J. Lynn-Grant (always known as Lynn) was thereafter one of my close associates.

At least one person, however, took a poor view of our "Extracts." From his eyrie in Ottawa, Colonel Duguid watched and disapproved; and in February 1944 he descended upon us for a "liaison visit." He arrived late in the afternoon of the 8th, and I made a handwritten note of his remarks that day:

The question of the circulation of extracts from War Diaries for general information was discussed, and Col. Duguid expressed the view that this was an improper practice; that operational information should be obtained through other channels; and that much of the information contained in the extracts was politically dangerous — i.e. if it "got into the wrong hands" and was "brought up on the floor of the House." Col. Duguid also felt that the Narratives prepared by Hist Sec, C.M.H.Q., were dangerous: they were, he said, "too good."

This was not all. Next day we had further talk:

We spoke of the danger of a cleavage between the two parts of the Canadian Army, at home and overseas; and in this connection he said that one of the matters which he had to discuss with the Chief of Staff was the "revival" of the link between his section and mine. He emphasized the fact that the *control* of the Canadian Army centred in Ottawa, and mentioned the recent removal of Generals McNaughton and Turner as an example of that control. He added that it would be too bad if the same thing happened to other people; these were not his exact words, but this was the sense of them. He went on to speak of an article on the Canadian Tunnellers at Gibraltar written by Major Stanley of my section. This article, he said, gave the impression that the Tunnelling Company was one hundred per cent General McNaught-on's work, whereas much of the credit was due to Canadian mining men. The arrival of the article was untimely owing to the fact that General McNaughton's status was then under discussion. The disposal of the article was still being discussed when Col. Duguid last heard of the matter.*

This looked like the outpouring of three years' accumulation of resent-ment. Now, I reflect that many officers of Duguid's generation, who had done well overseas in the first war, were hurt in the second by finding themselves in backwaters in Canada and superseded by younger men. This, I think, was Duguid's case. I kept my temper; after all, he was my superior officer, and I suspected that I still held the better cards. I went to my own superior, who was now Brigadier Penhale, and told him of the threats I had received. Pen's comment was, in effect, "Don't give it a

---

* The article finally appeared in the *Canadian Geographical Journal* for June 1944, four months after this interview.

second thought." I went back to my discussions with Duguid in better heart.

In one respect Duguid's arrival was timely. The day after he appeared in London the Canadian War Artists' Exhibition opened at the National Gallery in Trafalgar Square. This was the product of arrangements made by Vincent Massey with his friend Sir Kenneth Clark, director of the gallery. Pictures from all three services (including the army ones which Duguid had pronounced unsatisfactory) were on view; various generals graced the occasion, and the Duchess of Kent in a nice little speech declared the exhibition open.

In a meeting with Brigadier Penhale and myself, Duguid told us that he had obtained approval from General Stuart for two projects: a system of reports on operations, and a series of publications to be called "Episodes." The reports were an excellent idea; I would myself have been a bit backward about asking field commanders to prepare reports in addition to the rather elaborate war diary they were already required to furnish, but in fact the report system was to produce pretty fair results in practice.

Episodes was a different matter. Duguid at one time had been very much against "contemporary history," but now he had fathered this scheme. It contemplated publication of a series of pamphlets on the work of the army, "to comprise, basically, accounts by actual participants, subject to briefing and editing by Historical Section." It didn't strike me as much good (I knew enough about the army by now to know that the man who had the interesting experiences and the man capable of describing them interestingly on paper were rarely the same). However, it appeared that the higher authorities in Ottawa had approved the scheme so ours not to reason why. George Stanley and I spent some time with Duguid making plans. But Episodes shortly received its quietus. Duguid and I went to see General Crerar, who had now taken command of the army. While Crerar fully approved of the scheme of reports, with respect to Episodes he said firmly that no officer or soldier under his command would be permitted to participate in it as a narrator; he thought that the stories should be told by "outsiders" after the manner of the pamphlets by Hilary Saunders. Exit Episodes, and enter a series of pamphlets to be written by Stacey & Co.

Whether Duguid raised with General Stuart the question of our improper and dangerous "Extracts from War Diaries and Memoranda," or the relationship of his section and mine, I don't know. If he did he didn't get anywhere. The Extracts went on rolling out, to an increasingly wide circle of official readers. When the North-West Europe campaign opened, we started a new series based on the documents coming from there, and it went on to the end. I would like to think the information we circulated this way made a tiny contribution to winning the war.

From my point of view, at least one thoroughly useful result flowed from Duguid's visit: I got out to Italy. Duguid wanted to explain his scheme for reports to the commanders in the field, and I went with him, to see first-hand how our historical organization was functioning (and to see what a war really looked like). By now Headquarters 1st Canadian Corps and the 5th Canadian Armoured Division were in Italy in addition to the 1st Division, and our staff had changed. Gus Sesia and Will Ogilvie had come back to England to work up the material obtained in Sicily. Eric Harrison was now ensconced as historical officer at Corps Headquarters and Sam Hughes at 1st Division, and two war artists, Lawren Harris and Charles Comfort, were in the theatre. All these officers were now captains.

We flew out to Italy, of course. (I say "of course," but it is curious now to think that only recently had air travel begun to seem commonplace. When at the beginning of August 1943 I flew from London to South Wales with a party of officers to watch an amphibious exercise, I noted that it was "my first time in the air.") We went first to Naples, where the Canadian "1st Echelon" (the static headquarters in Italy) was located close to the Administrative Echelon of HQ Allied Armies in Italy. The Canadians' "A" mess was in apartments on the seafront belonging to the Prince of Caracciolo-Carafa, and we slept there in a room which might without exaggeration be described as palatial. Everything was laid on for us, including a spectacular eruption of Vesuvius. First Echelon was being run by that charming and efficient officer, Brigadier E. G. Weeks (a signaller). Bunny Weeks' staff arranged for us to push on by road to HQ 1st Canadian Corps.

The war was, for the moment, quiescent. In a few weeks the quiet would be shattered by the Liri Valley offensive, the Canadian Corps' first battle; but for the moment people had time to talk to us. We found Corps Headquarters located at Larino, far south of the fighting line, planning for the coming operation. It was commanded now by Lieutenant-General E.L.M. Burns, whom I already knew well. His Brigadier General Staff was

Nick McCarter. I had a reunion with Eric Harrison, who was set up in a tent adjacent to the general's mess; and he travelled north with us to visit the 1st Division, in the line near Ortona, which it had captured in desperate fighting at Christmas.

Divisional Headquarters was established on a hillside overlooking the Adriatic, a short distance south of Ortona. Major-General Chris Vokes and his staff were good to us and we had interesting talks with the general about the division's experiences. His aide-de-camp, Lieutenant Dickey (who was killed a few weeks later when his jeep struck a mine) took us on a conducted tour of the December battlefields, and particularly of the town of Ortona itself, ruined by the house-to-house fighting in which the Loyal Edmonton Regiment and the Seaforth Highlanders from Vancouver had gradually and painfully pushed the tough German paratroopers out of the place. A sign at the outskirts informed the traveller, "This is Ortona, a West Canadian town."

I could now say that I had seen the front — not the very front, it is true, but at least the back of the front. We did not see the infantry in the forward positions; but we did visit a field battery which was lazily lobbing shells at the Germans on a pleasant sunny afternoon which made it remarkably hard to believe that the shells were really being fired in anger. We also heard and saw German shells coming down, though none came very close to us. While at divisional headquarters I slept for two nights in a tent — the first time I had been under canvas in the war — and slept very comfortably, though on the first of the two nights I was awakened more than once by the whistle and explosion of distant enemy shells and the sound of our own guns.

One pleasant incident of our visit to the gunners was a meeting with Douglas LePan. Doug, an old friend who had been teaching at Harvard before the war, had succeeded J. B. Bickersteth as General McNaughton's adviser on education (he later published an eloquent memoir of the general which everyone interested in the Canadian personalities of the war period should read).[7] When that job folded up, Vincent Massey offered LePan an appointment at Canada House; but Doug had a deep desire to serve in uniform. He asked my advice, and I told him that it would really be a bit absurd for a person of his talents and qualifications to enlist as a private soldier; he could make a much greater contribution at Canada House, in a job for which suitable people were hard to find. He thanked me for my opinion and proceeded to enlist. I think my advice was good, but I admired Doug for rejecting it. So it was that on that sunny afternoon near Ortona I had a talk with Gunner LePan of the Royal Canadian Horse Artillery. (I was still glad to hear somewhat later that the Department of External Affairs had finally succeeded in winkling him out of the army and into Canada House.)

Sam Hughes and Charles Comfort were keeping house in a rather dirty little tent on the hillside below the farmhouse that accommodated Chris Vokes' mess, and Lawren Harris joined us there. We discussed our historical affairs, and Charles delivered a statement that would have done credit to a labour leader on the proper status of war artists. They had all been doing a splendid job, and anyone who wants to know what the Adriatic front was like in 1944 can look at the watercolours and canvases that Charles and Lawren produced. Sam for his part was operating as what I seem to remember Kipling calling "a decorator and colourman in words." The work of all three was to find expression later in the booklet *From Pachino to Ortona*.

When the time came to go I was sorry to leave the 1st Division. There was always something just a little special about the people who wore the red patch, and I had felt queerly at home there. I knew that the job I was doing was the one I was best fitted for, but I was not enthusiastic about going back to London. I would have liked to stay in Italy with these fine fighting men.

After a visit to the 1st Canadian Armoured Brigade (as the 1st Army Tank Brigade had now been renamed) we returned to Corps Headquarters, and from there we went on to the 5th Canadian Armoured Division, which had not yet been in action except for an unsuccessful minor operation by its infantry brigade on the Ortona front. Its headquarters was in Castelnuovo della Daunia. We met its new commander, Major-General B. M. Hoffmeister, and found him impressive. We then went back to Naples, and thence visited Avellino, a town which was being used as the Canadian base area. We had a long talk with Brigadier Eric Haldenby, commanding No. 1 Canadian Base Reinforcement Group, who told us much about relations with the Italian local authorities and population. The streets of Avellino had been given new Canadian names. There had been a moment of difficulty over one street, Haldenby said. The solution for the problem of prostitution had been to move all the prostitutes into a single street and then put that street out of bounds. But what was that thoroughfare to be named? Obviously it couldn't be called after a Canadian city or province. In the end, over the protest of an ex-stockbroker from Montreal, it was christened St. James Street. We visited 2nd Echelon, the Canadian records office for the theatre, which controlled the supply of reinforcements to units, had an enormous task of directing and redirecting mail, and incidentally was responsible for collecting and forwarding unit war diaries. After further interviews at 1st Echelon in Naples, we paid a visit to Headquarters Allied Armies in Italy, occupying the enormous palace of the Bourbon Kings of Naples at Caserta. Here I got a security clearance for carrying some war artist pictures back to England, and we left for home on the morning of 30 March.

The return trip to England was slow. We made an overnight stop at Catania in Sicily and then flew on to Algiers. Here we stayed. We had run into the problem of priority in air travel, which in Algiers was controlled by an American lieutenant from whose rulings there was no appeal. He evidently decided that Canadian historical officers were not a form of life that required rapid movement, and we spent a week in Algiers. It is not an uninteresting city, but I got rather tired of it. Luckily there was a rule that after a week you went automatically to the head of the queue, so we got away on 7 April. Our enforced stay was rendered much more pleasant by the hospitality of Major-General and Mrs. Georges Vanier at the Canadian Mission, located in what General Vanier called a "Hollywood villa" on the coast west of Algiers. There was a further delay of two days at Gibraltar, which at least gave us a chance for a good look at the fortress, including the tunnels built earlier in the war by Canadian sappers. We arrived back in England on 10 April.

We had found the Canadians in Italy obviously in good heart, and looking forward to further action. But they did not like the country. Complaints of its dirt and squalor were universal. They envied the troops preparing for action in England, and there was widespread interest in the prospect of the Second Front. The Canadian government policy that had split the army between two theatres did not commend itself to the people whom it condemned to play in the "Spaghetti League."

Colonel Duguid returned to Canada late in April. This visit had really improved liaison. I have made it clear that Duguid had arrived with blood in his eye. But I wrote Doris after his departure, "We parted good friends and he said that if he was asked about our show here there were really no improvements he could suggest." Doris was now in Ottawa, having found a war job in censorship, dealing with prisoner-of-war mail. (She remarked that she was encountering some German words for which her academic studies had not prepared her.) The Duguids invited her and Eric Harrison's wife to dinner, and she wrote to me, "I think you have really made a conquest of the Colonel. He couldn't say enough about how well you and Eric Harrison had looked after him on the trip."

It was now May 1944, and the great crisis of the war in the West was at hand.

Below: The author's mother, about the time of her marriage in 1898.

Above: The author and his big sister, in the backyard at 161 College Street, Toronto, about 1909.

Above: The staff of *The Varsity,* University of Toronto, 1927. All the names are to be found in *Torontonensis* for that year; the author, who was editor-in-chief, is front and centre (note the spats), and Helen Allen (now Stacey), is modestly lurking fourth from the left in the third row.

Right: At the Maison Canadienne, Paris, 1928. A group of students, chiefly visitors from Oxford. Seated at left, Hector Allard, later an eminent diplomat; on the higher level, Ross McLean (left), who became head of the National Film Board, and Arthur Jewett, who was later principal of the University of Bishop's College; standing Jack Pickersgill (left), who became a cabinet minister, and George Buxton later a professor at the University of Ottawa. The author is on the ground.

Above: Princeton Community Players, 1937. The author as Major Petkoff in Shaw's *Arms and the Man.*

Below: In the big cage at Princeton: the author lecturing to freshmen in McCosh Hall, probably in 1939. *(Picture by Elizabeth G.C. Menzies)*

Above: Meeting a Canadian troop convoy at Glasgow, July 1941. Left to right are Captain R.C. Harris, Ross Munro from Canadian Press, and the author.

Below: The Army War Artists' studio, Fairfax House, London, 1944: two Canadian war artists, Charles Comfort (left centre) and Lawren Harris, Jr. (right centre), show a picture to American war artists.

Christmas dinner at the Canadian Officers' Club, London, 1941. With the High Commissioner for Canada and Mrs. Massey are some of the ladies who helped Mrs. Massey run the club. The author is at the table in the right foreground.

London during the Blitz! Dinner given by officers of the General Staff branch, Canadian Military Headquarters, at Claridge's Hotel, February 14, 1941, in honour of Brigadier Maurice Pope when he left to take another appointment. Brigadier Pope is third from the left, with Lieutenant-Colonel Hugh Young on his left and the author next.

Right: Major W.A. Ogilvie, MBE, CM, painted against an Italian background after the war by Major Charles Comfort, OC, CD. (Courtesy of The Canadian War Museum.)

Below: ''Command Post, Assoro'': one of Will Ogilvie's splendid watercolours from Sicily, 1943. It shows the 1st Canadian Division's tactical headquarters beside the Norman castle on the Assoro hill. In the foreground General Guy Simonds watches the progress of the attack on Agira. (Courtesy of The Canadian War Museum.)

General the Honourable A.G.L. McNaughton, CH, CB, CMG, DSO,
CD, PC: from a photograph taken in England in 1940. (Courtesy of
Public Archives Canada.)

Right: "Young, hand-some, able and ambi-tious": Lieutenant-General Guy Simonds, CB, CBE, DSO, CD: a watercolour portrait by Major Charles Comfort. (Courtesy of The Canadian War Museum).

Below: Historical Officer at work in Italy: Captain (later Mr. Justice) Sam Hughes (right) interviews an officer of the 48th Highlanders of Canada. From a watercolour by Captain Charles Comfort. (Courtesy of The Canadian War Museum.)

Caen, August 1946. In front, left to right, the Mayor of Caen; Mackenzie King; M. Pasquier, Secrétaire Général of the Department of Calvados; Arnold Heeney; the author.

General H.D.G. Crerar, CH, CB, DSO, CD, ADC, from an oil painting by Lieutenant T.R. MacDonald, June 1944. (Courtesy of The Canadian War Museum.)

Dinner in honour of John Gray (seated centre right) on his retirement as president of Macmillan of Canada, May 1973; the author speaking.

Chapter 10

Fair Stood the Wind for France

A newer generation may not find it easy to comprehend just what the Allied landings in Normandy on 6 June 1944 meant to contemporaries, and particularly to people in England.

By then we had been through nearly five years of war. We had come desperately close to defeat in 1940, and had painfully fought our way back from that position with the help of powerful allies. Through those years the British people had been the target of savage bombing and had suffered many privations. They had lived uncomfortable and often miserable lives, of which the blackout was the grisly symbol. In 1942 and 1943 the tide of war had visibly begun to turn; light appeared at the end of the tunnel, a mere speck at first, then a little brighter. The enemy was cleared out of North Africa, the Allies landed in Italy. The enormous Russian machine was rolling forward. But the event that would proclaim the advent of deliverance, men felt, was the anticipated invasion of North-West Europe, the day when Allied armies would cross the English Channel and take tyranny by the throat.

As 1944 dawned the mood was euphoric — rather too much so, I in my wisdom thought. I wrote my wife on 2 January:

In this country — and, I gather, on your side of the water
too — everybody is terribly optimistic these days, and people are
beginning to talk about the invasion of the continent almost as if it was
already a thing accomplished. This troubles me a bit, as it would seem
that the disappointment will be pretty considerable if we should run
into any setbacks. All kinds of easy assumptions are being made. I was
amused at *The Times* yesterday: it quoted *Henry IV*:

> I will lay odds, that ere this year expire
> We bear our civil swords and native fire,
> As far as France; I heard a bird so sing,
> Whose music, to my thinking, pleased the King.

That sums up the present mood of easy and confident speculation
rather well. Of course, the talk from the States encourages it — the
"invasion within ninety days" sort of thing. Time will tell, as usual....

As it turned out, we pulled it off, though not within ninety days. Before
the actual day of invasion came, euphoria was giving way to nervous
excitement. My officers out among the assault force told me about an
ailment called "Channel fever"; it had led some soldiers to resort to the
device of insulting officers, or committing other military crimes, in the
hope that this would result in their being charged, placed in confinement,
and relieved of the necessity of taking part in the landing. The army,
needless to say, was on to them; they were duly charged and left with their
units, to be dealt with later, assuming they survived. These few faint-
hearted souls serve merely to emphasize the solid qualities of the vast
majority, who swallowed their inevitable fears and did their job.

The date of D Day, and the area of assault, were subjects of endless
public speculation. As in the case of Sicily, I was determined not to know
them, and managed to carry out this resolution, in spite of at least one
opportunity. Some characters who knew found the strain too much for
them, and broke out in foolish talk. One deplorable case became common
knowledge in the army. A brigadier in the Canadian assault force went to
a drunken party, and before the evening was over he and other members of
the group were out in public shouting the actual or approximate place and
date of the landing. Civilians reported the matter. It was too late to
remove the brigadier, for the operation was imminent. The punishment
he got was an interview with General Crerar. He was probably left feeling
that shooting would have been preferable.

On the morning of 6 June the BBC told us the day had come. The first news was a German report; the Allied communiqué followed. We knew that the 3rd Canadian Infantry Division and the 2nd Armoured Brigade were in the assault; First Canadian Army as a whole was in reserve. The avidity with which we at CMHQ read the reports of the landing and the fighting on shore can be imagined. Yet after all the tense expectation the English took it calmly. There was very little evidence of public excitement; the BBC, of course, gave the thing a lot of time, and the newspapers played it up, though in a rather restrained English fashion; but there was none of the feverish atmosphere one might have expected. No one, I think, wanted to cheer until the situation was a bit more solid. Nevertheless, optimism grew. I wrote after a few days, "We do seem to have begun well, and many people are now saying that the dividends of Dieppe are coming in at last." I went on, "It has been a remarkable week, with the invasion of France following hard upon the capture of Rome. The Canadians seem to have made useful contributions in both places; I hope my historical boys are all in good health."

The historical boys were, in fact, all in good health, for the moment. We now had a comparatively elaborate little historical organization in the field. There had been quite a bit of discussion as to the form that the organization should take; should the historians in the field be officially "on the strength" of the senior Canadian headquarters in the theatre, or of 1st Echelon, or what? The final decision was to form two little "self-accounting units," Nos. 1 and 2 Canadian Field Historical Sections, the former for Italy, the latter for North-West Europe. They must have been among the smallest units in the army. Ultimately these units provided an historical officer and a war artist for each of our five fighting divisions. I say ultimately, because in the beginning, partly to save manpower, partly because we were short of qualified people, we tried to avoid giving a full-time historian to every division. The divisions, however, were soon demanding one. Gus Sesia commanded No. 2 Section, and Eric Harrison No. 1, both as majors. And we still carried on our work at CMHQ, where apart from our staff of writers we had studio space to enable artists returned from the field to turn sketches into canvases. I myself ended up in November 1944 as what is called a "full" colonel, complete with the red tabs and red hatband that colonels wore in those days. Of course, I had no objection, but having never asked for a promotion in my life I didn't do it now; the establishment I submitted called for two lieutenant-colonels, one with a higher grading for pay than the other. My superiors directed that the submission be altered to provide for a colonel. When I went up, George Stanley went up too, to lieutenant-colonel, and Eric Heathcote to major. Our two senior artists, Ogilvie and Comfort, both in due course became majors, a rank which they had certainly earned. On the whole, Clio's servants were well treated in the Canadian army.

The system worked well in Normandy. The muse was represented in the Canadian assault force by Jack Martin as historical officer and Orville Fisher as artist. Both landed on D Day and were unscathed, and Jack Martin in particular did an extraordinary job. Our first series of "Extracts from War Diaries and Memoranda" from the new theatre, dated at CMHQ, 12 July 1944, contained interviews by him with the divisional commander, Major-General R.F.L. Keller, on the technique of the assault, and with all three infantry brigade commanders, as well as a detailed "lessons learned" paper by the 2nd Armoured Brigade. Looking now at these memoranda, clear, precise, militarily accurate, succinct and yet in essentials complete, I wonder how Jack did it in the conditions obtaining in the bridgehead. On 13 July a colonel in the training section at the War Office telephoned to say that our Extracts were "the best stuff we get." As the other divisions (the 2nd and 4th) came forward and into action, Joe Engler as historical officer and George Pepper and Will Ogilvie as war artists went to work with similar excellent results. We didn't have an historical officer specifically for the 4th Canadian Armoured Division until the establishment was amended, when John Spurr moved in.

Life in London continued to have its own little excitements. The early months of 1944 had brought some revival of German air activity against the capital; on 19 February we had an incendiary raid which was the heaviest attack since May 1941, and it was the first of several. Our attention, however, centred mainly on the prospect of the "secret weapons" with which Hitler was promising to destroy us. On 12 February we at CMHQ received instructions for Exercise "Rock" — the measures to be taken in case of heavy attacks on London with pilotless aircraft or rockets. The plan was to run the headquarters with a skeleton staff from the basement shelters, the rest of the staff being told to remain in quarters or, if necessary, to be evacuated from London. On further thought it was apparently considered that too much information had been given out, and I recorded three days later, "personnel already warned . . . concerning proposed action are now to be further warned to be silent about the warning."

The attack when it came was not so dreadful as had been feared. The first few flying bombs arrived on the night of 12 June, nearly a week after D Day, and three nights later the real business began. My diary for 16 June tells the story:

> Last night there was an "Alert" shortly before midnight. It was
> followed by sporadic aircraft noises accompanied by heavy bursts of
> fire. This continued at intervals. In the morning gunfire was still heard;
> there was a burst at 0640 hours, in broad daylight, and at 0730 hours I
> saw something I had never actually seen before — black puffs of flak
> above London in daylight. At about 0915 hours there was a heavy burst
> of fire in the vicinity of C.M.H.Q., followed by an "All Clear" at 0925
> hours and another "Alert" and gunfire at 0945 hours. By this time it
> was apparent to everybody that the enemy was using a new form of
> attack, and in the course of the day it was publicly confirmed that
> "Pilotless Aircraft" were being employed.

On Sunday the 18th I noticed that the four anti-aircraft guns at the A.A. site on the Hampstead Heath Extension, which had pointed northwest all through the war, had swung round and were pointing southeast; it was like a reversal of the course of nature. At noon there was a loud bang near CMHQ; a few minutes later Mac Hitsman appeared, his face bearing evidence of his having "gone to ground" suddenly and heavily. He had been nearby when a buzzbomb struck the Guards' Chapel at Wellington Barracks during church parade, killing many people.

The new offensive, although it didn't necessitate the sort of measures contemplated by Exercise "Rock," pushed London back into the front line. Personal planning became a bit unpredictable. On 30 June I had arranged to take Alison Coleman to the Aldwych Theatre to see the Lunts in *There Shall Be No Night*, but during the lunch hour one of the missiles came down in Aldwych near the theatre, again killing many people and effectively closing the show. As a substitute we went to *The Lilac Domino*, a rather pallid revival at His Majesty's Theatre in the Haymarket. The theatre was only about half full, and on the way home by tube we came to the conclusion that there were as many people sleeping in the tube stations as at any time in 1940-41.

By the beginning of October, thanks to the advance of First Canadian Army up the "buzzbomb coast" opposite, the doodlebug phase was about over, security was relaxed, and I was able to write home about it freely:

> Our first reaction, as I think I told you, was that the Hun had wasted a great deal of effort on a secret weapon that proved to be a damp squib. Our second reaction, as I think I didn't tell you, was that we weren't quite so sure; for the cumulative effect of the fly-bomb blitz was, as the English say, "lowering". . . . There were a number of noisy nights in which those of us who slept in bed didn't do a great deal of actual sleeping, as the things kept on coming over for considerable periods. I have never seen one in flight in daylight, but I have seen a number streaking across the sky at night with their tails flaming. In the distance they make a noise rather like an extra-large bee; but when they come close they make a loud booming noise which is really rather daunting. Quite recently one came over very low one evening when I was walking back from dinner. I didn't see it, perhaps because of fog, but I most definitely heard it. I lost no time in nipping rapidly up somebody's steps and taking shelter in a doorway. The thing, however, did what one always hopes they will do: it passed on to fall elsewhere. The worst danger from them is, actually, flying glass. When one came close at night I used to roll out of bed on to the floor, putting the bed (with my steel uniform-case under it) between me and the window. The creatures break glass at quite amazing distances. They were very tiresome; but they certainly were much less destructive than the "old blitz" and perhaps on balance rather less terrifying. As I look back, I think my most unpleasant experience of this war was the great all-night raid on London on 16 April 1941; *that* was a *very* "lowering" experience, and it was interesting to see how jumpy people were on the morning after. And yet I am glad, now, to have been through it, and sorry that I didn't see the first phase of the blitz in September and October 1940.

Before the buzzbomb or V–I phase was far advanced, we were worrying about V-2, the rocket. In mid-August schemes for evacuating large parts of our headquarters (and, undoubtedly, many other establishments) from London were being discussed. Again these plans came to nothing. When the V-2s began to arrive in September they turned out not to call for such drastic measures.

While these things went on I, in Cockspur Street, was being kept extremely busy. Correspondence with historians in two theatres of war, trying to advise them at long range and deal with the problems of their establishments, etc., took a good deal of time. The artist program, in England and on the Continent, was demanding. Our artists were nice people, but they *were* artists; and reconciling the demands of military procedure with those of the artistic temperament was not always precisely easy. With George Stanley's powerful help, I was always assisting and advising our neophytes in the art of historical writing, who were now beginning to write narratives of the campaigns. Believe it or not, I was still adding bits to the Dieppe record as new information came to hand. Finally, again with George's help, I was writing a booklet for publication. After a deal of cabling between the Sun Life Building and Ottawa, it had been arranged that we would initiate the booklet series (still sometimes called Episodes) with an item called *The Canadians in Britain*. We began writing it in July 1944, George and I sharing the job on a roughly half-and-half basis. By the autumn we had a completed manuscript, were collecting illustrations, were engaged in the usual argument with the British censorship, and faced the question of publication arrangements.

It had seemed to us that the Canadians' long sojourn in the United Kingdom, a unique episode in Commonwealth social history quite apart from its military significance, was a tale worth telling, and one which some British people as well as Canadians would be interested in. The main market would obviously be in Canada, but remembering the success of the British Ministry of Information's booklets it seemed sensible to mention our project to them. I had a connection with the ministry in the person of Cecil Day Lewis. He had often sought help from us, particularly in connection with Dieppe, so I felt I had a modest credit with him which I might now draw upon. I telephoned him and broached the matter. While I described the manuscript he was largely silent, but I was acutely aware that the temperature was going sharply down. The future poet laureate then asked who had written the booklet. I told him. By now the telephone receiver was almost too cold to hold. But he agreed to look at the manuscript. A fortnight or so later he informed me that he had read it. His view was that it was "of primarily Canadian interest"; for official publication in Britain it would have to be in part rewritten and materially shortened. I said that I assumed that we would have to make our own arrangements, and he assented.

I may as well tell the rest of the story here. A few weeks later I was in Ottawa. Duguid and I discussed the matter with the Wartime Information Board, represented by Mr. G. C. Andrew. Rather to my surprise, his attitude was not unlike Day Lewis's. The board felt that "the subject has only limited popular interest now," and in any case — a clinching argument — the board had no money. So the Department of National Defence had to do the job itself. Curiously enough, there was money in the appropriation — money for the publication of Duguid's unwritten second volume of the history of the first war! — which could be made available. On this basis the King's Printer embraced the project with enthusiasm. In our first interview in January 1945 he spoke of producing the booklet in two months. In fact, he proceeded with what I would come to know as characteristic deliberation, and *The Canadians in Britain, 1939–1944* appeared on 21 November. It would have been better if it had come out sooner; but it was handsomely produced and the price was very low. It and its two successors, *From Pachino to Ortona* and *Canada's Battle in Normandy* (of which more later) ultimately sold all told, in English and French together, some 94,000 copies. By Canadian standards, not bad.

On 26 August 1944, our fifth wedding anniversary, when the Normandy campaign was just finishing, and Paris had just been liberated, I wrote Doris, "My immediate schemes for the future have been a bit upset by the fact that a mutual friend of ours wants me to do a special job for him for a short time." This, I hoped, would convey to her the fact that General Crerar had sent for me and I was on my way to France.

The fact is that my career as what I have called writer-in-ordinary to the Canadian Army Overseas was entering another phase. The Army Commander wished to send to the Minister of National Defence brief dispatches on the army's operations as they proceeded. One of his staff had had a shot at writing the first of these, but General Crerar wanted "something in a different style." So I was sent for from London, leaving a mass of unfinished business in Cockspur Street for George Stanley to grapple with. Needless to say, I was delighted to get a glimpse of the theatre where our troops were fighting battles that would settle the fate of the world for generations to come.

I crossed the Channel by naval dispatch boat on 27 August. Conditions were very different from what they had been on D Day. The sky was blue and the sea as smooth as the proverbial millpond. I lay out on the craft's little foredeck and enjoyed the sunshine and the sight of the varied cross-Channel traffic: tank landing craft, tank landing ships, Liberty ships, naval escort vessels, and a big monitor steaming peacefully towards England, doubtless after completing a bombardment task in support of the troops on shore. I was well sunburned by the time we landed at the extraordinary artificial harbour that had been created at Arromanches. One of my fellow passengers was Colonel Bill Abel, the boss of public relations at CMHQ. A car met us and took us to Main Headquarters First Canadian Army at Amblie, a village between Caen and Bayeux.

The following day I had a talk with Brigadier Churchill Mann, who was now Harry Crerar's Chief of Staff; the general himself was at Tac Headquarters, in advance. Church explained the GOC-in-C's requirements and I spent the afternoon and evening drafting the dispatch, mainly on the basis of the account already put together by the staff officer aforementioned. On the 29th I revised it. On the 30th Main Army moved for the first time since its arrival on the Continent, and I moved with it. I drove by myself by way of Caen and Falaise, two ruined towns which we had bought with blood and high explosive. The battlegrounds I passed over were fascinating and appalling — devastated villages, fields ploughed up by carpet bombing, everywhere the debris of combat. Driving on eastward, although I did not actually touch the area famous as the Falaise Gap, I passed great numbers of German vehicles, Panther and Tiger tanks, half-tracks and many vehicles marked with the red cross, lying burned out in the ditches. Sometimes a particular concentration suggested a bombed traffic-jam. I found Army Headquarters in its new location near Brionne, where the Army Commander's mess was to be accommodated in a fine small chateau. The rest of the accommodation was rather muddy. At Brionne I saw the Army Commander, who approved the dispatch I had written for him, asked me to stay on to do another, and also asked me to nominate an officer for permanent appointment to his staff for the purpose of writing these reports. Here I must digress to speak of events in Italy. The commander of the British Eighth Army (Sir Oliver Leese) had not been pleased with the performance of 1st Canadian Corps' inexperienced headquarters in the Liri Valley battle. As a result, there were changes in the Corps staff. General Burns was left in command (in effect on probation — a devilish situation for any commander) but my friend Nick McCarter and the chief engineer were bounced.[1] Nick, passing through London, told me that part of the trouble was that the veteran 1st Canadian Division resented being placed under a corps headquarters that had never fought. He thought that he himself had been made a scapegoat for the Corps Commander. Major Eric Harrison, chief historian in the theatre and commander of No. 1 Field Historical Section, had done what I considered a first-class job; but he had got into difficulties with one of the new brigadiers. The first I heard of this was an intimation that the said brigadier was demanding that Charles Comfort paint his portrait in oils as a private commission. An opinion went back from CMHQ that this was contrary to policy (it was also contrary to good sense). Shortly I received a DO (demi-official) letter from the brigadier saying that he considered the administration of Major Harrison's "group" left much to be desired and suggesting that he be replaced. This Brigadier Penhale answered, to the effect that we had a high opinion of Harrison but that in view of the brigadier's opinion we would consider replacing him. Thus matters stood when the Army Commander asked for a historian.

I put forward two possible names: Jack Martin, who had done so well as historical officer at the 3rd Division, and Eric Harrison. I did not conceal Eric's difficulties with the brigadier. Evidently, however, this did not weigh heavily with General Crerar, for Eric got the job. With a personal appointment to the Army Commander's staff in question, the army wheels revolved rapidly. The selection was made on 1 September, a message went to London and another thence to Italy, and Eric arrived at Army Headquarters, breathless and having had no leave in England en route, on 16 September, in time for me to introduce him to the Army Commander before I went back to Cockspur Street. And before very long we were able to make him a lieutenant-colonel, an operation which gave me a certain amount of simple pleasure. In Italy he was replaced by Joe Wrinch, who did well. Before leaving Italy, Eric had recruited locally another historical officer, Lieutenant Tom Allen of the Patricias.

There is a small postscript. In October, at CMHQ, I received from Army Headquarters a draft dispatch written by Eric on the September operations, with a request that I revise it. Eric wrote beautiful English, but he was an Englishman and an academic, and his style might perhaps be called a bit elaborate (the word that came to me from Army was "flowery"). His draft would have delighted Brigadier "Bill" Williams, the Oxford don who wrote Monty's intelligence summaries; but I suspect that Harry Crerar found it a little puzzling. I did some crude surgery on it, and sent it back to Army, along with a note to Eric suggesting, in effect, that he emulate the example of Henry V approaching the French princess: "I speak to thee plain soldier." Eric knew his way around, and I never heard that he had any further trouble.

In North-West Europe the Germans were on the run, turning at intervals to fight skilful and deadly rearguard actions, but indubitably on the run. My time on the Continent was the period of the great pursuit across the Seine and up into the Low Countries. Our various headquarters were constantly on the move to maintain touch with their advancing units. I went with them, and luckily I was free to travel without restraint and watch the great spectacle that was unfolding. When I got back to London I tried to put my impressions on paper for the benefit of my family in Canada:

> It was a tremendous privilege to be in France during the great advance, and to accompany the victorious army, even in its rear echelons and as a military tourist. I cannot possibly convey the cumulative effect of passing for hours through a liberated countryside, with the wreckage of the beaten enemy — his tanks and vehicles, his dead horses and the graves of his dead men — littering the roadside ditches, and the population, free once more, welcoming the incoming troops with smiles and flowers and the V-sign. Don't allow anyone to tell you that the French were not glad to see us. Many people have told me that in the original bridgehead things were rather different (I suspect that the Hun had cleared a good many of the respectable Frenchmen out of that area); but in the districts liberated during August and September the warmth and obvious sincerity of the welcome were really most affecting.
>
> The scene in a liberated town is quite extraordinary. The place, of course, is festooned with flags. They always have plenty of tricolours; but the Union Jack and the Stars and Stripes are in short supply, and

had to be home-made for the occasion. (I even saw some versions of the Canadian Red Ensign, which would scarcely have pleased the College of Heralds but must have pleased a good many Canadians.) Everyone seems to be in the street, and no one ever seems to tire of waving at the troops passing in their vehicles, who likewise never tire of waving back (particularly at the female population). The young people wave and laugh and shout; the children yell and wave flags; the mothers hold up their babies to see the troops, and wave *their* little paws too; the old people stand by the roadside and look happy; and the Army rolls through. The whole thing is an astonishing experience for a man to have; and I am happier than I can say to have been there.

I got to Dieppe the day after it was liberated, and the reader can imagine how absorbing I found it. It was a remarkable and rather painful experience to look out through the slits of German pillboxes at the beaches where our people fought and died in 1942. A group of us, travelling in a jeep, went out of Dieppe by way of the Forêt d'Arques, southeast of the town. We were told afterwards that it was supposed to be full of snipers, but if there were any they didn't shoot at us. That sniper story was doubtless the reason for an extraordinary affair that followed. Driving along a secondary road east of the forest we gradually became aware that we were getting a more tumultuous welcome than usual; very few troops could so far have passed along that particular road, though we were far behind the front. One of the lads said, "If we get into a crowd, Heaven help us!" — and a moment or two later just that thing happened. We drove into the village of Envermeu, a little place with a wide up-tilted street with a big church across the end of it. As we turned into the sunlit street we saw what seemed to be the whole population standing in a crowd in front of the church. At the sound of the jeep they all turned towards us; and then, exactly as one person, they all began to run down the slope to meet us. It was precisely like a crowd-scene in a well-directed film — far too well stage-managed to be true. We told the driver to keep the jeep going at all costs; and for some minutes we ploughed slowly through a sea of people — men, women and children — whose sole idea seemed to be to shake us by the hand, tell us how glad they were to see us, and convey to us the fact that we were fine people. I don't know how many people I shook hands with, but it was all who could reach me. Only the fact that the top of the jeep was up, I suspect, saved us from kisses. When we crawled out on the other side of the village, breathless and amazed and rather humble, I found that somebody had thrown a big red flower into my lap, and another of the party was carrying in his hand an egg, which some well-wisher had pressed into it; fortunately, it hadn't broken! It was an experience we would all remember.

In addition to seeing the battlegrounds of the last few weeks, I caught glimpses of those of 1914-18. I still remember the thrill, when driving with other officers near Arras, of seeing two great pylons catching the sun on the northern horizon and knowing we were looking at Vimy Ridge. Shortly we were standing before the undamaged Canadian memorial and were all, I think, pretty deeply moved. And I told the family about an experience in Ypres:

> I had only two or three hours in Belgium, but I did get to Ypres, which I had never seen before. To-day it is a pleasant, peaceful, well-kept town, little touched by the present war. It has been thoroughly rebuilt after its ordeal last time, except for the fact that they left one wing of the Cloth Hall in ruins as a reminder. . . . One rather touching thing happened in Ypres. While we were looking at the Menin Gate, three nice children, two little boys and a girl a little bit older, came up and quietly attached themselves to us. One boy seized each of my hands, and the little girl attached herself similarly to Stu Cooper; and in this fashion we walked back towards the square. After a block or two the children decided it was time to go home, and after shaking hands ceremoniously all round (the little girl shook hands with me twice, first and last) they ran along. They didn't ask for anything, and they said very little; it appeared that they simply wanted us to know that they were glad we were there. I don't imagine this sort of thing happened to the Germans.

These three weeks on the Continent gave me an excellent chance for contact with the historians working there. Gus Sesia was working out of Headquarters 2nd Corps, and I had long talks with him and also with Jack Martin, Joe Engler, Orville Fisher and George Pepper. At my first meeting with Gus, on 31 August, he told me he was much concerned about Will Ogilvie; he had not heard from him for some time and feared that he had become a casualty. But on 6 September, to everybody's great relief, Will turned up at Army Headquarters, bringing with him a splendid group of watercolours and sketches, including some strikingly depicting the scenes of destruction in the Falaise Gap. He had been moving fast with the 4th Armoured Division and had had no chance to keep in touch with Gus.

After a final brief conversation with General Crerar (whose headquarters were now at Pihem, near St. Omer) I caught the courier plane for England on the afternoon of 17 September. We crossed the coast just south of Boulogne, where gun-flashes and smoke indicated that our assault was going on. Sussex was beautiful from the air. I found myself thinking a bit sentimentally of England and the fine things it had done in this war; and it was a satisfaction to reflect that its ordeal seemed to be almost over. At that moment we were viewing everything through rose-coloured glasses. But Britain's ordeal was not quite over. The day Boulogne was attacked was also the day the Arnhem operation began, and its failure suggested that the war was not going to end just yet. Moreover, when I landed at Gatwick Airport the people who met me said that for some days past the V-2 rocket had been coming down on London. Secrecy was being maintained about it. The Germans gave the new weapon no publicity, and the British refrained from telling them that it was reaching its targets. The Londoners enjoyed a sour little joke; when a bang was heard, people remarked, "another gas main exploding." The rocket was nasty, but on the whole less damaging and (to me at least) less terrifying than the V-1. You didn't hear it coming and if you heard the explosion you were probably all right. (If you didn't hear it, you were probably dead.)

There was a comic appendix to my continental trip. When I arrived at Army Headquarters at Amblie I was put into what was called the senior officers' camp. I remember it as a large marquee, empty except for a shallow slit trench supposed to shelter any occupants in case of bombardment. It was a cheerless place, and I was pleased when a distinguished deputation of half-colonels called on me formally and invited me to join their mess, known as No. 3. The food was passable in No. 3, and the conversation was better, especially when Peter Wright was there. Nevertheless, I was an old soldier by now and I was suspicious. I didn't believe that I was being invited into that mess out of sheer generosity or regard for my beautiful eyes. I was right. When the time came for me to return to London, another deputation asked me to undertake a small commission for the mess. It had a liquor problem. A supplier in London had ample booze for it, but there was a certain problem of transport. It was represented to me that all I had to do was to arrange to get a case a day, or every two days, on to the courier plane that came to Army daily; what could be simpler? I felt quite sure in my own mind that it wouldn't be nearly so simple; but I couldn't refuse. This is how I became involved in what used to be known as the liquor traffic.

A few days after my return to London the Provost NCO on the door at CMHQ telephoned up to me and announced, in a tone of polite amusement, that twenty-nine cases of assorted liquor had just been delivered addressed to me. I was shaken. Where could I possibly store it? Our efficient camp commandant, Bob Williams, had the answer: he had a vault. The first obstacle having been surmounted, I set about getting the stuff to Army. It turned out that it really could go on the courier plane, and in the course of the next day or two I got two cases off to France.

At this point, as I had fully expected, disaster struck. An American pilot was caught running a large cargo of French perfume into England. The result was an immediate order that no goods whatever were to be carried either into or out of the country in military aircraft. I was stuck with twenty-seven cases of booze belonging to a group of thirsty lieutenant-colonels serving their country in France, and no way of getting it to them. Part of the problem was the fact that the bottles were in the flimsiest of containers, which did nothing to conceal their contents. If they had been dispatched by ordinary surface means, they would have been pirated in the first mile. And in England in 1944 it was utterly impossible to get wood to manufacture more solid containers. I explored various avenues without success. Days passed; and in France the lieutenant-colonels grew thirstier. Emissaries began to arrive in Cockspur Street inquiring where their alcohol was. It was clear that they suspected I was drinking it myself, doubtless having wild parties at their expense. I explained the problem, but they clearly were not convinced. Everyone at CMHQ knew about my predicament and was convulsed.

I applied for help to everybody I could think of. Finally Movement Control produced a solution. The stuff could be sent to France by air through official channels if I would sign a certificate to the effect that it was material urgently required for the efficient prosecution of the war. I signed without a qualm, as I would have signed anything to get rid of that booze. The cases went off, and I heaved a sigh of relief. And they reached their destination; I know this, not because anybody thanked me for my efforts, but because the angry messengers ceased to arrive at CMHQ. How long the consignment lasted I don't know, but nobody ever again asked me to serve as an agent for wines and spirits.

From comedy to tragedy. On 6 October I heard from Gus Sesia that Joe Engler and George Pepper were missing. They had not been seen, he said, since they set out on 1 October to watch a bridging operation on the Antwerp-Turnhout Canal. Our troops had a bridgehead across this canal in the northern edge of Belgium and were extending it with difficulty. For a time it was thought that Joe and George might be prisoners, but on the 18th a letter from Gus told the story. Joe Engler was dead, and George Pepper had made his way back after ten days behind the enemy lines. They had accidentally driven into enemy territory, the result of a culpable failure on the part of our forward troops to block the road. When they ran into a German outpost, the course of discretion might have been to surrender, but Joe chose rather to fight against odds and was killed. In the confusion George managed to slip off and took shelter in a culvert just outside the German position. Here he remained for days, with no food except a chicken (and, he said, a wasp!) which he contrived to catch and ate raw. Finally he got away under cover of darkness, reached our lines, and was soon none the worse for his harrowing experience.

Joe Engler was our little organization's only fatal casualty of the war. He was an excellent historical officer, whose quality I appreciated more and more as I came to make use of the memoranda he left. His modest epitaph is a footnote in the history of the campaign, which states, with the restraint that I tried to make our trademark, that he "made a valuable contribution to this history."[2]

The work had to go on. As soon as Joe and George were reported missing, I arranged for Murray Hunter and Alex Colville to go out to replace them. Alex had lately had an unusual experience, when on Mr. Massey's suggestion we lent him to the navy (which was short of artists) and he spent some weeks in HMCS *Prince David* in the Mediterranean. He now set to work in North-West Europe; and George Pepper, after a period of recuperation, insisted on remaining there. There was no shortage of subjects; and it was now clear that we had to look forward to another winter of war.

Chapter 11

The End of the Affair

On 2 November 1944 a bombshell exploded at CMHQ. It came not from the Germans but from Mackenzie King. The resignation of Colonel Ralston as Minister of National Defence in Ottawa had not been wholly unexpected; but his replacement by General McNaughton certainly came as a great surprise. I remember meeting Bill Abel, the public relations man, in the elevator at the Sun Life Building. "Jeez!", he said. "Do you know what the last thing I said to that guy was? I said, 'I think you've always been wrong and I've always been against you.' Jeez!" I wrote that there was "much speculation as to possible further changes." No doubt Bill was speculating on his own account.

Nothing happened to Bill; but our Chief of Staff at CMHQ, General Ken Stuart, vanished instantly from the scene. He had gone to Ottawa with Ralston to support him in his recommendation to the government that the time had come for overseas conscription. We never saw him again; other people had to sort out the disorganized mass of important papers in his office. Lieutenant-General J. C. Murchie, the Chief of the General Staff at National Defence Headquarters, would have gone too had Mackenzie King not intervened with McNaughton. But the two men, whom Andy regarded as having done him mortal injury, and whom he had let me know he had it in for, had gone into eclipse. Stuart's rank of lieutenant-

151

general and his appointment at CMHQ fell to that great survivor, Price Montague.

McNaughton's motives in taking office were, I feel certain, very mixed. His notes of his first conversation with King on 31 October contain the words, "National Emergency. Not political," which indicate the grounds on which King based his invitation to him to join the cabinet.[1] McNaughton would always respond to an appeal to his sense of duty. But in this case he was also attracted by the prospect of taking the place of one man he had come to hate and of being in a position to dismiss another. I have no doubt too that he believed that he could succeed where Ralston had failed — that he could get the volunteers Ralston had not been able to attract. His characteristic optimism was at work, telling him that with his great reputation in the army and with the public he could not fail; and no doubt the kitchen cabinet, or what was left of it, was encouraging him. It must have been a very bitter pill when, like Ralston before him, he failed, and when the respect and indeed love with which the army had regarded him changed overnight to disgust and abuse when it became clear that he was supporting the voluntary system. Politics was not where he belonged, and it was I suspect with some bewilderment that he found himself going along with the sudden decision on 22 November to send a large group of conscripts overseas — a decision forced on King by the imminent resignation of important members of the government.

While the echoes of this conscription crisis were still reverberating in the corridors of Ottawa my job took me back to Canada for the first time in four years. The plans for the booklet series (at this time still referred to as "Episodes"), were still nebulous and it was desirable to get them into definite form. The best way to do this seemed to be discussion at the centre of authority. Naturally, I encouraged the idea for personal reasons; I had been separated from Doris for four years. Needless to say, the trip was long discussed before it actually materialized; and when the plan became definite it was further delayed by bad weather.

I left London on 3 December. The method of travel was by rail to Kilmarnock; thence by bus to Prestwick; and thence by Trans-Canada Airways Lancastrian aircraft (a Lancaster altered for passenger service) to Dorval. We flew by way of Lagens Airport in the Azores, our flying time being about eight hours Prestwick-Lagens, and about eleven hours Lagens-Dorval, where we landed about 1:15 a.m. on 5 December. I succeeded in hitching an immediate ride on an RCAF aircraft to Ottawa's Rockcliffe base. We landed there about three in the morning, and shortly thereafter I was throwing snowballs at my wife's window.

Officially speaking, this visit was notable for the fact that during it the first plan was made for an official history of the Canadian Army in the war. The war was not over, but now there was every reason for confidence that we were going to win it and, so far as Europe at least was concerned, win it soon. I have already remarked on the absence of anything like a national historical policy in Canada. In the light of later events, it is a fair assumption that if the government ever thought of a history at all they thought of it as a menace rather than as something to be desired. At any rate, it was evident that if a plan was to be made the initiative would have to come from the army historians themselves. Colonel Duguid had done nothing; and it seemed to be up to me.

When I suggested to Duguid that we make a submission suggesting a plan for a history he assented. We discussed the matter with Brigadier Penhale, who was now Duguid's immediate superior, and he asked for a paper. On 11 December I made a first rough draft. This covered both the booklets and an official history. After further conversation with Duguid and Pen the draft was revised and the recommendation for a history was separated from the booklet scheme.

The plan I suggested was quite different from Duguid's abortive scheme for a ponderous eight-volume history of the first war. I thought we should aim at a non-technical work of more modest dimensions aimed at a wider audience — "the intelligent general reader." Remembering also the well-founded criticism of the failure to produce anything before 1938, I sought to provide for meeting the presumed desire of the public for authentic information at an early date. I therefore recommended a two-stage history. The first stage would be what we called at this point an "Official Historical Sketch": a single volume of "about 100,000 words," which I blithely suggested would come out "approximately one year after the end of hostilities." (If I had known more about publishing, and particularly official publishing, I would have realized that this virtually implied having a completed manuscript in readiness for the printer on the day the last shot was fired, which was scarcely practicable.)

The second stage would be the history proper. I suggested four volumes. The first would deal with general military policy and development of the army, events in static areas and operations based on the United Kingdom, including Dieppe. The second would be concerned with the Mediterranean operations, the third with the campaign in North-West Europe, while the fourth would be devoted to Pacific operations (at this time everyone expected that the defeat of Germany would be followed by a bitter and perhaps protracted campaign against Japan). With magnificent optimism I said that this history should be completed within five years after the end of the war.

Naïve as this program was in some respects, and in spite of the fact that events rendered part of it redundant almost at once, it was followed in essentials, and the general principles laid down in December 1944 were never departed from. On 13 January 1945, General Murchie put the scheme forward to the minister; and General McNaughton (who was obviously operating now with less than the promptitude and decision I had once known) got around to writing "Agree" on it on 25 April. Duguid informed me of this and raised the question of whether overseas files (and historians) should remain overseas while the work was done, or be returned to Canada. Absolutely nothing was said as to who was to direct the work, or the basis of employment for historians. Again the matter was apparently left to me to pursue, if it was to be pursued at all.

Returning to Canada after four years of absence in the midst of war, I thought it worthwhile to set down my impressions of the country as I saw it in December 1944; and I should pass them on to the reader.

After four years in England, the first overwhelming sensation was the absence of the blackout. Driving into Ottawa in the small hours of a December morning, I marvelled at Rideau Street, with its quintuple lamp standards and its shop windows blazing. It was the first time I had seen a properly-lighted city since leaving Halifax four years before; Gibraltar was the closest thing to it, but that was nothing to this; and the contrast with London, even the slightly less gloomy London of the new "dimout," was stunning. The impression merely served to strengthen the belief that four miserable winters had rooted in my mind that the blackout was literally a major horror of the war.

A few days taught me, however, that while Canada had been spared that particular affliction it bore the marks of the war in many other ways. During the war I had heard many a Canadian officer, returned from the

Dominion to England, loudly upbraiding his stay-at-home countrymen and declaring, "People there don't know there's a war on." There may have been some justification for this at one time (though I always suspected that it was a bit artificial, owing something to the general unpopularity of the King government with the forces); but I found little evidence to support it in the winter of 1944-45. The desperate overcrowding of all forms of public transport — the Ottawa and Toronto streetcars as well as long-distance trains — was reminiscent of similar conditions in Britain. And when in my simplicity I sallied forth to buy some of the articles with which people overseas pictured shops at home as bulging, I got a rude shock. Such items as flannel shirts, socks, slippers and pyjamas were almost wholly lacking; thus the racks that in peacetime had held socks in endless variety of size and colour were now quite empty. After I returned to England I bought the things I needed with comparatively little trouble. (Luckily, I was not short of coupons; and this prompts the reflection that the conditions I found in Canada were partly the result of the absence of stringent rationing there.)

People, however, were suffering from more than little material inconveniences. There were many signs that here as elsewhere the long-continued strain of the war was taking its toll. My friends were four years older than when I had seen them last; but I felt that many of them had in fact aged far more than that. Men and women were tired of the war and anxious to see the end of it. One businessman told me what a bitter disappointment it was that more progress had not been made on the Western Front, and seemed surprised when I reminded him that a year before we would all have been very happy if we could have been certain that the coming year would bring such successes as we had actually won. The long casualty lists of the past couple of years had had their due effect, bereaving thousands of households and touching others with constant fear. And the bitter political controversy then in progress over conscription certainly added to the general sense of strain.

After living in a country where universal conscription was the accepted fact, it seemed strange to find Canadian cities full of mural advertisements calling for recruits. Queen's Park in Toronto had been defaced by a hoarding bearing the familiar poster representing a girl munition-worker holding out a new No. 4 rifle with the words, "It's yours — Good Shooting." (Later, I found that in the United States advertising for recruits was also the rule; but there it was limited to the women's services, which were evidently competing feverishly against each other.) One grew accustomed to the G.S. badge that general service soldiers wore to distinguish them from Home Defence "Zombies." I wrote, "Such things were easier to stomach (for me, at least) than the febrile and, indeed, psychopathic tone in which the conscription issue was being discussed in the newspapers, and particularly the unmeasured abuse which was being hurled at General McNaughton, the new Minister of National Defence, by the opposition press. Politically the state of the country was tragic."

In Ottawa I had two conversations with General McNaughton. The main one was limited largely to the matter of his files; he now asked me to return to him those he had left with me, making photostats of those I needed in my work. In a more casual talk, at the Governor General's New Year levee, he emphasized that Duguid was to have access to everything, including files on future operations (which seemed to me rather unnecessary). We had no talk about his political position and difficulties; of this I was glad. I heard one penetrating remark on the subject from my old friend General Maurice Pope, now military staff officer to the Prime Minister, who one day joined Brigadier Penhale and me at lunch at the Rideau Club. He said that he thought the importance of McNaughton's appointment as minister, succeeding the conscriptionist Ralston, was that it gave Quebec three weeks to make up its collective mind to accept overseas conscription, which in the end it did, though with the greatest reluctance.

Doris and I had a week in the United States, visiting my sister in Providence over Christmas; we got to Princeton for a day. In the nature of things, I had so little real contact with Americans that it was hard to form any worthwhile opinion of the state of the country. My Canadian colonel's uniform excited considerable speculation (I was called everything from "Captain" to "General") but seemed to be regarded with a generally friendly eye.

The food situation at the time of our visit was much worse in the United States than in Canada, and the general level of prices there was very much higher. (It seemed to be universally admitted that the Canadian price controls had worked extremely well.) On the other hand, supplies of manufactured goods appeared to be much better than in Canada; the stuff was to be had — at a price. In the matter of food, Canada was infinitely better off than Britain. Such rationing as still existed in Canada (it had been more stringent earlier) was no great hardship; and to a man who had seen just one shell egg between his return from France on 17 September and his departure from London on 3 December it was astounding to be able to order (and get) as many eggs as he wanted. And there was an unlimited supply of grapefruit and oranges, a tremendous boon. Britain, of course, had not been much of a fruit country at the best of times; but now the contrast between the situation there and the Canadian fruitstore windows, packed with scarlet and gold delicacies shining under the bright lights, was painful.

We had heard, at earlier stages of the war, stories of soldiers being abused in the streets of Canadian cities (particularly cities predominantly French) and had been told that the population in general was less friendly to the King's uniform than in Britain. I saw little in 1944 to support this — though once in a street in Lower Town Ottawa I did hear a soldier jeered at by some young civilians (he automatically replied, "Yellow rats!"). One instance of consideration for the uniform contrasted strangely with practice in the United Kingdom: on the crowded trains of the Christmas season servicemen were given priority, and civilians got seats afterwards if any were left. In Britain, troops were forbidden to travel during the holiday week, and civilians had the train to themselves. As a soldier, I preferred the Canadian system.

I went back to the United Kingdom by sea. (I thought at the time that the fact that a place could not be found for me on an aircraft perhaps reflected the state of feeling between National Defence Headquarters and the army overseas.) I sailed from Halifax on 11 January 1945 in the new *Mauretania*, a fine ship, now stripped to accommodate the maximum number of troops and carrying a very heavy armament of anti-aircraft guns and rockets. My voyage this time was a contrast with that of 1940. Then I had the good luck to travel on a ship which had her peacetime fittings; but such a fortunate lot was not to be expected late in the war. I was lucky, as the result of a bit of mild wangling: I got half of a very small two-berth cabin, thereby removing myself from another cabin which until then had held three colonels and four lieutenant-colonels. Everything was highly regimented, as was probably necessary in such conditions; everyone without exception was pushed out on deck at certain hours, and pushed below at certain other hours; at times I had the sense of being an inmate of an unusually well-conducted penitentiary. You got only two meals a day (nothing at all in between); but the meals you did get were large and excellent. We soon learned to carry a bun away from the breakfast table; and this, combined with the odd apple or orange and a bit of chocolate, enabled one to carry on comfortably until the far-distant evening meal. But it was not, on the whole, a comfortable passage.

The ship sailed unescorted, relying on her speed to protect her against submarines and (presumably) her armament in case of air attack. However, as we neared the United Kingdom a Coastal Command aircraft kept an eye on us, and on the last night two destroyers joined us. There was another contrast with the voyage of 1940. Then, I recall, a fatherly RNR officer had told us, "In case the ship should be torpedoed, there's nothing to worry about. Destroyers will be alongside in a couple of minutes, and all you have to do is climb down the scramble nets on to their decks." (The reassuring effect of this was of course reduced when the destroyers failed to find us.) In the *Mauretania* all anybody said in the way of comfort (I think it was the unpleasant RAF group captain who was the permanent ship's commandant) was, "The North Atlantic at this season is so cold that nobody lasts in it for more than a couple of minutes."

My fellow passengers included the second group of conscripts being sent overseas under the new policy. I must say that these notorious "Zombies" were on the whole better disciplined and better behaved than the 2nd Division volunteers who had crossed with me in the *Capetown Castle* four years before. The headquarters of the 15th Infantry Brigade was on board, and from its officers I heard a good deal about this brigade's troubles (the nasty word "mutiny" was being officially avoided) at Terrace, B.C., late in November, after the decision to send the conscripts overseas was announced. They emphasized how well organized the "dissidents" were; and they all as one man reported that the prime movers in the affair were not French-Canadian soldiers. The people responsible, they said, were Central Europeans from the prairies, including a certain number of actual Germans.[2]

Back in Cockspur Street there was plenty to do. Our various narratives marched on. Duguid had agreed with me that it was desirable to get to work in Ottawa on a policy narrative concerning events in Canada parallel to the overseas one on which we had been engaged so long, and was anxious that George Stanley, with his skill and experience, should be made available to do this job. This made sense, but other commitments prevented George from getting away to Canada until the summer. (When he did reach Duguid's establishment, he told me afterwards, he was treated as if he didn't exist.) Jim Conacher was putting the final touches to a narrative of Sicily which not only made an important contribution to our history but also helped get Jim a Harvard Ph.D. And to our miscellaneous writing jobs was added an unusual assignment when we were asked to help write a booklet to explain to all ranks, in simple language, the army's plans for repatriation and demobilization.

In February we finally got authority from Ottawa to produce the second booklet in the series that was now to be called "The Canadian Army at War"; this was to deal with the fighting in Sicily and the first phase on the Italian mainland. Sam Hughes and I shared this job between us; I drafted the section on Sicily, and he, with the benefit of first-hand knowledge, wrote the later chapters. We wrote it in less than two months; *From Pachino to Ortona*, text, maps and illustrations, went off to National Defence Headquarters by air on 12 April. I think, in retrospect, that this modest little effort gained rather than lost by the speed with which we produced it. Looking at it now, it seems to my prejudiced eye a rather lively and interesting piece of writing. The credit, I think, is largely Sam's.

One of the curious tasks that fell to me at CMHQ was lending assistance to Emil Ludwig. A German Jew by birth and a Swiss citizen by choice, Ludwig was a popular biographer whose books had enormous sales; his subjects included Lincoln, Bismarck, Napoleon and Jesus Christ. He was living in the United States in 1943, when something moved him to approach Mackenzie King with a request to sit for a literary "portrait". King was nothing loath, and *Mackenzie King: A Portrait Sketch* appeared the following year. It was extremely thin both in size and content; it is interesting that Ludwig did not include it in any of the bibliographies of his works that I have found in reference books. For King, however, the connection with Ludwig was tremendously important. When he was planning his memoirs in 1948, the first chapter heading that occurred to him was "My friendship with Ludwig" (the second was "Relationship with Sovereigns of Britain").[3] In these circumstances, it is not surprising that when Ludwig came overseas early in 1945 to look at the Canadian army, he was preceded by a cable from Ottawa instructing us to roll out the red carpet for him.

On a day in April I was called to General Montague's office, introduced to the distinguished visitor and told to be good to him. I took him to my own office and we talked. I remember him as an agreeable little man of rather owlish appearance. I soon discovered that he knew almost nothing of military matters, of Canada, or (curiously enough) of Mackenzie King, about whom he had just written a book. In an attempt to give him a glimpse of reality, I mentioned that Mr. King was very unpopular in the army. He registered surprise and said "Why? Is it because he is in favour of conscription?" At that point, I fear, I gave up. What he wanted from us was an outline of Canadian operations in North-West Europe. This we provided, and he went away, I trust happy. What distinguished literary production, if any, resulted from his visit to the Canadian army I never heard.

The big news in the Canadian Army Overseas in the late winter and early spring of 1945 was the reunion of the army (though it was news that the general public did not hear for a long time). It had not taken the government long to discover that it had made a fundamental error in dividing its army, and it was asking for the 1st Canadian Corps back from Italy before it had fought a real battle. Reuniting the army, however, was slower than dividing it; the Combined Chiefs of Staff made the necessary decision only early in February 1945. Between late that month and the end of March the Canadian formations from Italy were arriving in the Low Countries, and the 1st Corps, now commanded by Lieutenant-General Charles Foulkes, came under General Crerar on 15 March.[4] The move was very popular with the Canadians from the southern theatre; though the complaint was sometimes to be heard that the brick buildings of Holland offered much less secure cover from fire than the stone ones of Italy.

The reunion of the army meant that we could and should reorganize our field historical services. The two little Field Historical Sections could now be thrown into one. I felt that there was no great need for continuing permanent historical representation at the two Corps headquarters; the whole show could be directed from Army Headquarters. The really vital elements, the historical officer and the artist at each division, with the irreducible minimum of transport and clerical help, remained as they were. Eric Harrison would be in command as a lieutenant-colonel, and would still be able to look after the Army Commander's dispatches; Gus Sesia would be his second-in-command.

It seemed a good idea for me to travel to the Continent to discuss these new arrangements with the commanders there and with my own officers. Also, I wanted another look at the war before it folded up. I set off accordingly on 12 April. At Main Headquarters First Canadian Army, which was in a Dutch army barracks at Grave, I found Eric Harrison, and we were joined by Joe Wrinch and the historical officer for the 5th Canadian Armoured Division, Captain Ralph Currelly, who had been recruited in Italy and whom I had not met before. We proceeded to plan my tour, which took me to both Corps headquarters and all five of our divisions and gave me a good look at large portions of the liberated Netherlands and occupied Germany.

Once again I wrote down my impressions for the benefit of my family back in Canada:

> Holland — the parts I was able to visit — showed fewer signs of misery and privation than I had expected. There has certainly been much misery under the German occupation (and every so often one would hear in messes of evidences which our troops had discovered of Gestapo atrocities); but the eastern part of the country was not starving. I suspect that a farming community never starves; it can always produce the essentials of life for itself. It is presumably in the great port cities (still in German hands) that we will find real famine [we did]. And it was quite extraordinary to see how neat and prim the Dutch have contrived to keep their country under the conditions of the past few years. There can have been no shortage of paint in the Netherlands; every house seems freshly painted, and (except in the numerous places that have been devastated in action) towns and countryside alike are bright and shining, as neat as a new pin. The contrast with Britain, where for years past there has been no paint worth buying and the country has been getting steadily shabbier, was very striking.
>
> But there was no doubt about the attitude of the Dutch people; they were terribly glad to see us. As many Canadians said to me, they are less demonstrative folk than those of Brussels and other communities where the liberators got wonderful receptions last year; in spite of this, the atmosphere of the newly-freed towns was very like that of Upper Normandy last September, and as we drove through them with the population waving and shouting and smiling I recaptured some of the wonderful exaltation of those days. . . .

A liberated Dutch town is — very literally — a riot of colour. Holland, I think, must have been a great country for flags in peacetime; for now every house seems to have its flag — and they are all large and all clean. The proper way to display the national colours seems to be to fly the red-white-and-blue flag with an orange swallow-tail pennant above it; and frequently one sees a version of the flag with orange substituted for red. The whole country has decked itself with the royal colour of Oranje-Nassau: every little girl seems to have an orange hair-ribbon, and many have orange dresses; and their elders usually wear a little bow of orange ribbon. . . . Incidentally, one sees almost no flag except the native one. In Normandy we used to see plenty of British and American flags; but in all my travels about Holland I saw, I think, only one British and three U.S. flags. The explanation, I suspect, is that whereas the French in many cases had to make flags . . . the Dutch all owned flags already, and of course the flags were all Dutch. I was glad to find that one of our War Artists — Alex Colville, who has been doing very fine work — was doing a picture which will record the scene in a Dutch town as the people greet the liberating troops. The picture is full of colour and animation, and strictly true.*

Our troops liked the Dutch and were getting on very well with them, and incidentally preferred the people in the northern part of the country to the southerners among whom they had spent the winter. I had heard many officers say that after the war there would be a new and special relationship between Canada and the Netherlands; something which has certainly come to pass. It was a good moment in history. "Things are happening in Holland these days," I wrote, "which are like the happy ending of a fairy story. One of our divisions which I visited [the 3rd] . . . had its headquarters on a lovely Dutch estate. The owner, the local nobleman, was a Dutch patriot who had to go into hiding two or three years ago to save himself from the Germans. During all that time his wife had had (so I was told) only one letter from him, and had given him up for dead. But the night before my visit he came back — and sent one of the Dutch women living nearby

---

* Alex, I gather, didn't like this picture. Civilian mob scenes lacked reality for him compared with the grimmer facts of war. (And yet liberation was what the war was all about.) He did not turn the picture in with his other productions, but presented it to the Canadian Legion in Sackville, N.B.

into the house ahead of him to tell his wife, so his appearing would not be too severe a shock to her. Later the Canadian general [Holley Keefler] tried to apologize for ruts which our vehicles had made in the Baron's lawn. The Baron refused to hear of any apology. 'General,' he said, 'those ruts will never be disturbed. They will be left forever as memorials of the liberation of my country by the Canadians!' "

In Germany things were different. The bright banners of Holland gave place to plain, chaste, simple white; "There is a white flag on almost every building," I wrote. "I need hardly say, moreover, that the reception by the populace, where there is a populace, is quite different. They watch you pass by without betraying any emotion, either friendly or hostile. One group of children waved at our car in quite the Dutch manner; on the other hand, one little girl, obviously quite unreconstructed, put out her tongue at us and said "Bah!" before her (very) slightly older sister, who was clearly badly scared, could drag her into the house. We did *not* shoot the child and burn the house." Our men, remembering what the Germans had done to other people, took grim satisfaction in seeing what had happened to some German towns. "Cleves, where Anne came from (also called Cleve, Kleve and Kleef) is really an extraordinary scene of destruction; but even so it is probably better off than Emmerich, on the other side of the Rhine, where a great part of the place is literally flat. And there is always somebody to tell you of some town which is still harder hit; when I spoke of Emmerich, some Englishman immediately spoke up and said, 'But have you seen Wesel, sir?' (I hadn't, and still haven't; but I am prepared to take it on trust.)"

There was very little apparent disposition on the part of the German civilians to offer resistance to our troops. However, at one place, Sögel, on the 4th Canadian Armoured Division front, investigation established that civilians had taken part in the fighting; in reprisal, the centre of the town was systematically demolished. Four days later, at Friesoythe, the Argyll and Sutherland Highlanders of Canada of this division lost their popular commanding officer, Lieutenant-Colonel Freddie Wigle. Apparently a rumour was going round that Colonel Wigle had been killed by a civilian sniper; as a result a great part of the town of Friesoythe was set on fire in a mistaken reprisal. This unfortunate episode only came to my notice and thus got into the pages of history because I was in Friesoythe at the time and saw people being turned out of their houses and the houses burned. How painfully easy it is for the business of "reprisals" to get out of hand! I am glad to say that I never heard of another such case. That day at Friesoythe was, I think, the only day in the war when this Whitehall warrior got close enough to the front to hear small-arms fire; the 4th Division was preparing to attack across the Küsten Canal to the north.

During this nine-day trip to the Continent I did a lot of business. I saw General Crerar and discussed the new historical arrangements in the theatre. He said he liked the way in which our overseas Preliminary Narrative (the one on which George Stanley had been engaged) was being done, and warmly approved the idea of a similar narrative to be written at Ottawa; and he agreed that the future official history should be directed at *the public*. At 2nd Corps I had a long talk with the Corps Commander, General Simonds. He, too, accepted (after some doubt) the idea of a history directed at the public; and he said that it should bring out unmistakeably the fundamental lessons of the war, particularly the facts that it is utterly absurd to try to fight a major war on a basis of limited liability; and that you cannot merely put a Canadian into uniform and expect him at once to become a first-class soldier. The Canadian fighting formations in both great wars were effective because of their high standard of training. The Canadian Corps of the first war was, in the later stages of the war, an extraordinarily well-trained and experienced formation; while the Canadians in this war were, by the time they went into action, better trained than any regular troops had ever been. It was not the first time I had heard these or similar ideas from Guy Simonds; he had said much the same thing on the first occasion I met him, in his closing address to the Canada War Staff Course held at Ford Manor in 1941, of which he was commandant.* In 1945 he threw in the additional opinion that after this war Canada should adopt some form of universal service, which would simplify our problems in any future war. Guy was an impressive and incisive talker, in public or in private.

At 1st Corps I didn't see the Corps Commander, Charles Foulkes, but I talked with his Chief of Staff, George Kitching. Both Corps headquarters were unwilling to lose their resident historians (Major Wrinch at 1st Corps, Major Sesia at 2nd), and I undertook to try to leave them there for a time, Joe Wrinch being "on command" from CMHQ At 2nd Corps I had good

---

* The reader of *The Canadian Army, 1939-1945*, page 310, will find that I incorporated this very sensible suggestion of General Simonds verbatim, adding that our troops, however well trained, found that they still had something to learn on the battlefield.

conversations with two old friends, Elliot Rodger, the Chief of Staff, and Fin Clark, the Chief Signal Officer.

Going the round of the divisions, I saw the whole roster of historians at work. At the 1st Division (lately from Italy) I met Tom Allen; there was no artist there at that moment, for Tom MacDonald had lately been brought back to England and not yet replaced by Orville Fisher. At the 2nd Division were Murray Hunter and George Pepper, now a veteran; at the 3rd, Bob Gray (who had come to us from public relations) and Alex Colville; at the 4th, John Spurr and Bruno Bobak; while at the 5th (also fresh from Italy) were Ralph Currelly as historical officer and Campbell Tinning as artist. These were the "second generation" of our men in the field; the pioneer workers of earlier days were mostly back in London now, writing up or painting up the events they had been present at in earlier stages.

During this tour I was struck, and not particularly favourably, by the increase in pomp and ostentation at our senior headquarters, and particularly at Army. Every general, like every cabinet minister, is exposed to sycophants who are always ready to suggest expedients to enhance the comfort or magnificence of the great man. These people, I suspect, had been at work. Army Headquarters in McNaughton's time had been a simple place; it still was in Normandy, where the Army Commander's visitors' mess at Pihem was a tent in a messy farmyard. How different now! I wrote home: "This trip was definitely *not* a case of roughing it. I slept two nights in tents and one night in a caravan [trailer]; but the others I spent in magnificent houses, taken over as visitors' messes. So this is war! I felt that the whole apparatus was absurd, and all the other visitors felt the same way. (It is all of a piece with the Army Commander's guest caravan 'The Viper's Nest',* the captured vehicle which was described in the papers and which is really an incredible object.)" Harry Crerar's "A" mess became more and more a holy of holies; I was never invited there during my visits to the Continent, though General McNaughton had always invited me to a meal there when I was doing business with him. Just before I returned to England Army Headquarters moved to its final operational location at Delden; I remember seeing sappers at work building an imposing brick fireplace for the "A" mess marquee. At Delden, the last night before my return, I ate a

---

* VIP = Very Important Person. Needless to say, I never made the Viper's Nest. That was for visiting cabinet ministers and the like.

meal in a mess tent pitched in really idyllic surroundings in a lovely Dutch park, while a band played soft music nearby. The food and drink, while not sybaritic, were good. It was very pleasant; but several of us remarked that it was definitely not warlike.

London's blackout ended officially on 23 April. This was conclusive evidence that the war with Germany was nearly over. A fortnight later we Londoners, permanent and temporary, celebrated VE Day — the day of Victory in Europe.

The news that all German forces had surrendered came on 7 May. The London streets rapidly became a mass of colour. Any flag except the enemy's was all right to use for decoration, and there were some funny combinations and juxtapositions; owing I suppose to some freak of the supply situation, the South African flag was in evidence in particularly large numbers, and I am sure that a lot of the people who carried it or hung it out hadn't the faintest idea what it was. I had arranged to go to an early evening showing of the film *Henry V* with my neighbour David Patey. When we came out of the theatre we were surprised to find the streets comparatively quiet; it had been announced that the next day, the 8th, would be the official VE Day. It was to be a holiday, and Winston Churchill would broadcast at three in the afternoon.

Next day — a fine and warm day, exactly right — I went down to the office in time for lunch, which I ate in Mrs. Massey's club across the street. A little before three I climbed to the roof of the Sun Life Building, went across on to the roof of Canada House and looked down into Trafalgar Square. It was crammed with people (perhaps 20,000, we thought) waiting for Churchill's speech to come over the loudspeakers. From the roof we heard him with difficulty. At the end of the speech a bugle sounded the *cease fire*, then came "God Save the King," and the crowd sang it. For the rest of the afternoon the West End streets were full of good-humoured people making cheerful noises. Curiously enough, the American soldier, who had been such a *very* prominent feature of the London scene for so many months past, seemed to have become submerged; in the hour of victory the English had got their country back — even the West End of London. Someone said later, when I mentioned this, "When the East End comes up everything else is submerged" — but there were a lot of people there besides the East Enders.

I had dinner at the East India Club, and at nine o'clock I went out into Trafalgar Square and listened to the King's speech come over the loud-speakers, in circumstances very different from those in which I had listened to him in Montreal in September 1939. Thereafter, with untold thousands of other people, I made my way towards Buckingham Palace. The great open space in front of it was absolutely jammed with people; but by follow-ing in the wake of one of the improvised processions which were a feature of the day I penetrated to the south side of the Victoria Memorial just as the King, the Queen and the two princesses came out upon the balcony. Back in Pall Mall, the scene was really rather thrilling. The great gas torches that decorated the fronts of so many of the clubs were flaring brightly, shining on the bright flags and the streets teeming with happy people and making an extraordinary picture. In Trafalgar Square there were searchlights and a bonfire, and overhead a low-flying Dakota (I think) was circling in the gath-ering darkness. I got into the queue for the tube at the Strand Station and made my way home to Hampstead, where I had a date with a local bonfire.

It turned out to be quite a good bonfire. It began rather tentatively, but as it went on and the flames lighted up the street the highly respectable and very retiring residents of the region gradually and timidly began to come out of their shells, appearing one by one and blinking at the fire in pleased surprise. Neighbours who had probably never spoken to each other became acquainted that evening; and people began to vie with each other in pro-ducing fuel for our fire. At last it developed into a ceremonial burning of blackouts: an admirable symbol of the ending of the country's long ordeal. And then out of the night there came a group of young people with a piano accordion, and they stood about and sang, and danced in the firelight, while the respectable local residents looked on in a mixture of pleasure and embarrassment. The evening ended with sandwiches and drinks at the Pateys' and some time between one and two I pushed off home to bed, reflecting that my total drinking for the day was a pint of cider and two glasses of sherry, and that nevertheless I had contrived to have a very good and interesting time.

The thing that I remember most vividly, that made the most lasting impression on me, was the behaviour of the vast crowds that thronged the West End: so cheerful, so happy, so utterly pleased with life, and yet so utterly harmless, so invincibly well-behaved. There can have been few peo-ple who hadn't had a drink or two; but there were extraordinarily few drunks. I never felt so strongly the greatness of the English people as I did that day.

And so the shooting, in Europe at least, was over. The second war with Germany was passing into history. The Canadian Army had played its part. The time had come to get down to writing the story. Who was going to do it, and how? Getting an answer to those questions was the next task.

Chapter 12

Launching a History

As the echoes of the last shots of the war with Germany died away, we had an approved plan for a history of the Canadian army's part in it. What we didn't have was a historian to write it; and even before the fighting ended the members of the able historical staff that I had gradually assembled overseas were beginning to mention their urgent desire to get back to their civilian jobs at the earliest possible moment. The universities, faced with the prospect of a great influx of students coming out of the forces, wanted their professors back. Like everybody else, I myself was worried about the immediate future.

The job I had been doing for the past four and a half years made me an obvious candidate for the position of official historian, and there was no blinking the fact that the post interested me. In a sense, I had been in training for it since October 1940. At this point, there ought to have been some initiative from Ottawa — a proposal to appoint either me or somebody else. There was none; and with our wartime historical organization beginning to fade away the question had to be raised from overseas. I discussed it with my superiors, who were also I can say my friends, putting on no pretence that I was not interested, but emphasizing the element of urgency and mentioning that I had a job waiting for me at Princeton. I also put my ideas in writing as to the conditions that should govern the job:

169

My own opinion is . . . that if the History is to be worth anything the Official Historian must be placed in an independent position, which should be defined in advance by Order in Council. The formula used in the last Official History, — to the effect that the author has been given full access to official documents, but that inferences drawn and opinions expressed are those of the author himself, for which the Department is in no way responsible — would be a sound guide to procedure and should be taken literally. I think that any individual would be unwise to undertake the responsibilities involved without an understanding that he would be fully responsible, that he would have an adequate staff, and that his work would not be subject to censorship except on grounds of military security.

General Montague sent this memorandum to the Army Commander, adding, "My own thought is that Stacey is the logical and by far the best qualified person to undertake this task, but I certainly would not advise him to do so, or even suggest that he should do so, unless the conditions outlined . . . were fully fulfilled by the Government in advance." General Crerar fully agreed, and in consequence a letter making strong recommendations along these lines was sent from Canadian Military Headquarters to the Department of National Defence on 30 June 1945. Looking at the correspondence now I see that a tactical error was made. This letter should have been a personal communication addressed to the Chief of the General Staff. Instead, it went as a routine letter signed by the Deputy Chief of the General Staff and making no reference to the fact that it expressed the views of the Chief of Staff and the Army Commander. This made it much easier to brush off.

At any rate, on 17 August the Chief of the General Staff, General Murchie, signed a reply that was not very satisfactory from my point of view. It ran in part:

2. The Minister [General McNaughton] has decided that the work will be carried out within the framework of the Active Army and by Army personnel, as an Army project.
3. Approval has been given by the Minister for the continuance of Colonel C. P. Stacey in his present post, with rank and grading not less than he now has, as Official Historian, in charge of Production of the History of the Canadian Army in this war. This appointment will be

subject to the normal conditions under which all staff officers are employed. No Government can waive control of material contained in official publications. Colonel Stacey should be so informed.

It was only some years later, accidentally leafing over the file in Ottawa, that I discovered who had drafted this pomposity: it was Colonel Duguid.

This came close to ending the whole thing so far as I was concerned. After all, there was no shortage of jobs for professors of history in 1945. But people (I particularly remember Brigadier Penhale) suggested that I had a certain moral responsibility to stay with the ship if decent conditions could be obtained: and I certainly wanted to do so.[1] What was more, the guard was changing at National Defence Headquarters. Andy McNaughton's sad venture into politics ended with his resignation of the National Defence portfolio on 21 August: simultaneously the wartime overseas army was taking over at Ottawa, in the person of Lieutenant-General Charles Foulkes as Chief of the General Staff. This appointment, which some people thought strange, I shall have something to say about in a moment. Andy's loyalties to his old friends (among whom I think we must number Duguid) ceased to influence the situation. On 14 September another cable, drafted by me, was sent to Ottawa by the new Chief of Staff at CMHQ, General Murchie (note, please, that Murch, as C of S CMHQ, was replying to a communication sent by himself as CGS Ottawa). It went personally to General Foulkes:

> Para I   Stacey while interested in seeing the work through states that he would not care to assume responsibility proposed without obtaining clarifications serving to give him assurance quote that I shall have means of performing task with credit to the army and the country and without discredit to intellectual honesty and status as historians of my associates and myself unquote.

> Para II   He believes task can be carried out within framework of active army provided special requirements are recognized and work protected against interference and interruptions. Considers following requirements essential.

> Para III   Status of official historian. (A) official historian should have access to CGS when occasion arises. (B) volumes of history when completed and recommended by official historian for publication should be

subject to approval only on CGS and ministerial level. This analogous to Australian practice. Object is not to prevent circulation and discussion of drafts which is clearly desirable but to guard against possible petty or interested interference and speed up work. (C) staff employed in preparing history both at CMHQ and DND should be exclusively responsible to official historian and required to perform no other tasks. This entails separate staff to deal with inquiries and miscellaneous historical work but would eliminate a major cause of delay operative in case of 1914-19 history.

Foulkes' reply could hardly have been improved on: "Your para three: (A) agree (B) agree (C) agree." It also held out the hope of conditions favourable to the continued employment of our competent people, and asked that I should be sent for a visit to Ottawa as soon as possible. The result was that Colonel Duguid and I had an interview with General Foulkes on 5 October. The Chief told us that he proposed to appoint me director of the Historical Section at once. Duguid was to be given a separate directorate and staff with no responsibilities except completing the history of the first war. The old gentleman accepted this situation very cheerfully, but I may as well say at once that no history resulted. He was, I think, past the point where he was capable of a real effort of production.

I proceeded to draft a revised plan for the Second World War army history. This substituted for the volume on the Japanese war which had been "overtaken by events" a volume on general military policy, events in and around Canada, and operations based on Canada. The plan for a preliminary sketch history was retained, and I still talked of writing the whole works in five years, while admitting that actually getting it into print would take a little longer. Very fortunately, as it turned out, this scheme was submitted to the new Minister of National Defence, Mr. Douglas Abbott, and by him approved.

Clearly, all this involved a fundamental change in my scheme of things. I was now to earn my living as a regular soldier. I was not abandoning my vocation as professional historian; but for the present at least I was saying good-bye to university teaching. This involved ending my long and pleasant connection with Princeton.

I had been exchanging letters with various of my Princeton colleagues throughout the war. The university had undertaken that at the end of the war I could expect to return to Princeton for at least one year at my rank and salary of 1940 (i.e., assistant professor and $3000 or thereabouts). When it began to appear that I might be offered something attractive in Ottawa I felt that I should inquire of Princeton whether the prospect there was likely to improve. On 24 August I wrote to Joe Strayer, the eminent medievalist who was now chairman of the History Department, explaining how things stood: that the offer of an important and relatively lucrative position in Canada seemed possible, but that the conditions in other respects might not be attractive and that I should like to know how Princeton saw my future. Joe replied that while I could certainly count on an advance in salary if I returned he could not say more until he had a chance to consult the senior members of the department. Before I heard from him again General Foulkes made his offer and called me to Ottawa.

On 9 October, in Toronto, I wrote my letter of resignation from Princeton. I described the arrangements made at the Department of National Defence and said that, all things considered, I had felt that I could not refuse the proposition that had been made to me. I asked Strayer to tell the president and the department how sorry I was to be taking this step. Either for want of time, or perhaps from reluctance to take this final irrevocable step, I did not post the letter the day I wrote it, and next day in Ottawa I found a letter from Joe Strayer, sent on from London. It was one of those communications containing the phrase, "This has been a hard letter to write." Joe said I could return to Princeton as an assistant professor "at a sizable increase in salary but with no promise of immediate advancement." One reason was that "The President is unwilling to promise advancement to men who left here as assistant professors until he sees what the war has done to them." As for the department's own attitude, there were three other men more or less in my position and it was as yet unwilling to give me priority. Joe observed, "I think there is a feeling in the Department that your work lies on the fringe of our interests." In other words, they were not interested in Canadian history, which was no news to me.

I suppressed an unworthy impulse to inquire whether any information was available as to what four years' hard service on the home front had done to President Harold Dodds. I simply added a postscript to the letter I had already written:

> 10 Oct. On returning to Ottawa I found awaiting me your letter of 25 September which had been forwarded from London. This of course merely demonstrates the soundness of the decision I had already taken.

So ended my official association with Princeton, which I still remember with affection and gratitude.

Turning to my new career, I should tell the story of how Charles Foulkes became Chief of the General Staff.

Most officers of the Canadian Army Overseas would have rated Guy Simonds well ahead of Foulkes as a commander. Simonds had few friends, I think, but many admirers. He was generally accounted our best tactician and probably our most genuinely brilliant senior officer. People particularly remembered his improvisation of armoured personnel carriers in the breakout operation in Normandy. This was the first appearance of the APC on any battlefield; today it is in every army. Foulkes' record was less sparkling. He had, I suspect, not many more friends than Simonds (though I think I would number myself among them) and definitely fewer admirers. The 2nd Division's performance under his command in Normandy was not distinguished (there were those who said that the division had never fully recovered from Dieppe). Later he commanded the 1st Corps competently in Italy and the Netherlands. He lacked Simonds' dash and *panache*. When he was appointed Chief of the General Staff over Simonds' head in 1945, many people no doubt said "politics"; but there was more to it than that. Foulkes was appointed because General Crerar, the Army Commander, considered him the better man for the job at that moment.

When Mackenzie King was in England just before D Day, Crerar told him that in the event of his becoming a casualty the best man to replace him was Guy Simonds. King recorded that the Army Commander called Simonds "A very good soldier, though he might not be the best man for post-war planning."[2] This was still Crerar's view after the German surrender, when the Department of National Defence formally sought his advice about the future employment of the two Corps Commanders. I saw the cables at CMHQ. The Army Commander's reply was long and measured. As I recall he wrote first about Simonds, speaking warmly of his success in command of the 1st Division in Sicily and the 2nd Corps in North-West Europe. He said that he was an officer primarily of operational type, but was also a highly trained and very experienced staff officer. Passing on to Foulkes, he gave a similar review of his record; he concluded, "Would consider him exceptionally qualified for very senior staff appointment." That presumably did it. The junior Corps Commander became

Chief of the General Staff, the senior one found himself for the moment merely commander of the "Canadian Forces in the Netherlands," the troops awaiting repatriation.

Guy Simonds was undoubtedly deeply hurt. It was reported that he asked for an appointment in the British Army, only to meet with a cool reception from Lord Montgomery, who offered him the rank of major-general, no prize for a lieutenant-general with a long and brilliant record as a corps commander. The British, of course, had their own people to look after. Subsequently Simonds, remaining in the Canadian army, was given a senior appointment at the Imperial Defence College, London.

In the face of much contrary opinion, I am inclined to think that Crerar was right. He obviously thought that Simonds, a first-rate battlefield commander, was not temperamentally suited to deal with politicians in a period of retrenchment. Some years later, when Simonds had become CGS, one of his senior subordinates said to me that what he particularly admired about Guy was that he never gave advice based on other than strictly military considerations. Under ideal conditions this is certainly an admirable trait in a soldier, but conditions are not always ideal, and to refuse to take note of political realities is likely to end merely in a general finding himself on the retired list. Simonds was fortunate in that his tenure as Chief coincided with the Korean War and the beginning of activity under the North Atlantic Treaty Organization, a period of military expansion. In four years he built up a powerful Canadian regular army, over 50,000 strong, which was much respected by our NATO allies (it is now largely a thing of the past). Nevertheless, it was believed that he got into difficulties with his political masters; it has been stated that when he retired Lord Montgomery asked for him for a senior NATO appointment in Europe, but the Canadian government refused.[3] He certainly left the service in a very bitter mood.

When I left London for the interview with General Foulkes in Ottawa I took with me the text of the third and last booklet in the "Canadian Army at War" series, *Canada's Battle in Normandy.* I had written this myself, beginning in May 1945, and the job brought me into discussion with General Simonds, and ultimately was somewhat affected by the new relationship between him and General Foulkes. On 28 July I sent a copy of the draft text to General Simonds in Holland for his comments. Two days later I had a cross-Channel telephone call from him (the war really *was* over) complaining rather strongly about certain passages, particularly those relating to Operation "Spring" (25 July 1944).

"Spring," which thus raised its unprepossessing head as a historical problem, was to be with us for a long time, and I had better explain it. Perhaps the best way is to quote the account of it which I finally published in *The Victory Campaign* in 1960. It was the final episode of the long pounding battle which the British and Canadians fought on the eastern flank of the Normandy bridgehead to keep the German armour tied up there and so assist the Americans to break out in the west. It was in fact on this very 25th of July that the Americans launched on their front the attack that was to result in the encirclement of two German armies. The Canadians' contribution was to run their heads against the formidable defences south of Caen held by the crack German divisions that otherwise would have been available to check the American offensive. It was, I wrote, "A bloody day":

> It is impossible to give a precise total for the Canadian battle casualties of Operation "Spring". . . . The most extreme case is that of the Canadian Black Watch. . . . It . . . seems evident that the Black Watch . . . had 307 casualties on 25 July. Five officers and 118 other ranks were killed or died of wounds. . . . Except for the Dieppe operation, there is no other instance in the Second World War where a Canadian battalion had so many casualties in a single day.
> . . . We should not be far wrong if we estimated the total battle casualties of Operation "Spring" at about 1500, and the fatal casualties at about 450. Again excepting Dieppe, it was the Canadian Army's costliest day of operations in the Second World War. The 2nd Canadian Corps attack had struck a stone wall. The result is not surprising, in view of the strength of the German positions and the powerful force of high-category troops which was holding them.

I no longer have the draft of *Canada's Battle in Normandy* that I sent to Guy Simonds, but the account of "Spring" in it was certainly generally similar to that just quoted, though in 1945 we didn't have the precise casualty figures that the statistical experts later ground out for us. Guy didn't like it, and he particularly didn't like the emphasis on the losses. A booklet described as "based upon a preliminary examination of official records" was not the best place for arguing with an ex-Corps Commander smarting under a recent slap from his government, so I modified the text by removing the comparison with casualties in other battles, while at the same time emphasizing the inexperience of the 2nd Division (which had been less than a fortnight in the line) and the importance of the one objective (the village of Verrières) which we had taken and held. This satisfied Guy.

However, it did not end our special problems about "Spring," and I may as well tell the rest of the story here. In the autumn of 1945 our minister, Mr. Abbott, came under pressure from his constituents in Montreal to issue a statement about the disaster to the Canadian Black Watch, a Montreal regiment. In the end he did not do so — a wise decision, since a statement would merely have turned a knife in old wounds and led to demands for similar statements about other misadventures. In the meantime, however, we were occupied in interviewing every survivor of the affair we could find still in England and some in Canada. (I remember George Stanley interviewing one of Mr. Abbott's ministerial colleagues, Major Walter Harris, the Minister of Finance, who had commanded the tank squadron supporting the battalion and was wounded. He wasn't very communicative.) It was a grim tale; we gathered that of some 300 officers and men committed to the attack against the west end of the Verrières Ridge, only about fifteen got back to our lines. I remember one private soldier saying to me that when the storm of fire from dug-in German tanks struck them on the summit of the ridge, "We just pushed on, sir; we had been told that was the Black Watch way."

This affair had involved both Simonds and Foulkes: the former as Corps Commander, the latter as commander of the 2nd Division which included the Black Watch. The subordinate of July 1944 had become the Chief, and this did nothing to sweeten the controversy that took place between them now. It flared up again when I sent them copies of the draft of our preliminary one-volume history for comment. Foulkes resented Simonds' tendency to blame the inefficiency of our troops for our misfortunes; and although Simonds said "Spring" was a "holding attack" — a term which could be applied to the whole series of operations on the British front — Foulkes said *he* had never been told it was a holding attack (it had been represented to him as a break-through operation with prospects of success) and he doubted whether Simonds had been told either. Here is a passage of my notes of an interview with General Foulkes on 27 June 1947:

> ... Gen Simonds was at Gen Foulkes' headquarters most of the day. He issued orders late in the afternoon for the renewal of the attack on the 26th, and it was only when Gen Foulkes visited Gen Simonds' headquarters on the evening of the 25th, intending to report that it was out of the question to renew the attack, that he found that orders had been

received from Gen Dempsey [commanding the Second British Army, under which the 2nd Canadian Corps was still serving at this time] that the further attack would not take place. Gen Foulkes incidentally mentioned that at this time Gen Simonds had gone to bed and would not see him, but he got the above information from members of the staff.

When I took over the Historical Section the arrangement was that in the interest of getting on with the job as rapidly as possible the records then overseas should remain there for the present, and a small historical staff should be kept in London to work on them. I myself for a year or so commuted between Ottawa and London, spending a few months in each place alternately.

Staff was the constant problem. A quotation from my Ottawa diary for 21 June 1946 tells what was going on:

Capt. L. P. Harris, War Artist, took his leave of D.H.S. [Director Historical Section]; he is now returning to civil life. Capt. J.E.A. Crake, Narrator, did the same. Capt. J. B. Conacher, Narrator, left us a few days ago. Our excellent wartime staff is rapidly melting away; the attractions of academic life are apparently too great to overcome, although we would be glad to have these narrator officers remain with the Section.

George Stanley, fortunately for me, stayed on for a year as deputy director in Ottawa, finally leaving us for the University of British Columbia at the end of 1946. Eric Harrison went back to Queen's, but returned to us for a summer of work overseas. Jim Conacher also came back for a time later. Sam Hughes, a lieutenant-colonel in the final stages, held the fort for me in London until the law called him too loudly to be disregarded. The war artist program came to its final end when Major Charles Comfort, who had latterly functioned, to its great profit, as officer in charge of it, said good-bye at the end of June 1946.

Luckily, some of the veterans stayed. Particularly important was Major Gerald Nicholson, who had been recruited by Duguid and had spent some time with us in London. A Saskatchewan high-school principal in civil life, he was an excellent writer and researcher and a very pleasant person: the obvious replacement for George Stanley as deputy director. I was lucky also that Murray Hunter, with his sound academic training and field experience, stayed by the ship. When we cut down the section in London to a liaison post, as we shortly did, he was our representative there for some time, and had his full share of problems. Both Nicholson and Hunter drafted parts of our preliminary "Summary." Mac Hitsman carried on with us as a civilian, defying his growing physical disability. Charles Lynn-Grant came back to Ottawa in the role of executive officer and took charge of the administration of our considerable staff and of miscellaneous tasks such as dealing with inquiries; the public seemed to have an insatiable appetite for odd military historical information. Some wartime officers fortunately became available to work in the directorate for limited periods; Captain R. A. Spencer joined us late in 1945, and Captain B. Legge soon afterwards. Like Conacher, Spencer later became a colleague of mine in the Department of History at the University of Toronto. It is quite impossible to name all the officers who worked in the section for longer or shorter times, as researchers or administrators. Courtney Bond drew our excellent maps, which many other authors have since paid him the compliment of pirating. John Porter, later noted as the author of *The Vertical Mosaic*, drafted a chapter of *The Victory Campaign*, and surprised me long afterwards by saying that in our shop he learned a lot about writing. Fred Steiger, first as an officer, later as a civilian, made a unique and indispensable contribution by his work on the German documents. Doug Cunningham, Dave Fromow, Archie Huestis, Reg Roy, Roy Oglesby — the list could be made much longer, and indeed many other names of people to whom I owe debts can be found in the prefaces of my various books.

Our attempts to find suitable narrators among the officers of the regular army were only moderately successful. I wrote later, "My experience, over the years, in trying to teach young army officers with BA degrees and an alleged 'interest' in history to do historical research left me with a higher respect for my own profession that I had had before. I had always thought the job was rather easy; but many of these people simply could not do it."[4] On the other hand, I found that there were people without university educations who were natural researchers; Captain L.R. Cameron, whom we inherited from Duguid, was one of these. The tendency as the years passed was for the directorate to become increasingly civilian. Nevertheless I would emphasize that writing military history is difficult for anyone who has not had at least some tincture of military training or experience.

Gibbon talked sense when, recalling his unregenerate early years, he said that the captain of the Hampshire grenadiers had not been useless to the historian of the Roman Empire.

With the three little booklets out of the way, we settled down to our first major historical task: writing the one-volume preliminary history. We called it at first an "Official Historical Sketch," but at Brooke Claxton's instance the word "Sketch" was later changed to "Summary." I began work on it in Ottawa late in October 1945, the same month in which I was appointed official historian, and we pushed it on with more than convenient speed. When I wrote later that we achieved publication on 5 May 1948, the third anniversary of the cease fire in Europe, only by "taking no leave and working, one might almost say, nights, Sundays, and holidays," I exaggerated, but not by much. During these years the Historical Section, or at any rate the members of it closely involved in the production of the book, worked almost at wartime pitch.

I may as well describe the book. I called it simply *The Canadian Army, 1939-1945*. It amounted to just over 350 printed pages, with a dozen illustrations in colour (reproductions of pictures by our war artists), and numerous maps. In a preliminary work of this sort documentation seemed unnecessary, though I noted in the preface that in many cases "the sources of quotations and statements made are identified in the text." As I have already mentioned, Gerry Nicholson and Murray Hunter drafted portions of the text, Gerry the latter part of the story of the Italian campaign and Murray part of that dealing with North-West Europe. As we carefully explained to the reader, the book was necessarily an interim report, "a Summary, not a History." My tattered old office copy of it is pockmarked with emendations, additions and corrections, particularly where statistics are concerned. Nevertheless, I think, the book has not worn too badly, and while the person who wants a precise account of the Canadian army in the Second World War should read the three-volume history which we produced later, the old Summary still affords a fairly satisfactory bird's-eye view of the struggle and the achievement.

Chapter 13

Swanning with Rex*

In the summer of 1946 there was a brief interlude whose story I cannot fail to tell, for I dined out on it for years. I found myself conducting the Prime Minister of Canada, the now legendary Mackenzie King, over the Canadian battlefields in France.

At this time I was still working in London. Across the Channel in Paris a so-called "peace conference" was in progress. It was not much of a conference; essentially, it consisted of representatives of the great Allied powers revealing to their smaller partners the arrangements they had made for making peace with some of the enemy countries, and giving them an opportunity to offer comments. Mackenzie King headed the Canadian delegation to this rather curious exercise; and someone apparently suggested that he might use a couple of week-ends during the meeting to visit some of the fields where his countrymen had lately shed their blood. The

---

* Two explanations are needed here. The verb *to swan* is defined by the newest *Concise Oxford Dictionary* as meaning to move "aimlessly or majestically (*around*) like swan." This has much to commend it, but in the wartime army "swanning" connoted slightly illicit travel, journeys which were certainly not, in the phrasing of the official posters, "really necessary," and were undertaken at public expense. Rex was the name by which Mackenzie King was known to his intimates, of whom the author was not one.

result was that I received a message asking me to prepare an itinerary, followed almost immediately by a firm invitation to act as guide.

Naturally, I was not sorry to take on the job. I had seen King but had never met him; for a historian, this was an opportunity. I could not claim to be really well acquainted with the battlefields of Normandy, but I certainly knew more about them than King did; and this was a chance to improve my knowledge. Luckily, I had lately dispatched an expedition composed of Bob Spencer, Bruce Legge, and a borrowed public relations photographer to take photographs of those same battlefields and make topographical notes about them before the terrain changed too much; and Bob was able to brief me on certain special areas that might be of interest to the Prime Minister. On 7 August, I set off for Paris by civil aircraft. I had been bothered to discover that international currency regulations prevented me from carrying with me a single penny in either French or English money. Being by now a confirmed pessimist, I felt sure that this was the time army arrangements would break down; there would be nobody to meet me at Orly Airport, and Parisians would see the undignified spectacle of a Canadian colonel carrying his bedroll (I had brought it with me as a precaution) into the city on his shoulder. My fears were groundless; awaiting me were two cheerful Canadian soldiers with a jeep, which whisked me rapidly to the Crillon in the Place de la Concorde, a better hotel than I had been wont to inhabit in Paris in my student days.

In the hotel lobby I immediately encountered money trouble. A bellboy seized my bedroll. How was I to remunerate him? I looked wildly round for a Canadian face, and providentially saw one: that of James Gibson, one of Mackenzie King's secretaries. I rushed up to him and said, "Jimmy, for God's sake lend me a little money to pay this bellboy!" I still remember the look of pain that came across Gibson's handsome features; but he reached into his pocket and produced the necessary currency. (I am almost certain I paid him back after contacting the delegation's paymaster.) I found myself billeted in what had once been a truly splendid three-roomed suite. The phrase for it now was tarnished magnificence. I got it because Mike Pearson had just moved out, and General Pope had not yet arrived, and the delegation wanted to hold on to the suite. It had a gold-plated shower, which didn't work, and a gold-plated telephone; it didn't work either. The day after my arrival I talked the proposed expedition over with various eminent people, notably Brooke Claxton, the Minister of Health and Welfare, and Arnold Heeney, the Secretary to the Cabinet. It was arranged that on 9 August I should journey down to Caen to make arrangements with the local authorities. Claxton and Heeney explained to me that Mr. King was old and tired, and that ceremonies should be kept to a minimum to avoid fatiguing him further. It was on that day, I think, that I saw Edouard Handy, the P.M.'s confidential secretary, carrying his notebook into King's corner suite, and somebody remarked, "The old man is going to dictate his diary." This, I believe, was the first time I ever heard of the Mackenzie King diary.

On arriving in Caen I betook myself to the Préfecture. The prefect of Calvados, it turned out, had gone fishing as soon as he heard Mr. King was coming; he was reported to be a Communist. The person left in charge was the *secrétaire général*, a delightful and obviously competent youngish civil servant named Monsieur Pasquier. I made my arrangements with him in my best (and rather broken) University College French (it was only later that it came to light that he was much too polite to allow it to be known that he spoke at least as good English as I did). We laid on the itinerary, I duly explained that the elderly P.M. must be spared too many ceremonies, and we parted good friends.

The next morning the official caravan set out from Paris for Normandy. As it formed up outside the hotel I was first introduced to King, saluted him and shook the prime ministerial hand. He was most affable, as indeed he was to be throughout. At this stage I was not in his car; I rode in the leading vehicle with Arnold Heeney, Brooke Claxton, Dana Wilgress and the military attaché. The Prime Minister rode in the second car with the ambassador, General Vanier. (For the actual tour of the battlefields, the ambassador and I changed places, and I rode with the P.M.)

Reaching Caen at lunchtime, we proceeded to the Mairie. Here there was a *vin d'honneur*, a form of entertainment with which we became only too familiar during the next two days. The maire read an eloquent address of welcome. Then King drew from his pocket a half-sheet of notepaper on which somebody had written for him three short paragraphs in French. These he read in an accent so excruciatingly bad that I suspect most of his hearers thought he was speaking English. He then finished the speech in actual English, which Georges Vanier gracefully translated. When King had finished his remarks he folded the half-sheet of notepaper and put it in his pocket. Throughout the rest of the tour he kept producing it (it got grubbier and grubbier mile by mile) and reading one of the three paragraphs to whatever audience happened to confront him at the moment. Sometimes it was the middle paragraph, sometimes it was the last one, sometimes it was the first one; the one thing you could be absolutely certain of was that it would have no relationship whatever to the business in hand. This procedure put a distinct strain on the politeness of quite a number of French mayors; their looks of astonishment were something to see. The time came when we all winced when the P.M. reached for his pocket.

I must pay a humble tribute here to dear old Georges Vanier. The tour must have been very difficult for him, constantly dancing attendance on the Prime Minister and called upon for mediation and translation at a moment's notice. But his courtly good humour never failed. We were all grateful to him for one particular achievement. Arnold Heeney, in the memoirs he wrote on his deathbed, said of Georges' translations of King, "The brief and pedestrian sentences in English were transmuted at some length into deliberate and moving French."[1] Except for the excellence of the French, Arnold got the facts precisely reversed. As the tour proceeded, King's speeches got no shorter, but Vanier's translations shrank and shrank. In the end, he would render ten minutes or so of King's English into about a minute and a half of flowing French, without, it seemed, leaving out anything material. I never admired Georges Vanier so much.

From the Mairie in Caen we repaired to the Préfecture, where we sat eating and drinking until four o'clock, and left for the battlefields, merely snatching a cup of coffee and a glass of brandy as we left the Préfecture.

Stacey's careful time-table for the tour already lay in ruins, but worse was to come. With true French *insouciance* the municipal authorities of the little places south of Caen had decided to disregard the directive that there should be no *cérémonies* in honour of the distinguished visitor. Was he not the chief executive of that country far away from which young men had come two years before to drive the *Allemands* out of this countryside where they had no right to be? There was no question of getting through the villages with merely a wave to the people in the street. The roads were blocked — blocked by the people waiting for *les canadiens*. Always there was the mayor with his tricolour sash and his address of welcome, and always of course there was the reply — sometimes a paragraph from that awful piece of paper, sometimes a short speech in English followed by a translation by the ambassador.

And let no one think that it was not moving — far more moving than the pomps of Caen. I remember more than other places Fontenay-le-Marmion, still half in ruins — the tiny hamlet below the Verrières Ridge that had been the objective of the Canadian Black Watch when they were cut to pieces in Operation "Spring." A streamer across the street said in flowers "Honneur au Canada." The mayor (I think he was the local shoe-maker) came running, adjusting his sash, to read his address and give Mr. King a present. A little girl handed the Prime Minister a bouquet, and he kissed her on both cheeks. And the youngsters from the village school, eight or ten in number, sang (under their teacher's careful supervision) "O Canada," "God Save the King" (in English) and the "Marseillaise." I stood saluting in the street, very close to disgracing my uniform with tears.

My time-table was increasingly wrecked as we went on our way, wrecked by the determination of the local people to engage in acts of wel-come, wrecked by the Prime Minister's enjoyment of the whole thing and refusal to be hurried. The official story I had been given to tell, that he was old and tired and must be spared all unnecessary ceremonies, was shown up as an absurdity; the more ceremonies there were the better the old gen-tleman liked it, and indeed he seemed to grow steadily younger as the miles rolled by and the cheers of the populace resounded. After all, he never got this sort of reception in Canada! Late, late in the afternoon, hours after our schedule called for it, we reached Falaise. This town, so famous in 1944, had been utterly ruined by the Allied air forces. Almost alone in surviving intact were the *Hôtel de Ville* and in front of it the eques-trian statue of William the Conqueror, Falaise's most celebrated son. How they escaped destruction seemed hard to fathom — unless perhaps the RAF and the USAAF were using them as aiming marks. The *vin d'honneur* here was in a large upper room of the *Hôtel de Ville*. I was troubled. Our party were to be the guests of the Republic at dinner at a château outside Falaise at eight o'clock. My still unfulfilled itinerary called for a trip to the area of the Gap of 1944, and it was out of the question to do this and still be on time for the official dinner. I was sure that the Prime Minister had only the vaguest idea of the terrain we were covering or its relationship to the events of 1944. I looked about, observed that King appeared to be engaged in conversation on the other side of the room, and said to one of our party that I thought it would be wise if we quietly dropped the Gap trip from the program. To my astonishment a voice said sharply in my ear, "What's that? What's that? We are going to do the whole tour just as planned." To this day I don't know how King heard me or just how he arrived beside me so suddenly. It was as if he had travelled underground. At any rate, I had had an object lesson in the difficulty of putting anything over on Mackenzie King.

And so it happened that as the soft August dusk fell, at a time when we should have been sitting down to dinner, we (or some of us) were in fact speechifying in the village street at Chambois, where the 1st Polish Armoured Division met the 90th U.S. Infantry Division on the evening of 19 August 1944 and closed the Falaise Gap. Actually, we had more speeches than usual, for it occurred to King to give Brooke Claxton a chance to show off his French. Brooke, who I suspect had prime ministerial ambitions at this period, was assiduously studying French (as an English-speaking Montrealer, he had naturally known little of the language). He had acquired a sound vocabulary, but he had no ear at all and his accent was unbelievable. In any case, King felt it necessary to introduce him at some length; the introduction then had to be translated by Georges Vanier; so on that occasion we had three speeches instead of the customary two. We finally sat down to dinner at 10:30 p.m. (I imagine the chef had shot himself) and rose from the table at 1:30 a.m. I need not say that it was a magnificent repast, with, I seem to remember, at least six kinds of wine. (To these, I noted, the Prime Minister did justice, though in moderation; the war was over, and his self-denying ordinance against alcohol had been revoked.)

The next morning we set off to see the beaches on which the Canadians had landed. The mayor of Courseulles-sur-Mer was one of the few officials who had paid any attention to the directive about avoiding ceremony. He received the Prime Minister quite informally, though very politely, while the town band (the local *sapeurs-pompiers* doubling in brass) played softly in the background. But King was not pleased. He said to General Vanier, "George, ask him to say a few words so I can reply." Georges, looking exquisitely unhappy, did so; and the mayor, overcoming his surprise, said a few well-chosen words. Then the P.M. reached into his pocket, pulled out that very tired piece of paper, and read an unusually unsuitable paragraph. We saw Bayeux and the tapestry, we saw some more of Caen and Falaise, and that night we drove back to Paris. We had reverted to the arrangements of our original drive from the capital, and Claxton, Heeney,

Wilgress and I, relieved of the presence of the Prime Minister, sang all the way.

Mackenzie King, it had been pretty obvious, was not very much interested in the battlefields as such. I did my best, and he listened politely, but I feel sure that he still had no real idea of what went on in Lower Normandy in 1944. What interested him was crowds of people. Bob Spencer had discovered that the British Columbia Regiment's tanks were still on the spot east of Estrées-la-Campagne where the regiment, after losing its way, was virtually destroyed on 9 August 1944. To me it was a very moving scene, with the rusting Shermans standing shot through and through by the German Panthers and Tigers that had concentrated against them after they had taken up their mistaken position. I took King there, but he wasn't interested. I couldn't get him out of the car. Here in the heart of the Norman countryside there was no crowd to cheer: nothing for a politician. I rather think he resented being taken to this dull place, and that this is the origin of one of the few references to me in his diary, not a particularly friendly one: "It interested me to see how Stacey, the historian, seemed to pick out each particular class of tank by name. One felt it was almost a sort of worship of these various instruments of destruction. Horrible looking things. All rusted. Piled up."[2] At the moment my feelings towards King were no more friendly than his to me.

I was struck by the fact that King made no attempt to pick the brains of the people he met. Pasquier, for instance, might well have had interesting things to say about contemporary France; but King showed no disposition to draw him out. The Prime Minister's conversation, I remember saying later, was just what you might have heard from any old gentleman on the back of a Toronto streetcar. I wrote to my family, "After two days' riding in his car, he defeats me. He is not without political virtues (obviously!); he made some very good impromptu speeches; and yet there is a total absence of any impression of intellectual force or vigour. His conversation is of the most commonplace — he talks about the harvest and sympathizes in vague general terms with the bombed-out people, particularly the children; and one is left wondering how he reached his present position and held it for such a long period. But he is a hard man to know and understand, and one should doubtless reserve judgment. One should remember, too, that he is probably past his best; he is 72, and his suite are constantly remarking that he gets tired easily and needs to be protected. (Yet, as you will have gathered, this tour was no rest-cure; and he stood up to it extraordinarily well.) And I suppose I should not be talking about him in this vein; for he was really very kind and affable to me." Later in the same month I was moved to set down some notes on King as I had seen him. I wrote among other things that his "delight in the adulation of the French public inevitably left an impression of vanity," and that in my less charitable moments during the tour "I found myself feeling that I was acting as bear-leader to a vain and rather foolish old man."

I flew back to London the day after our return from Normandy; but I had not seen the last of King. Almost at once I was told that I was wanted again in Paris. The Prime Minister was to pay a visit to Dieppe. The fourth anniversary of the great raid of 19 August 1942 was upon us.

The Prime Minister and his group (including me) drove to Dieppe from Paris on 17 August. A very considerable Canadian official party, including the senior officers of the three Canadian services in Britain, and a number of survivors of the raid, came from England for the anniversary observances. The ceremonies were numerous, and I shall not bore the reader by describing them all. On the 18th there were religious services at the village of Puys, east of Dieppe, which was the scene of the most tragic episode of the raid, where the Royal Regiment of Canada was destroyed on the beach, suffering the heaviest casualties that any Canadian unit took in a single day in the whole war. I was standing close to King on the shingle as he looked at the tall sea-wall and the narrow gap in the cliffs that the battalion had been supposed to penetrate. Only a combination of good luck and surprise could have brought success there, and the unfortunate Royals had neither. I found myself remembering President Truman's outburst at (I think it was) Salerno: "What squirrel-headed general had the idea of landing here?" King was not Truman. He said nothing; but that he was thinking was obvious, and it was not hard to divine his thoughts. And since he set them down in his diary, we know exactly what they were: "I really felt as though the men who had planned that raid ought to have been cashiered ... It was sending men to certain death without a ghost of a chance ... It just made one indignant beyond words."[3]

Later that day there was an incident which struck me as singularly unhappy. The Canadian Minister of Agriculture, Jimmy Gardiner, was a member of our party. He had lost a son flying at Dieppe. The boy and his wingman were both buried in the village churchyard of St. Aubin-le-Cauf, some miles inland. We went there so that wreaths could be laid on the graves. There were few Canadian troops left overseas in August 1946, but we had brought a little detachment of the Canadian Provost Corps over from London to lend a military touch to the anniversary. Four men under a sergeant were posted at the graves. As the Prime Minister and Mr. Gardiner went forward to lay their wreaths they presented arms. One might have thought that at that point a moment of respectful silence would have been most in order; but politicians have little use for silence. To my astonishment, King launched into a speech. He was, of course, quite oblivious to the fact that the soldiers were still standing painfully at the present. I watched the rifles beginning to waver; and then I caught the unfortunate sergeant's eye and signed to him to do something, and with a half-whispered command he brought them down to the order. It was my one useful contribution that day. The affair was not over. Georges Vanier, of course, had to translate King's speech, and then Jimmy Gardiner was moved to speak too. Georges translated him also, and then, God help us, the Prime Minister remembered some things he had forgotten to say and we had yet another oration.

An event that evening I recall with more pleasure. After the obligatory official dinner we adjourned to a beautiful little eighteenth-century theatre on the front of the town overlooking the sea. Luckily it had survived the raid, though there was some fighting in and around it. In honour of the visitors, who were seated in what in a monarchical country would have been the royal box, there was a concert of Canadian music. The music, I am sorry to say, I do not remember; but one thing I do remember. Among the guests from England was Major-General Ham Roberts, the Military Force Commander at Dieppe, who had been little in the public eye since he lost the command of the 2nd Division in 1943. At the climax of the entertainment the mayor of Dieppe rose and addressed the gathering. He spoke with a force and clarity that riveted his words into my memory. "Mesdames, messieurs, je vous présente le général Roberts, qui commanda le débarquement canadien sur les plages de Dieppe, le 19 août 1942." The whole theatre rose up with a roar of applause; and old Ham, blushing, stood up and took a bow. It was, I suspect, the best moment of his life; and I was delighted to see some honour paid to a soldier who had played his part and suffered, as Ham certainly had. Quite enough, I thought to myself, had gone to a confirmed civilian who had run no risks save political ones and had hated the army all his days.

The next day was the actual anniversary of the raid. The high point of the program was to be the laying by the Prime Minister of the cornerstone of a monument which the city of Dieppe proposed to erect to commemorate the raid and the liberation of the city by the 2nd Canadian Division in 1944. The site was at the west end of the promenade, below the castle and facing the sea. The local authorities had prepared the ceremony with characteristic care. In front of the site of the monument a large space had been kept clear. There was no guard of honour; but formed on the left was a splendid French army band, which I was told was the *Musique militaire de la région de Lille*. The dignitaries and citizenry of Dieppe were present in numbers. Our party drove up in a *cortège* of cars, King in the first one. The cars stopped. King alighted and stepped forward on to the open space, followed by General Murchie, the Chief of Staff at CMHQ, and the rest of us. At that moment the band struck up "O Canada."

Murch halted and saluted with such dignity as a man of his considerable tonnage was capable of. We all halted and saluted. All, that is, except the Prime Minister. Mackenzie King was ahead of us and did not see us stop. But I also feel quite certain that he didn't recognize the tune. At any rate, while his suite stood stiffly at attention honouring what we used as a national anthem, King went toddling forward, smiling happily at the assembled populace. And as he drew abreast of the band, as God is my judge, he *waved* at the bandmaster. (I have never seen a more astounded young French soldier.) It was about then, I think, that General Murchie was heard to say, not in a particularly low tone, "Oh, God damn it!" He ceased saluting and wandered after the Prime Minister. And then the rest of us did the same. What the French onlookers thought I still wonder. Perhaps they thought they were witnessing an old Canadian custom. It all seems funny now; but at the moment it was acutely humiliating.

The ceremony then proceeded. I cannot help recalling that it had been impressed upon us that precise timing was essential, for to begin the observance a Spitfire wing of the Royal Air Force was to fly over from England, honouring the fourth anniversary of the RAF's greatest air battle of the war; it lost more aircraft over Dieppe than on any other single day.* The

---

* I had had some trouble in getting the Air Ministry to admit this, but they finally did.

moment came; and there appeared — one Spitfire, which engaged in a few aerobatics. Various people in brown, I regret to say, stood around saying, "How bloody characteristic."

Nevertheless, the afternoon ended with a certain touch of glory. The Canadian party — a fairly large one, including the senior officers, the dozen or so Dieppe veterans, the Provost detachment, the miscellaneous military types like myself, and, of coure, the Prime Minister and his hangers-on — marched through the town. The band took the head of the motley little column, playing "Sambre et Meuse" (roughly the French equivalent of "The British Grenadiers"). The streets were thronged; every window of the tall houses was full of people, applauding and throwing flowers. It was a considerable moment. And certainly Mackenzie King was in his element. He was as cheerful and active as a schoolboy, returning the citizens' plaudits with waves and smiles. He picked up a bouquet that somebody had thrown and brandished it gleefully at the cheering people in the windows. In his diary he described it all with typical awkwardness: "No expression of rejoicing could be more touching than this expression of love and rejoicing, this afternoon."[4]

I said good-bye to Mackenzie King that day before hitching a ride back to England in a RCAF aircraft. I never met him again, and my only contacts with him were a couple of telephone conversations when he was seeking advice about help with the memoirs which he never wrote. He impressed me as being indeed the enigma that so many people called him. A week after the Dieppe visit, I wrote, "There was no sense of a forceful penetrating mind at work; and one was left wondering just how the Prime Minister concealed the qualities which he must have possessed in order to rise to the highest office in an important state and retain that office for so long a period."

Fate decreed that in later years I should spend quite a bit of time reading his extraordinary diary, which I first heard of in the Crillon that day in August 1946, and trying to gain a fuller understanding of the man with whom I had a passing acquaintance at the time. One impression which those contacts in 1946 left with me the diary confirmed. King struck me as curiously unsure of himself, insecure. I remember something that happened when we visited the place at the Château d'Audrieu where the men of the Royal Winnipeg Rifles murdered by the S.S. had been temporarily buried. The group of us approached the spot with some uncertainty:

what does one do at an empty grave? We military people waited for the Prime Minister to set us some example. We then realized that he was waiting for an example from us; in fact, he was craning forward to see what those of us on each side of him were doing. We saluted; and King then removed his hat. Other incidents left a similar impression on me. At the time I attributed this to the fact that he was ill at ease with soldiers. After I had read the diary I realized that it was in fact an inbred insecurity, rather remarkable in a man with such a tremendous record of political success. One place where it appeared was in his attitude towards the preparation of speeches. He was unwilling to speak without a complete manuscript before him. He revised and revised; and he made life hell for the members of his staff who were assisting in drafting. And yet I can testify that he was capable of very effective impromptu speech when circumstances forced it upon him. The day of the ceremony at the Dieppe monument we had an official luncheon. King was to speak, and he had a prepared manuscript. But we ran late; the Spitfires were supposed to arrive at a precise moment; and the proceedings had to be shortened. King threw his manuscript aside and made a brief extempore address. It was excellent, the best speech I heard him give during that visit. yet this was the sort of thing he feared to attempt.

Chapter 14

The Fight for the History: Phase One

I t is time to get back to the mundane affairs of the army history, which passed through a serious crisis early in 1947.*

Mackenzie King, as I have noted, had always hated the army, and he didn't like the other fighting services much better. He had undoubtedly resented the apparent necessity in the period immediately following the war to maintain larger forces than those before 1939, and at the first opportunity he attacked them. Late in 1946 he moved Brooke Claxton into the Department of National Defence. Claxton, it is clear, was put in as a hatchetman to cut the defence budget. On 3 January 1946, as we now know from his diary, the Prime Minister told the cabinet, "What we needed now was to get back to the old Liberal principles of economy, reduction of taxation, anti-militarism, etc." These grand old principles now got me into bad trouble.

By working like galley-slaves we had made considerable progress in writing what was still called the Official Historical Sketch. In order to

---

* In this chapter and the following one I lean heavily upon the article entitled "The Life and Hard Times of an Official Historian" which I contributed to the *Canadian Historical Review* of March 1970.

speed publication I decided to submit the book for approval piecemeal, not waiting for a complete manuscript. By the beginning of 1947 I had three chapters ready to show the Chief of the General Staff. It was at this point that the roof fell in. On 16 January the new minister addressed the senior officers of the three services in Ottawa. He made rather a pleasant impression on me, in spite of talking of economies. He said that no one need worry about his security; all contracts and agreements would be carried out. That afternoon, however, the blow fell. I was summoned to General Foulkes' office where I presented my three chapters. He then proceeded to produce the bad news. All work on the Canadian Expeditionary Force history of 1914-18 would cease on 31 March next. No real objection could be taken to this; it was common knowledge around our directorate that Colonel Duguid was making no progress. But Foulkes went on to say that the cabinet had decided that no money would be spent on *any* histories after 31 March 1948. He said that there would still be useful work for a Historical Section after that date and was kind enough to say that he hoped I would stay in the army.

He suggested that we concentrate, during the time allowed for the completion of historical work, on the Sketch, perhaps developing it into a slightly more complete book. The government, he said, had felt that the recent slight improvement in relations with Russia permitted them to cut the defence services (appropriations for the three, next year, would be less than for the army alone this year). The government had concluded that it must cut taxes or lose the next election, and social services could not be cut. The general promised that my section's establishment would not be meddled with during the coming year. I told him I would think the matter over.

Thought brought only the conviction that there was nothing to do but get out. The day after the interview I wrote my friend Professor R. G. Trotter of Queen's University, Kingston, who had suggested I might go there when my army work was done. But on 20 January, as the result of an intervention of which at that moment I knew nothing, the situation changed dramatically. General Foulkes told me that the minister wished to see me; and he and I went to Mr. Claxton's office. As we walked down the corridor he told me to "hit hard."* With nothing to lose, and remembering

---

* Long afterwards, leafing through a file, I discovered that Foulkes had in fact told the minister that he could use the money allotted to the history to better advantage elsewhere. He did not mention this to me at the time.

Claxton's talk about contracts and agreements, I took him at his word. Here is the account in my diary:

> ... I told Mr. Claxton frankly that I considered the new policy on histories a breach of faith, two Ministers having approved our programme in detail, and that one short volume was absurd as a record of the Cdn Army in the War of 1939-45. He asked questions about the histories of the other services and showed (a) a desire to cut them short, while continuing that of the Army, and (b) a tendency to suggest a greater degree of co-ordination. He suggested in particular that our projected Vol IV on policy shd be converted into an inter-service policy volume. He appeared to accept the fact of a commitment on the Army history. He asked the C.G.S. to discuss the matter further with me and see him again tomorrow.

The corner had been turned. I gather that General Foulkes, facing a greater crisis than mine with the minister, got considerable quiet pleasure out of my accusing Claxton of a breach of faith. He obviously reported the remark, for shortly the Vice Chief, Church Mann, was heard saying, "Once more unto the breach of faith, dear friends, once more."

What had happened to change the situation? I recorded, "The C.G.S. told me that he considered the apparent change of heart was due to representations from Mr. L.B. Pearson of Dept of External Affairs, who suggested that foreign powers might be impressed by the fact that Canada apparently was not sufficiently interested in her armed forces to write a history of their achievements." This was in fact only part of the story. Mike Pearson, who on suitable occasions liked to advertise himself as a historian, had not leaped to the defence of history without being pushed. What had really taken place I found out three months later, when I visited Toronto and talked to an old friend, Professor George W. Brown of the University of Toronto's History Department. George told me that while in Ottawa on 15 January he had gone to see a former colleague, Gerry Riddell, now in External Affairs. Riddell had taken him to see Mike Pearson, likewise a former colleague. According to George's account, Mike "mentioned the decision to stop work on the war histories, merely making the observation that this might mean that there would be documents available for graduate students, etc." George expressed astonishment, said he thought the decision very unsound and added that he was sure I would resign at once.

Pearson, "who had apparently not thought of these matters," picked up the telephone on the spot and spoke to Claxton, arguing that the decision should be reversed. No doubt this chance meeting of Brown and Pearson was what saved the army history. If the history we wrote has any national value, the country should be grateful to the memory of George Brown, crediting Mike with an assist.

The histories of the other two services, which were not covered by the ministerial approvals that, by good luck, I had obtained for the army plans, didn't fare so well. Claxton didn't like the history Gilbert Tucker wrote of the navy's shoregoing activities (my recollection is that Gilbert had a volume dealing with the first war about ready for publication at the time of the 1947 crisis, and that Claxton took particular exception to the fact that it began with a very detailed account of German naval policy before 1914; this was deleted before the book appeared). In the end, Tucker's two useful volumes on the non-operational side of the navy's work in the two wars were duly published; I was told that Admiral Nelles, a wartime Chief of the Naval Staff, intervened strongly to save them. Tucker refused to attempt to write the history of naval operations until the German documents were available. Claxton himself, I think, arranged for Joseph Schull to write a popular history of Canada's naval fighting on the basis of narratives Tucker's people had compiled. This book *The Far Distant Ships*, is in many ways admirable, but is essentially introductory. If there is never a scholarly and critical history of Canadian naval operations based on all the records, including the other side's, blame this on Brooke Claxton.

The air force came off worse than the navy. Its historians had made the mistake of planning a vast history (I think, ten volumes); and I suspect the chiefs of the service gave them little support. Claxton once said in my hearing that the RCAF fought with the RAF and it was up to the British to tell the story. I should have told him that it would be a very cold day indeed when the British put themselves out to tell the story of the battles and problems of the RCAF; but I was busy with my own fight and assumed that somebody in light blue would tell him the facts of life about the air. If anybody did it had no effect. The air force history was shot down and stayed shot down. Again, the responsibility is Claxton's. When in 1965 I found myself presiding over the "integration" of the three service historical sections, I made it my business to get authority for the production of a history of the Royal Canadian Air Force. For a time it looked as though the people entrusted with the job were going to equal Colonel Duguid's record for cunctation; but in November 1980 I had the pleasure of attending a party to celebrate the publication of Volume One.

Brooke Claxton was certainly a very able man, but not quite so able as he thought he was. He reminded me of Sydney Smith's famous remark about Lord John Russell: "There is nothing he would not undertake. I believe he would perform the operation for the stone — build St. Peter's — or assume (with or without ten minutes' notice) the command of the Channel Fleet; and no one would discover by his manner that the patient had died — the church tumbled down — and the Channel Fleet been knocked to atoms." Brooke undoubtedly considered that he knew more about running the army than the Chief of the General Staff, and more about writing history than I did. Dealing with him was not rendered easier by the fact that he had a rather unfortunate manner. I hesitate to use the word uncouth, but he was certainly not one of the couther people I have known. In 1945 Mackenzie King, assessing his party colleagues as possible future leaders, wrote, "if Claxton had a better style of address, of speaking, etc., he would, in some ways, be the best of all to take on in the post-war period."[1] Indeed, his style of address left something to be desired, though I never knew him to be intentionally rude. As for his judgment, he told me at least twice that nobody would be interested in reading about the Second World War after about 1948. When one thinks of the hundreds of books about that war that have poured from the presses ever since, one wonders how anybody, even a politician, could be so remarkably wrong.

In his unpublished memoirs, which have served posthumously to give a favourable impression of him to historians who did not know him, Claxton left a fairly cordial reference to myself, describing me as "exceedingly thorough and sharp and independent."[2] For this I suppose I ought to be grateful, but it does not wholly erase the effect of my successive discussions with him about our project.

His suggestion that the policy volume of the army history should be converted into one on general war policy was thoroughly admirable. On the day after our first interview he approved a new plan incorporating this feature. Thereafter the problem was to get his approval for the text of our one-volume history. My running fight with Claxton over what he decided should be called the Official Historical Summary began in July 1947 when

I received from him four closely typed pages of comment on the opening chapters. One point that particularly disturbed me was a passage that presumably I had not been intended to see. I had quoted Sir John Dill as writing to General McNaughton about the Canadian involvement in the events in France in June 1940, "It is all rather a sorry tale but I am sure in the circumstances you will realise what our difficulties were . . ." Beside the words "rather a sorry tale" Brooke had minuted, "Should he be allowed to say this?" The attitude this suggested would have made any writing of history impossible, but fortunately it did not prove to be typical. (The quotation, incidentally, is in the book as published.)[3] On 11 August I had an hour's interview with Claxton about these comments. I wrote in my diary, ". . . I agreed to modify phrasing on two or three points. On all important matters the Minister agreed to my representations — notably in the act of Gen McNaughton's resignation. It transpired that he had not realized that the draft had been widely circulated and that General McNaughton had seen it. . . ."

On 29 September I saw the minister again about another batch of chapters:

> He made many points, among them the following: (a) He now dislikes the word "Sketch"; (b) He wishes either to sign the Preface or contribute a foreword (I got the impression that the former is his idea); (c) He thinks the introduction to the question of Gen McNaughton's resignation, as at present framed, likely to cause undue comment; (d) He wd like the ref to Seaforth Xmas dinner in a *church* at Ortona eliminated, as likely to cause difficulty, among Protestants or Catholics; (e) he is worried about the reference to a "Christmas truce" in 1944 in Italy, evidently feeling this could lead to criticism from various points of view; (f) He took exception to a quotation re bulldozers being used to cover common graves of German dead on the Gothic Line, saying it was "too brutal." He made a great many detailed comments on verbal points, etc. He began the conversation by saying that he was still convinced that there would be no interest whatever in Official Histories after 1948.

On 2 October I had another talk with Claxton:

> . . . I had made emendations (mostly minor) to meet his various specialized suggestions. He accepted all these except the only one that cd be

said to touch policy closely (the para introducing the section on Gen McNaughton's reputation): to this he said he wished to give further thought. (I suspected that he intended to show it to the P.M.) He was quite affable and made no further suggestion re the Preface.

Readers of the book will find that the church in Ortona, and the Christmas truce, survived; but the brutal Gothic Line bulldozers were cut out. I advised against the minister writing a foreword, arguing that traditional practice was against it; Charles Foulkes said to me that the name of an active politician on the book would damn it in the eyes of old soldiers and other readers. Claxton did not persist.

The fact that Claxton clearly disliked frank statements of the failure of an operation reminds me of what was literally the only direct instruction I ever received from anybody on how to write the official history. It was verbal, and it came from General Charles Foulkes. I have found no note of the date, but the words are very clear in my memory: "We must on no account conceal our failures." For this, if for nothing else, General Foulkes deserves to be remembered with esteem.

Claxton was particularly troubled by the reference in the Summary to General McNaughton's retirement from the command of the army. In the original version the introductory paragraph to this section read:

> The events which led to General McNaughton's retirement from the command of the First Canadian Army cannot be dealt with in a volume which is primarily an account of operations. That very complex crisis requires lengthier treatment than is possible within this set of covers; nor has investigation of it yet been completed. We can mention here only those aspects which are directly related to the question of the employment of the army.

This bothered the minister more than anything else in the book. At first he accepted it when assured that General McNaughton had read and accepted it; but later he re-opened the question. He felt the middle sentence of the paragraph was provocative. On 22 October he himself suggested an alternative version: "In a volume which is primarily an account of the operations of the Canadian Army, it is not possible to discuss fully the changes in command which from time to time occurred with the Army. Mention is made of the retirement of General McNaughton as

Army Commander in so far as that retirement affected its overall operational role." I agreed to this, subject to substituting for Claxton's last five words "was related to the Army's operational role."

A yellowed hand-written memorandum among my papers reminds me of an incident shortly before the publication of the Summary. In February 1948 a tremendous foofaraw was raised by George Drew, Tory politician, Mackenzie-King-hater, and counsel for the parliamentary opposition before the royal commission that had investigated the ill-fated Canadian expedition to Hong Kong in 1941, over certain secret cables from the British government which had been referred to in the course of the inquiry. Drew asserted that these cables (which the British authorities refused permission to publish) indicated that London had some foreknowledge of the intended Japanese attack and that the Canadian force was sent in spite of this. The commissioner had said that the cables would not have offered any reason for Canada withdrawing from the Hong Kong commitment.[4] I had not worried about these cables before, but with violent controversy raging in the press, I now felt that I should see them to satisfy myself that nothing in them invalidated statements made in the forthcoming Summary. General Foulkes and I went together to see Claxton and explained my problem. Claxton said he would consult the Prime Minister. My memo proceeds:

> The same evening I received a telephone message asking me to see the Minister in his office at the Parliament Bldgs.... I went to his office accordingly. He said that he had talked to Mr. [Louis] St. Laurent [Secretary of State for External Affairs] (presumably in the absence of the Prime Minister who was reported in the press to have a cold) and Mr. St. Laurent felt that I should not see the cables. With respect to a remark I had made in the afternoon (after Mr. Claxton had described the contents of the cables) that it might be well if I was in a position to say that I had seen them and took the same view of them as the Commissioner, Mr. Claxton said [I am sure he was reporting a remark of St. Laurent] that if this was done the opposition would merely say that this was a certificate from the Government's "paid apologist" ...
>
> Mr. Claxton said that he would *read* the cables to me, if I desired it, for my own satisfaction and protection. I said I should be grateful if he would do so. He then read five cables, ranging in date from 20 Sep 41

to 30 (?) Oct 41, from a ministerial file. I watched closely and felt satisfied that he read them in full.

Without going into details, the British appreciation as presented in these cables was that any Japanese attack was more likely to be directed against Russia than against the western democracies; a possible attack on Thailand was also mentioned. I summed up, "There was certainly no apprehension of such a broad and general offensive as actually began on 7 Dec 41; the tone in fact was almost complacent." The documents were far from creditable to British Intelligence, but they did nothing to support Mr. Drew's overheated imaginings, or to invalidate the account given in the Summary. I felt better, but I was not allowed to insert the statement about the cables that I had wished to do. I was left with the impression that Uncle Louis St. Laurent was a gentleman of obscurantist tendencies, an impression which was to be heightened by a later experience.

The best of the story remains to be told. Quite soon after the events I have just described, somebody at National Defence Headquarters cleared out his safe, found a lot of secret documents of the war period which presumably now had only historical interest, and very sensibly sent them to the Historical Section. When we examined them, we found among them four of the five famous Hong Kong cables! I could now examine them at my leisure — they fully confirmed the impressions I had already formed — but could not of course use them in print. When we came to produce the official history proper I was able to include the footnote that I would have liked to put in the Summary, stating that they fully supported the commissioner's conclusions, which indeed were substantiated by a variety of documents already published elsewhere.[5] For example, the American congressional inquiry into the Pearl Harbor attack had published — without any consultation with Britain — numbers of highly secret British papers that made the British appreciation of the situation quite clear.

Even after we had Claxton's approval, the production of the Summary was not altogether easy. The King's Printer chose to contract the job out to *Le Soleil* in Quebec City. The people at *Le Soleil* were willing, but we got the impression that they had never made a book before. Certainly we had to tell them everything, and Charles Lynn-Grant, who dealt with them, had many headaches. The book when it finally appeared in May 1948 was not particularly handsome, but it could have been worse.

We had sent portions of the draft to a good many participants for comment — this is one way of achieving accuracy — and these people and some others had to get copies of the book. And there was one person who certainly had to get an advance copy, suitably inscribed. Mackenzie King was still Prime Minister, though he retired later that year. Wording the inscription gave me a bad hour or two. The reader will have gathered that my admiration for King was not unlimited (I think I feel more kindly towards him a generation later). I had to be polite, but I did not want to be either an obvious sycophant or a liar. In the end, I wrote this: "To The Rt. Hon. W.L. Mackenzie King, O.M., Who as Prime Minister of Canada led the nation in the Second World War." That, I thought, would do, particularly as I had not specified whether he led the nation well or badly, or forward or backward. After two or three weeks with no acknowledgment, I began to think that the P.M. was going to take no notice of my effort; but I did him an injustice. Shortly I received a very pleasant note thanking me for the book "and for the words with which it is inscribed," and, while remarking with the cunning of an old book-receiver that he had so far had the opportunity "merely to glance through its pages," saying some kind things about the historian.

I think I can say with honesty that the book had a good reception from the public. The press, both in the news and editorial columns and the book review sections, was pretty uniformly kind. *The Legionary* said, *"The Canadian Army 1939-1945* is just what the veterans and the people of this country have been waiting for." And the notices in the serious and professional periodicals could not be complained of. I think the one I read with most pride was the review in the *American Historical Review* by my American opposite number, Kent Roberts Greenfield, late of Johns Hopkins. I quote a few sentences: "Writing combat narrative is a difficult art. Conscientiously practiced, it cannot produce breath-taking literature. But Colonel Stacey always writes clearly and, at certain points, inspired by his theme, he has written some of the finest pages of English prose that I have read in years." Even in those days, comparatively few academic reviewers commented on the style of the books they discussed. The practice is even rarer today, and I find myself suspecting nastily that the reviewer sometimes doesn't know good writing from bad. The late Harold Innis, so much admired, was a supposed expert on communication who was quite unable to communicate. But what use is research in history if the researcher cannot make his results clear and interesting to the reader? At any rate, I have put a good deal of myself into *The Canadian Army, 1939-1945*, and while I knew that Bob Greenfield was over-kind I was pleased to know that a good judge thought that it had merit as a book and not merely as a report.

Also, the book sold. In May 1955, when it had pretty well shot its bolt, the Queen's Printer told us that he had sold 15,040 copies, by Canadian standards a very good sale for a serious book. And it is worth mentioning that it had been given the Governor General's Award for Academic Non-Fiction for the year 1948. All told, my idea of a one-volume history to give Canadians at the earliest possible moment a rapid authentic sketch of what their army had done in the great crisis seemed to have worked out pretty well. So far as I know, Canada was the only country to attempt such an enterprise.

While we were working on the Summary, we were also getting a medical history under way. There was a tradition that the doctors should have a history of their own; a rather idiosyncratic history of the Canadian medical services in the first war by Sir Andrew Macphail was published in 1925. In the latter part of the second war a senior army medical officer was employed overseas in travelling, interviewing and collecting material for a history, but the result seems to have been nearly nil and at the end of hostilities he returned to civil life. In 1946, however, Lieutenant-Colonel W. R. Feasby of the Royal Canadian Army Medical Corps, who had been editing the *Journal of the Canadian Medical Services*, took on the job of editing an army medical history, being provided with a small research staff in my office. He worked for a modest stipend on a part-time basis. When Claxton came on the scene the army medical history was transformed into a tri-service one, Bill Feasby remaining in charge. My own responsibility for this project was purely administrative; I stayed as far away from the question of its content as possible. (As a doctor's son, I knew that a layman was wise to be cautious in dealing with the medical profession.) Bill Feasby had medical problems of his own — diabetes and failing eyesight — but he persisted courageously with a task that was complicated by personal and professional as well as inter-service jealousies. In the end, with the aid of many contributors on special subjects, he produced what seems to my ignorant eye a very respectable *Official History of the Canadian Medical Services, 1939-1945* in two volumes, one dealing with "clinical subjects," the other with organization and campaigns. They were published respectively in 1953 and 1956.

The decision to put the medical history on a tri-service basis was characteristic of Claxton, who had a strong bias towards integration, if not unification. If he had had his way, we might have had much sooner the absurd unification of the services carried out in the 1960s under Paul Hellyer; though perhaps it is unfair to Brooke to assume that he would have gone so far. But a number of measures in his time indicated the trend of his thinking; notably the fact that when the cadet colleges were re-opened in 1948 it was as joint services schools, training officers for all three services. The three historical sections came close to amalgamation. It appeared at one point in 1947 that a decision had been taken that this should be done, with me in charge. The plan was always vague, and it finally died. I would have taken the thing on if asked to, but I took no initiative in the matter. I think it may have been Charles Foulkes who finally killed the scheme; I remember him saying to me that if there was anything wrong with the naval history, we would get the blame. I was quite happy, and very busy, with the army history, and wanted nothing more.

In the final stages of producing the Summary, we became involved in an international dispute over access to what were called the Combined Records. The story has never been told before, but over thirty years have passed since the affair was amicably adjusted, and the Commonwealth Relations Office file on the matter is now available in the Public Records Office in London for all to see.[6]

The Combined Records were the high-level strategic records of the Grand Alliance — essentially, the records of the Combined Chiefs of Staff. The Combined Chiefs was an exclusively Anglo-American committee which ran the war on behalf of the Western Allies. During the war Canada and the other lesser members of the alliance accepted, with a more or less good grace, the fact that strategic direction rested with Great Britain and the United States, and their forces were employed in accordance with the decisions of the Combined Chiefs, the most important of which were taken in the great strategic conferences at which President Roosevelt and Prime Minister Churchill were usually present. Mackenzie King was at Quebec during the conferences there, but was not a member of them. It went without saying that while the war continued we Canadian historians had no access to the Allied strategic records, and did not expect it; but we assumed that when the fighting was over we would be able to consult these papers in order to give the Canadian public authentic explanations of how and why the decisions were made in accordance with which Canadian servicemen risked their lives. The people I dealt with in the Historical Section of the Cabinet Office in London assumed this too, and said so. It was the more astonishing when after the shooting stopped it became clear that this was not going to happen. Somebody on a high level decided that the papers would not be opened to Dominion historians. We would be allowed to submit questionnaires, to which the British or Americans would give such answers as they thought proper; we would not be allowed to see the files. This was no basis for scholarly history. When my liaison at the Cabinet Office, Brigadier H.B. Latham, told me about this, I could hardly believe my ears; I said that they were treating the great Commonwealth partners like minor foreign allies; we might have been the Dutch. Latham did not dissent, but there was nothing he could do.

The matter came to a head at a conference of American and Commonwealth official historians at Washington in February 1948. I had seen the fight coming, and General Foulkes, after consulting Claxton, had told me I could "wave as big a stick as I liked." Gerry Nicholson and I attended on behalf of Canada. The British representatives were Latham and Professor J.R.M. (later Sir James) Butler, a Cambridge don chiefly noted for a book on the Reform Bill of 1832, who had been appointed chief military historian. We had invited them to visit us in Ottawa either before or after the Washington meeting, but the invitation was declined on budgetary grounds. Butler said little during the Washington discussions. It seemed clear that the civil service was fully in control, and I was left with the impression that the voice of scholarship was muted in Whitehall.

The Americans had not been particularly aware of the Combined Records issue (they told me they had assumed that the Dominions had access to these papers) and they were largely passive and surprised spectators of the sanguinary skirmish that took place between the members of the Commonwealth. The main encounter was in the office of Brigadier-General Harry J. Malony, the U.S. army's chief of military history, on the morning of 7 February. (It may be explained that the U.S. army had a soldier as chief of military history and a civilian chief historian, Bob Greenfield. In Canada I combined the two jobs in myself.

The British organization was entirely civilian, though it included many retired officers, of whom Brigadier Latham was one.) The brief diary record I wrote later ran, "Rather acid exchanges between Brig Latham and myself, he claiming that in asking access to these [Combined Records] we were breaking 1947 agreement.* I dissented strongly." I got powerful support from Major-General Sir Howard Kippenberger, the very distinguished soldier who was the chief New Zealand historian. (His *Infantry Brigadier* is one of the very best personal memoirs of the war.) The Australian and South African representatives apparently couldn't see the issue at all; they sat like bumps on logs. The only decision we could come to on the Combined Records issue was that the matter would have to be settled on a higher level. As the business part of the meeting appeared to be over, and I had commitments in Canada, I returned home that night, leaving Gerry Nicholson to watch over Canadian interests.

The next day, however, something more happened. The Americans kindly arranged to take the visitors to see the battlefield of Gettysburg. Nicholson went on this expedition. But at least some of the British and American delegates remained in Washington; and that day they signed between themselves, behind everyone else's back, an "agreement." This dealt with the exchange of draft histories and narratives, but it also accepted the exclusion of Dominion historians from the Combined Records. This we would not have acquiesced in. In any case, we had no use for an agreement arrived at in such a manner.

General Foulkes, when I reported the situation to him, was inclined to favour trying to resolve it by informal action. I tried a letter to Latham, with no result. On Foulkes's suggestion I wrote on 14 July 1948 a letter to a member of the British High Commission staff in Ottawa, explaining

---

* This agreement is referred to in my diary for 2 June 1947, which notes that after talking to the navy and RCAF I prepared a letter to External Affairs, advising that the Department of National Defence was willing to accept a United Kingdom proposal for exchange of information, "on understanding that we will in practice be given access to diaries of Army Groups." Army groups were the highest purely British formations with which we had dealings. I feel sure that it never occurred to me that this agreement could be interpreted as excluding us from papers held jointly by the U.K. and U.S. — especially as these could not be disposed of by a purely British agreement.

that in my view this question "closely affects the integrity of our Official History as a record upon which the public can rely." I said we desired access to the records of the important wartime strategic conferences; other records of the Combined Chiefs of Staff affecting the employment or operations of Canadian troops; and the records of SHAEF and AFHQ, the Allied headquarters in the two theatres in which large Canadian forces were employed. I wrote, "While I think there is no question but that our government would press the matter with considerable firmness if it were placed before them in a formal manner, we should, as I have already mentioned to you, much prefer to avoid the necessity of formal correspondence on this question." Again there was no result. When we sought the assistance of the East Block, where External Affairs and the Privy Council Office had their bases in those days, those establishments seemed less interested than I expected. The great Norman Robertson, once Under-Secretary for External Affairs, whom the current game of musical chairs among the mandarins had now made Secretary to the Cabinet, yawned in my face (which I didn't especially appreciate) and said he was sure External had all the strategic records we wanted. It hadn't, of course; the Combined Records were in London and Washington and nowhere else.

There was no use making an official approach to Washington; it was clear that the source of our troubles was London. While in Washington again in December 1948 I talked about the business with my American friends. In this conversation General Malony mentioned that General Kippenberger had written to the Secretary of the Combined Chiefs of Staff on his recommendation, but he believed that he had never had a reply.* It was made quite clear to me that the Americans considered this an issue between the British and ourselves, and they did not wish to get involved in it. Malony, in fact, said that it was analogous to an argument between the United States and Puerto Rico, in which *we* would not care to interfere! I did not attempt to explain the constitutional status of

---

* At this time the Combined Chiefs of Staff still maintained an official existence, though the war this committee had been set up to direct was long over. It is interesting that I have found no reference to General Kippenberger in the British records; their consistent story is that no Dominion except Canada showed interest in the Combined Records issue, and that Canada's interest was almost exclusively the work of Stacey.

Canada, as this would probably have been a long task and might not have affected the issue very much.

Months passed and we got nowhere. We told the Cabinet Office in London that what we needed most was the minutes of the "big conferences"; they replied that these in themselves would be little use to us — we would need all the background documents too. There was truth in this, but nevertheless it was a quibble; as we found when we finally got them, the conference records by themselves were enormous and very informative. I know now that in 1949 the Cabinet Office was expressing a very poor view of me. An undated and unsigned memo reviewing the matter avers that the Washington agreement was accepted "by all the Commonwealth historians who were present at the Washington Conference" and notes that I left Washington before the meeting was over. (The Gettysburg expedition is not mentioned; this little bit of sharp practice, I am sure, was never reported by the British delegates to their superiors in London.) I particularly like a passage which was deleted from the draft, presumably because it was considered too frank, but which certainly expresses a real British view:

> Although it has been hinted that these requests would in the last resort be strongly pressed by the Canadian Government, it is significant that they appear to have shown only a perfunctory interest in the question, in spite of the length of time since it was first raised. In short, Colonel Stacey is dissatisfied with the results of the Washington Conference, and the United Kingdom and United States Governments are being asked to modify its conclusions on his personal representations.

The awkward fact remained that Canada had never accepted the Washington agreement, and therefore it had never come into effect. On 8 August 1949 Sir Norman Brook, the head of the Cabinet Office, wrote Sir Alexander Clutterbuck, the United Kingdom High Commissioner in Ottawa, enclosing, it appears, the revised version of the document just quoted, and asking him to talk with "the appropriate person in the Department of External Affairs" about this "rather troublesome question." He complained that Colonel Stacey had asserted the right to see the combined records, a claim which the British authorities found embarrassing because "the real reasons for decisions" were often found in "national" documents lying behind the combined records, which it was out of the question to open. Here is Brook's picture of proper historical procedure:

> He [Stacey] has argued that, unless he can have a free run over the records, he cannot know which specific document to ask for. But in practice it need not work like that at all. He can perfectly well ask whether there is anything in the combined records which has a bearing on this, that or the other question arising on the Canadian History. If there is nothing, we shall tell him so. If there is something, we can tell him (without disclosure of documents) broadly what it is and can indicate any documents which it might be valuable for him to see. If he then decides that he ought to see any of these, for the purpose of his historical work, we shall be quite willing to seek the consent of the British and United States Chiefs of Staff for the disclosure of that particular documents, or documents in accordance with the 1948 Agreement.

Apart from the vital fact that this procedure would have enabled a group of British civil servants to decide what papers the Canadian historian could see, and thereby damned his history in the eyes of scholars and everybody else, it was ludicrously cumbersome. If we had had to follow it our history wouldn't have been finished yet.

Brook's letter concluded:

> I am afraid that all this has become a point of prestige for Colonel Stacey. I am anxious that it should not become a point of prestige for the Canadian Government. It would be most unfortunate if they should assert a claim that, for the purposes of writing the history of Canada's part in the war, their historian should have the free run of his teeth on the top level documents of the United Kingdom Government. For this, I am sure, is a claim which could not possibly be conceded.

It was also a claim which we had never made, and which we would not have dreamed of making. We well knew that the British would not open their domestic secrets to us.

On 19 December 1949 Clutterbuck wrote a "Dear Mike" letter to the Canadian Secretary of State for External Affairs. He enclosed a memorandum (undoubtedly the one received from Brook), and remarked, "In the circumstances I have been asked to make an appeal to you that the matter

should not be allowed to become a point of prestige either for Colonel
Stacey or for the Canadian Government, but should be approached from
the purely practical considerations involved." He said he would like to
discuss the matter when Pearson had had a chance to consider it. It was a
delicate invitation to the Secretary of State to disavow Stacey.

Clutterbuck got no firm reply. During the next few months there was
correspondence between National Defence and External in which the
latter showed itself reluctant to take up the cudgels strongly on our behalf.
In February 1950 Arnold Heeney, who was now Under-Secretary at
External, wrote Brooke Claxton a letter that betrayed considerable sym-
pathy for Clutterbuck's argument. It concluded, "I think we should try, if
possible, to achieve a satisfactory solution without allowing the matter to
become a point of prestige for the Canadian Government." Claxton fired
back a long letter, drafted by me, in which he described the funny business
that had gone on at Washington during the 1948 meeting, and pointed out
that I had acted under instructions throughout and that this was not "a
controversy between the United Kingdom on one side and an officer of the
Canadian Army on the other." He said that unless External had strong
views to the contrary, he proposed to ask the Prime Minister to raise the
question with the Prime Minister of the United Kingdom. Mike Pearson,
who was now of course Secretary of State for External Affairs and a
cabinet colleague of Claxton's, then wrote to him deprecating such
extreme action.

Early in May 1950 I prepared at Claxton's request a paper on the
subject which could be a basis for discussion by Pearson with the British
government during a forthcoming visit to London. General Foulkes sent
this to Claxton covered by a letter of his own which dealt with the matter
in crisp soldierly terms:

> You may recall that when Mr. Pearson replied to our request for
> immediate action to be taken on the clearance of these documents, Mr.
> Pearson challenged the right of Canada to have access to documents of
> the Combined Chiefs of Staff or other agencies of which we were not
> members. It appears to me that this argument is not valid, as surely the
> attitude we must take is that throughout the war Canada did not once
> surrender her sovereignty or any right to make her own decisions in
> regard to any action she took in the war, but in order to expedite the
> winning of the war Canada was prepared to have the Combined Chiefs

of Staff, and other agencies, act on her behalf, as well as on behalf of
Britain and the United States. In other words, the decisions taken by
the Combined Chiefs of Staff were not only decisions to be acted on by
the British and American Governments but also on behalf of the
Canadian Government. Therefore, in reality they were acting as our
agents. If they were acting as our agents surely we have the right of
access to the documents.

I feel very strongly that we should insist on these documents being
provided by the British, who were only too anxious to have Canadian
formations fight under their command and to act for us whenever they
saw fit.

This paper went to External along with mine, and I have a feeling that
it may have done the trick. At any rate, while in London Pearson
mentioned the matter to Patrick Gordon-Walker, the Secretary of State
for Commonwealth Relations, who, Mike wrote later, "understood our
position and said he was anxious to make a suitable arrangement." This
was doubtless the turning point, and gave an opportunity to the one
person in External (I thought at the time) who fully appreciated the issue:
our High Commissioner in London, Dana Wilgress, who had as adviser
my old friend Major-General Fin Clark, the head of the Canadian Army
Liaison Establishment, who in turn was briefed by Murray Hunter.
Pearson asked Wilgress to follow the matter up with Gordon-Walker, and
on 9 June Wilgress saw Gordon-Walker and left with him a very firm
aide-mémoire. It said, "The Canadian Government feels that it should be
entitled to access, by its official historians, to 'combined records' which
deal with operations in which Canadian forces and resources were
employed. . . ." It was thus made clear that this was not merely the
tiresome Stacey talking, but Canada.

The opposition now caved in at once. The British discovered that they
could in fact overcome the difficulties that had been represented as
insurmountable. Early in August 1950 an *aide-mémoire* presented to the
Department of External Affairs by the United Kingdom high commissioner in Ottawa said that they were prepared to approach the United
States authorities to seek their agreement in releasing the records of the big
conferences and the other records of the Combined Chiefs of Staff bearing
on the employment and operations of Canadian troops. With respect to
the records of SHAEF and AFHQ, there were practical difficulties; there

were millions of documents, not yet catalogued in detail, but if we would supply the Cabinet Office from time to time with details of the period or operations in which we were interested, efforts would be made to meet our needs, and documents might be released subject to American consent. Since it was understood that I might be attending a conference of official historians in Amsterdam in October, it was hoped that I would come to London, where the British authorities would welcome an opportunity of discussing the matter with me.

With matters thus arranged, my conversations in London were virtually a love-feast. On 22 August Major Hunter and I went to the Commonwealth Relations Office for a meeting with Mr. A. B. Acheson of the Cabinet Office and Mr. R. R. Sedgwick of the CRO. Everything was amicable, but at the end of our discussion there was a curious development. The British representatives politely inquired whether, with the practical difficulties pleasantly adjusted, it would now be possible for Canada to sign the "Washington agreement." At this point I told the story of how that agreement was made by the British and American delegates, behind everybody else's back, on the day of the trip to Gettysburg. Acheson and Sedgwick had clearly never heard this before. They said little, but one sensed that they were shocked. We never heard of that agreement again.

On 15 September I went, by invitation, to Sir Norman Brook's office and had a rather long conversation with him, which again was most amicable. We dealt with practical problems. I assured him that we had no desire to pry into British cabinet papers, and would always be ready to use the questionnaire method in connection with them. He told me (not without a touch of pride, I think) that he was the custodian of Mr. Churchill's papers; he might be able to give us special help as a result of this connection, and invited me to communicate with him direct on this or other matters. Sir Norman's note of the conversation concludes, "Sir Norman Brook told him [Stacey] that on matters ... which he felt might raise some question of principle, he might if he wished, write direct to him — indeed, he rather encouraged him to do so and Colonel Stacey seemed pleased at the suggestion." I am sure Brooke was absolutely right about my pleasure, but I don't recall that I ever needed to avail myself of the privilege.

On 23 September I was able to report to the Chief of the General Staff rather euphorically that the long controversy had terminated satisfactorily and that we could expect to receive at an early date, on a loan basis, copies of the printed records of the ten major Allied conferences that were important to us. I wrote, "It will be observed that we have not obtained any general acceptance of the principle that we are entitled to these documents *as of right*; however, there is presumably no point in raising theoretical questions of this sort when we can, in practice, get access to the documents that we require."

I might say one word about that conference in the pleasant and expensive city of Amsterdam. The Dutch were hospitable (though, characteristically, government parsimony set limits to the hospitality). The meeting gave me an opportunity of visiting the battlefields of the Scheldt estuary, which I had not seen before. The conference was notable for the active part taken by the French; this was the first chance I had for observing at first hand the interesting phenomenon of the extent to which the French sought, and with some degree of success, to take over the international organization of the study of the Second World War. The dominant figure in this historical offensive was Henri Michel, who was active at the conference and who finally produced one of the largest and heaviest single volumes dealing with the conflict. When one considers the extent of the contribution that France made to the defeat of Germany, this is all a little surprising. I always remember with pleasure the title of one conference arranged by M. Michel's organization. It ran (approximately): "The Liberation of France (Apart from the Military Operations)."

Chapter 15

The Fight for the History: Phase Two

*T*he Canadian Army, 1939-1945 was an interim report, intended to hold the Canadian public (presumed to be avid for historical information about the war) at bay until we could provide a more detailed history. Producing this turned out to be a task neither easy nor short, for reasons many of which were beyond the control of the historian. I began dictating Volume I on 9 July 1948. Volume III was not published until January 1960, when I had retired from the army.

I have not so far described the plan for the history in detail. Volume I was called *Six Years of War*, and sub-titled *The Army in Canada, Britain and the Pacific*. It was in the main a story of organization, training and garrison duty; but it had two great operational highlights — the Dieppe raid and the defence of Hong Kong, the two most controversial and tragic battles our army fought. I wrote this volume myself, with a great deal of help from other people, who drafted six of the sixteen chapters, as explained in the preface. I fear, however, that the only one of these drafters whose work survived my revision almost intact was Jim Conacher. The other volumes dealt with our two great campaigns. Volume II, *The Canadians in Italy*, I turned over to Gerald Nicholson, my deputy. He, too, had drafting help, and I read his chapters in their initial form and offered comments. He produced a notable and distinguished volume, though I felt that it might usefully have been a little shorter.

Volume III, *The Victory Campaign*, dealing with the fighting in North-West Europe in 1944-45, I again wrote myself, again with much assistance which is acknowledged in detail in the book. The title of the book was arrived at only after much thought. I must admit that my decision was somewhat influenced by the attitudes of our British friends. It became apparent before the war was long past that they — historians and public alike — were most conscious of the (admittedly glorious) phase of the struggle when "we stood alone." (Canadians have been kept busy reminding them that "we" means the Commonwealth, and not just the United Kingdom.) Our British opposite numbers were clearly far more interested in the days when we were gallantly losing the war by ourselves than in the campaigns in which we won it with the aid of powerful friends. Those later episodes were the ones in which the Canadian army saw most of its active service. Hence *The Victory Campaign*.

The volume on general national war policy we simply had not the means of tackling until the army history was out of the way, although of course material for it was collecting steadily over the years. In the end, since I had accumulated more information about the business than anybody else, it was arranged that when I retired in 1959 I should write the book on a part-time basis while teaching at the University of Toronto. In the nature of things, this was a slow process, and there were special reasons for delay which I shall describe. This book's title too was a matter for much head-scratching. In the end, I called it *Arms, Men and Governments*, with the sub-title *The War Policies of Canada, 1939-1945*. This weighty tome of 681 pages was finally published in 1970, a quarter of a century after the end of the war. Well, at least nobody can take away from us the fact that we did publish a comprehensive short history of the Canadian army's part in the affair just three years after the last shot in Europe. If more of our wartime stable of well-qualified historians had stayed on after the shooting stopped, we could have achieved our final goal much sooner. As it was, I felt, rightly or wrongly, that, while we had a number of excellent researchers in our postwar team, only Gerry Nicholson and I were equal to the task of writing a volume for publication. The early volumes of the army history proper also ran into political obstruction, and this was one important reason for the delay in publication.

Nevertheless, even in the best of circumstances, drafting a detailed history based on an enormously wide range of sources is in the nature of things a very slow business. The documented preliminary narratives compiled during and after the war were enormously valuable, but their authors, being human, were not infallible, and whereas in theory one should have been able to write the history on the basis of them alone, in practice one was always going back to the original documents. The chapters or portions of chapters drafted for me by other people often had to be rewritten by myself. And I could give only part of my time to writing history. I had a fairly large directorate to administer, with the inevitable personnel problems to iron out. And certain official jobs descended upon us which were unconnected with the history and which pretty well had to be done by the director himself.

One of these was that connected with the classification and naming of the engagements our army had fought in and the award to regiments of battle honours resulting from them. To soldiers and units these things are important. The classification job was done on a Commonwealth basis; this was agreeable to most Canadian soldiers, I think, not merely because it was traditional but because it was felt that Commonwealth-wide honours would command more respect and because there was a suspicion that if it were done on a Canadian basis special interests and "politics" (in more senses than one) might creep in. So a Battles Nomenclature Committee met at the War Office in London under the chairmanship of a British general (Sir Harold Franklyn), with all the Commonwealth countries represented. The Canadian representative was the senior officer at the Canadian Army Liaison Establishment in London, but naturally the real work fell upon my staff and me. I attended several meetings of the committee. It often happened that a senior officer who had been involved in the operations under consideration was invited to attend when available; I remember Guy Simonds' impressive performance when Sicily was being discussed.

The job was complicated by the fact that no decisions had been made about the basis on which battle honours were to be awarded. We wasted much time discussing whether various affairs should be classified as "battles," "actions," or "engagements," simply because we did not know whether an engagement would qualify a regiment for an honour, or whether only a battle would be so recognized. (In the end, the decision was that battles, actions and engagements were all equally eligible for being inscribed on the colours or "appointments" of regiments awarded them; but that decision did not rest with the Battles Nomenclature Committee.) We Canadians were again somewhat amused by British attitudes which we thought we observed in the proceedings of the BNC. It seemed to us that it was rather easier to get a scrap recognized as a battle in the early stages of the war (when "we stood alone," remember?) than in the later stages when the operations were really big and important. We sniggered quietly up our sleeves during the discussion of the easy victories over the Italians in North Africa in 1940. And we got ourselves mildly disliked, I fear, by our tendency to judge an operation by the butcher's bill. We took the view that an important encounter was one in which a fair number of people got killed. The British regarded this, I think, as a bit crude. We also had an occasional difference of opinion about naming operations. No Canadian thought of calling the 1st Corps' great attack in Italy on 23 May 1944 anything but "Hitler Line"; but the British didn't want that evil man's name on their regimental colours. We settled the matter by calling the action on the Canadian front "Hitler Line" and that on the British front off to the right "Aquino." (That was all right with me; after all, it was on the Canadian front that the line was broken.) In spite of these little tiffs, the whole operation was amicable and the net result pretty satisfactory.

Not until 1956 were the results of these labours promulgated in Canadian army orders.[1] At that time we had another job. Few Canadian regiments, particularly in the militia, were equipped for historical research, and though they were supposed to claim the honours to which they considered themselves entitled, we had to help them. So we produced a draft list for every regiment and left it to them to accept it or make further submissions. Most accepted our suggestions; but I remember one case where a successful claim was made for an additional honour. The Toronto Scottish had served in the war as a machine-gun battalion. We looked at the figures for their participation in the Dieppe raid, noticed that they had only 125 officers and men there, and too hastily decided that that did not qualify for the honour. The Tor Scots came back at us. Not only was their regimental headquarters there, they said, but also their whole main armament: every one of their Vickers medium machine-guns was there and firing. The argument was unanswerable, and the Toronto Scottish now carry "Dieppe" on their colours with proper pride.

The point of all this is to explain, in part, why it took so long to write the army history. The plain fact is that it took me nearly five years to write the volume called *Six Years of War*. By 1953, however, the job was done; and on 20 March I sent it to the Chief of the General Staff (who was now Guy Simonds, Charles Foulkes having moved up to be permanent chairman of the Chiefs of Staff Committee with the rank of general). I recommended the volume for submission to the minister and publication. Guy took his time, but he sent it on to the Minister of National Defence (still Brooke Claxton) on 15 July. On 26 November I sent the Chief Nicholson's Italian volume, and he passed it on to the minister a couple of weeks later.

In the light of the experience with the Summary, it was interesting to speculate what was now going to happen. Would Claxton again proceed to discuss these volumes with me line by line? I decided, if that happened, that the best course was to be flexible on minor points and absolutely firm on major ones. I was not at all prepared for what actually happened.

What actually happened was absolutely nothing. The weeks passed, and there was no word from the minister. Late in September Claxton's defence secretary told me that the minister wanted to look further at the first volume before authorizing printing (he mentioned particularly what he called the introduction, meaning presumably Chapter I, on prewar planning and preparation, an area which might be considered particularly sensitive politically). In January 1954 the minister, telephoning me on another matter, said he would deal with the history as soon as possible. In April I wrote a rather strong draft memo for Simonds to send the minister; he said he would take the matter up at a suitable opportunity. On 24 June (when Claxton had had Volume I nearly a year) the defence secretary told me that the minister would "clear up" the histories over the weekend). I waited with interest. All that happened was that one week later Claxton resigned from the government. The histories were left as a legacy to his successor, Ralph Campney.

As to Claxton's motives I can only speculate. Apart from the fact that he had many other things to think about, it was common talk that Brooke could see a political implication where nobody else could perceive anything of the kind. I suspect that he glanced at my draft, noticed some of its modest revelations on such things as the country's state of preparation in 1939, and took fright: what might this do to the Liberal party? I think he knew that a serious attempt to censor the book would bring on a crisis with me, and it was easiest to do nothing, leaving the volumes of typescript to gather dust in his office.*

As they say nowadays, I was back in square one. I had never met Campney and it was clearly out of the question to bother him about the histories until he had time to get his feet under his desk. Further delay had probably to be accepted. However, on 14 July, a fortnight after he took office, General Simonds sent him a memo drafted by me explaining the background and mentioning the undesirability of another historical fiasco of the sort that had followed the first war. Nothing happened. In October (when Volume I had been in the minister's office for fifteen months) I spoke to Campney's executive assistant and explained my embarrassment. He was friendly, but still nothing happened.

In December 1954 we made some progress. I urged Guy Simonds to go at the minister again. He did so, had a long discussion with him, and obtained his consent to an arrangement I had proposed when the draft was first submitted: let us get the type set, and provide the Chief of the General Staff and the minister with galley proofs in lots which would make it easy for them to read with a view to (I hoped) approval. I wrote in my diary on Christmas Eve: "Volume One . . . goes to the printer at long last after a year and a half of quite unnecessary delay." Early in March 1955 I introduced myself to Ralph Campney at a meeting of the Ottawa United Service Institute which he had addressed, and he assured me that there would be no further delay. Next day I sent him the first batch of galleys, through the CGS.

We were not yet out of the woods, and at this point I have to introduce a new complication: the use of Canadian cabinet records.

Back in 1947, when Brooke Claxton first suggested that we convert the proposed volume on army policy into one dealing with policy covering all three services, he remarked, very sensibly, that this would involve access to the minutes of the Cabinet War Committee. These I had then never seen. I should explain that the Canadian cabinet proper began to keep minutes

---

* My feelings towards Claxton are best summed up in the fact that when he became the first chairman of the Canada Council, set up to encourage development in literature and the arts, I made a private pact with myself that I would never ask for a grant from the council while he was there. Nor did I; then, or for some time afterwards. In due course, however, I lined up with the other pigs at the trough.

only on 14 February 1944 and even then they were for a time extremely exiguous and frequently totally uninformative. However, the powerful Cabinet War Committee, over which the Prime Minister presided, kept detailed minutes throughout the war, and they are a source of fundamental importance for the history of Canadian war policy.

In July 1948 I followed up the minister's suggestion, asking General Foulkes to move him to obtain access to the minutes for me. Claxton wrote the Prime Minister making the recommendation, and with what seems rather surprising alacrity Mr. King assented. His letter was dated 12 August:

> My Dear Claxton:
>
> Replying to your letter of August the 4th, I quite approve of the official historian and senior members of his staff being given access to the minutes and other records of the War Committee of the Cabinet, 1939-1945, for the purposes mentioned in your letter.
>
> I am sending a copy of this communication to Mr. Heeney, Clerk of the Council.
>
> Yours sincerely,
> W. L. Mackenzie King

It is clear that Arnold Heeney, by this time a very important mandarin, was distinctly upset by the audacity of the two cabinet ministers in going over his head and failing to consult him in this matter. There was a flurry of excitement; Claxton's office called for the file, and it appeared that Heeney wanted some alteration. I heard from one of Claxton's secretaries that she was taking the P.M.'s letter off the file, and anticipated that another letter (presumably making conditions and reservations?) would be received in its place.

I had cannily made a copy of the letter before returning the file. No other version of it ever reached me. I should dearly like to think that King declined to withdraw the letter, but I have looked at his diary without finding any reference to the matter. (At this time he was deeply involved in political calculations arising out of his impending retirement, and the details of public business get short shrift in the diary.)

Whether King rebuffed Heeney or not, Arnold did not abandon the fight to maintain the barrier of official secrecy against the danger represented by official historians. Contrary to what seems to be a widespread opinion today, I myself believe that a degree of secrecy, at least in current matters, is essential to the functioning of government; but I really think that Heeney and the people he had trained believed that secrecy was an end in itself. On 19 October I recorded:

> 1500 hrs. interview with Mr. Heeney (Sec of Cabinet) re cabinet minutes (War Cttee). We agreed (a) everything will be put at my disposal; (b) no agreement or conditions will be put on paper at this moment, but a memo written later; (c) when I have drawn a. sufficiently detailed plan for the [policy] volume, I will go over it with Mr. Heeney & he will indicate those subjects which are so delicate that they cannot be treated or must be treated with special care. He said there wd be few such subjects.

Although (b) and (c) were never actually carried out, the problem did not go away.

The immediate development was that I began reading the War Committee minutes. The process started on 25 October. In all the circumstances, I had to do the whole job myself. I went through the record of 339 War Committee meetings, plus three subsequent meetings of a special committee which in effect continued the War Committee for a short time after its demise, and a good many other Committee documents. I made extended notes in longhand, working month after month as other business allowed, in the office of W.E.D. Halliday, registrar of the cabinet, looking out on the green lawn of Parliament Hill. Bill Halliday was long-suffering and we became very good friends. I learned from my reading a great deal about war policy, and a good deal about Canadian history at large. (Those invaluable minutes, for which the country owes a debt of gratitude to my friendly enemy Arnold Heeney who kept them, are now available to all scholars in the Public Archives in Ottawa.) All this provided an essential basis for the future volume on policy, but it didn't do anything to advance the writing of those volumes of the army history for which, presumably, Canadians were waiting with bated breath.

The question of the use that could be made of these sacrosanct cabinet records in public print arose rather prematurely in 1954. An able young American army officer named Stanley W. Dziuban, who was employed in the Pentagon in Washington, wrote a thesis on Canadian-American military relations during the late war for Columbia University. His military superiors allowed him to use, apparently, all the official records in the Pentagon for the purpose (something we would certainly not have done for a Canadian officer in parallel circumstances, especially as many of the papers Dziuban used were of Canadian provenance and were opened to him, and used in the dissertation submitted to Columbia, without any reference to Canada). However, when the thesis was ready for publication Dziuban turned up in Ottawa seeking clearance for it. This was embarrassing, in view of the restrictive Canadian practice; but it really did not represent any threat to the public interest and, chiefly on my recommendation, I think, the clearance was given.* It struck me that since the book contained a great deal on the wartime functioning of the Canadian-American Permanent Joint Board on Defence which had not previously been published, there might be criticism in Canada if the first information on these things appeared in an American thesis. I suggested that I might write for publication in Canada an article that would forestall such comments. This was approved, and the article duly appeared.[2] But the text of it caused difficulty. I had referred several times to decisions made by the Cabinet War Committee. This stirred up the high priests of secrecy in the East Block. They insisted that no distinction should be made in print between cabinet and War Committee; all decisions should be referred to merely as made by the "Canadian Government"! This was absurd, but there was no time to argue; I accepted the absurdity for the moment, reserving my fire for a more important occasion. And with the publication of the first volumes of the army history proper imminent (I hoped!) that occasion was at hand.

After collecting all the information on British practice I could, I made a submission recommending that approval be given to the principles I had followed in drafting the history, which were in fact the same followed in

---

* Stanley Dziuban, I think, thought he-had a book which American publishers would eat up. He soon found out that they had not the faintest interest in relations with Canada. The volume finally appeared as part of the U.S. army official history: *Military Relations between the United States and Canada, 1939-1945* (Washington, 1959). My impression is that Dziuban knew next to nothing about Canada when he undertook the thesis; but he learned while doing it, and the book is very useful.

London. The main points were: except for actual decisions, the records of the cabinet or its committees were never either directly quoted or cited, but were presented in paraphrase; opinions expressed in discussion were never attributed to individual ministers; cabinet *conclusions*, as distinct from *discussion*, might be directly quoted, with dates; finally, factual reports made verbally to cabinet or committees might be reported in paraphrase form. Subsequently, I pointed out that the secretive Mr. Heeney himself had published a very full account of cabinet procedures during the war (including a detailed description of the role of the War Committee) in the *Canadian Journal of Economics and Political Science*;[3] I remarked, "In my opinion an official history could not disregard the War Committee, and refer to decisions as made simply by 'the Government', without incurring criticism and perhaps even derision."

Eventually the Privy Council Office essentially accepted my arguments and position, but the matter of use of cabinet records got involved with the question of authority to publish the history. Through the spring and early summer of 1955 I continued to press through various channels for a decision on this, and continued to hear talk from members of Ralph Campney's staff about an interview with the minister; but the interview did not happen.

By July I felt I was about at the end. It was over twenty-seven months since I had put Volume I forward for approval. I had lately become sufficiently doubtful about the outcome that I had been doing little work on Volume III, but had been devoting myself to the day-to-day work of the directorate, which was always plentiful. I had been patient, and was beginning to think I had been cowardly.

At this point, as in 1947, good fortune and a good friend came to the rescue. On or about 13 July I had lunch at the University Club of Ottawa — a cheerful little institution of which I had been president, and which now no longer exists — with some other people from National Defence. I boiled over about my troubles. Campney was shortly leaving for an extended visit to his home in British Columbia, and I said that if he left without seeing me I was going to resign from the army, sacrifice my pension and tell the whole story to the public. One of my companions was Air Commodore C. F. Johns, who, though I think I did not realize it, was in regular touch with the minister. Apparently Freddie Johns went straight from our luncheon to Campney's office and urged him on no account to leave for Vancouver without seeing me. That was the turning point this time. I got my interview with the minister on the afternoon of 15 July.

It was quite a pleasant interview. Ralph Campney was a straightforward man with no pretences and none of Claxton's self-importance. He apologized for the long delay and talked frankly about what troubled him about the history: its official status (he had absolutely no background on this), the use of cabinet records, the treatment of individuals. On this last point, he was relieved when I told him that the drafts had been widely circulated, that people prominently mentioned had had opportunities for comment, and that their comments had been incorporated where they seemed to have substance.He asked me to provide him with a general memorandum for the information of his cabinet colleagues. He felt that, since the publication of the history might have repercussions, he should not authorize it without reference to those colleagues; he would take it up with them on his return to Ottawa. I told him that all my experience suggested that the history could be published as it stood without causing any great excitement or public controversy.

Feeling a great deal better, I set about composing a two-page paper on "Official Histories." I wrote privately, "It is rather appalling to have to be outlining first principles in words of one syllable at this stage!" The paper was ready for the minister when he came back from his holiday. Here are the most important parts of it:

> The underlying considerations leading to the production of official histories are the need of governments for a record of experience for future guidance, and the assumed right of the public, after the lapse of a reasonable period of time, to authentic accounts of great national crises as revealed in the official records.
>
> The requirement for producing such histories on an official basis arises from the difficulty of permitting free access to government records of recent date to private researchers; combined with the fact that the task of writing the history of a great war is so vast that it could not possibly be undertaken by a private researcher unless he had at his disposal a great deal of time and the means of hiring a large staff. The result is that detailed and authoritative accounts of such episodes as the Second World War must be compiled and published by governments or not at all. . . .

The basic problem in planning an official history is that of combining provision for the requirements of security and the general interests of government with that degree of objectivity in presentation which alone can protect such histories against the charges of "dishonesty" which are frequently levelled at them. The usual expedient is to appoint to take charge of the work a qualified historian who has the confidence of the government and whose reputation will at the same time serve in the eyes of the public (and particularly of the country's historians, who are the group most directly interested) as a guarantee that the history will be an honest presentation of the facts.

It is usual to include in the volumes a disclaiming note to the effect that while the historians have been given free access to official documents, the interpretation and commentary are entirely their own.

Mr. Campney had another talk with me on his return to Ottawa, and on 16 August the matter of official histories was discussed by the cabinet. Late that day Bill Halliday told me that it had been decided that the history "would be published without editing," though there were some minor reservations. I got the details shortly. The basic decision was that the Minister of National Defence was not expected to take responsibility for editing the history, and the book was to carry the traditional disclaimer stating that the opinions expressed were those of the historian.

The reservations, which had been laid down by the Prime Minister, Mr. St. Laurent, concerned the use of cabinet records. These generally followed the lines I have already described, but there were additions. No report was to be given on what was said at cabinet or committee meetings by official guests of the government from other countries. Nothing should be cited to indicate that there had been any disagreement between ministers or between a minister and his advisers (but in the light of the accepted rule forbidding attribution of opinions to individual ministers, this was not likely to be an additional embarrassment). The most peculiar provision was to the effect that there could be some indication of the subjects discussed at a meeting but not of the details of such discussion nor of the tone and atmosphere, and never in such a way as to indicate that the writer had been present! This I thought plain comic. Had the Prime Minister, I wondered, ever read any history? I never met Louis St. Laurent except for being introduced to him at Mrs. Massey's club in London early in 1946; and I am sure I am quite wrong in letting this paragraph in the cabinet record influence me to the extent of thinking of him as a silly old man.

However, the main battle had been won. At long last, we had authority to publish those volumes that had lain in the minister's office so long. Volume I appeared in December 1955 and Volume II in September 1956. Political pusillanimity had held them up for well over two years, but the decision of 16 August 1955 meant that we had no difficulty with later volumes.

Of course, by the time Volume III was ready for the press, any likelihood of difficulty had been vastly reduced by a change of government. No reader will be surprised to learn that I voted Conservative in the famous election of 10 June 1957; yet I don't believe that I was primarily motivated by my own troubles with a Liberal administration. I had certainly voted Liberal in 1958, if only because I couldn't bear George Drew, who was then leading the Tories; and I think I was moved in 1957 chiefly by the conviction that it was time, and more than time, for a change. I had no particular regard for John Diefenbaker (though I didn't realize, of course, what a buffoon he was going to turn out to be); but I was tired of a government that seemed to regard the country as its private property, as if it had been granted to it as Prince Edward Island was to the British absentee proprietors in 1767. I felt that if Canada was not to be a one-party state the time to act was now; and as it turned out some millions of other people felt the same way.

I have two particular memories of that election. One is of *Maclean's* magazine, printed before the election but published after it, assuming that the Liberals had won again (the editor, Ralph Allen, whom I had known as a war correspondent, said ruefully, "Somebody goofed; and it was me"). The other is the night of the poll in the house at 703 Parkdale Avenue where Doris and I were living. The so-called Learned Societies had been meeting in Ottawa, and Donald Creighton had come to watch the results on our television set. Donald put on a show that was far better than the one on the television screen. The picture of him repeatedly bouncing out of his chair with hoots of unholy joy as the CBC reported successive unbelievable Grit disasters is still with me. (One of the Liberal casualties was my minister, who was defeated by a Chinese Canadian whom the wits at National Defence immediately dubbed "The Chink in Ralph Campney's armour." I was rather sorry. I remember Ralph Campney with some gratitude. His Conservative successor, Major-General

George Randolph Pearkes, VC, I didn't have much to do with. This I didn't regret, as I had never liked him since he had thrown me and another CMHQ staff officer out of a conference following an exercise in 1941. He was generally considered a bad minister.)

There were certainly advantages from my point of view in the fact that the party that had been in power during the war was finally out. So far as I know, Volume III of the army history, though submitted "through channels" like its predecessors, was never read on any level above my own. Pearkes had been sent home to Canada long before the North-West Europe campaign broke out, and presumably had little interest in it; and Lieutenant-General S. F. Clark, the Chief of the General Staff when it was submitted, though he had served with distinction through the campaign, would not have dreamed of interfering with the book.

It is worth while to remark that, by the time I came to write the volume on policy, St. Laurent's rules were no longer a serious embarrassment. The availability of Mackenzie King's diary had provided a source of information almost as comprehensive as the War Committee minutes and much franker — and not subject to Uncle Louis' pettifogging rules. It was directly quotable, which the minutes at that time were not; there is no backwardness about describing tone and atmosphere; and it records in detail the disagreements of ministers and the remarks of visitors from other countries. King was secretive in his lifetime, but his private record effectively defeated, for the historian, the secretiveness of his successor.

I turn briefly to more personal matters. During the war, while working overseas, I had largely severed my connections with the academic historical world. I had kept in touch with my friends by letter, but that was about all. I had almost entirely stopped writing for publication, except in connection with my army job. I didn't keep up with historical literature, and rarely read a historical journal. (Some of my associates did rather better at living in two worlds; only long afterwards did I hear that Major Gerald Graham of my staff — we had finally got him away from the navy — was regularly broadcasting to Canada as "Professor Graham," military regulations notwithstanding. As someone remarked, the boss is like the wronged husband: always the last to know.)

I was officially "struck off strength" CMHQ, London, in October 1946, when I turned in my ration card and caught the *Aquitania* for Halifax. I now ceased to be peripatetic between Canada and Britain and based myself in Ottawa. Doris had found us a flat at 400 Second Avenue, where we camped until October 1948, when we bought the nice little house on Parkdale Avenue which was our home until I left the army in 1959 and moved to Toronto. In Ottawa I was more in touch with the Canadian historical world at large. I became active in the Canadian Historical Association (a small organization in those days compared with what it is now). Rather to my surprise, I was made president of it in 1952-53. One project of my time which I am glad to remember is the initiation of the C.H.A.'s Historical Booklet series, intended to be helpful to teachers of history. We had planned that George Stanley should write the first one, *Louis Riel, Patriot or Rebel?* But the Ontario Department of Education, on which we were counting for some support, thought that too controversial a subject (how times have changed!). I was obliged to write the first one myself — *The Undefended Border: The Myth and the Reality.* This theme was presumably considered safe. The alarm having subsided, George's pamphlet came next. The series still marches on. My chief recollection of my C.H.A. presidential address is that the public address system didn't work.

I found myself receiving a good many books (this too is an activity that still marches on). I reviewed for the *Canadian Historical Review* the two volumes of Donald Creighton's immensely impressive biography of Sir John A. Macdonald, saying that it *was* immensely impressive, but also picking a few nits. Donald always said that he didn't read reviews of his books, but he must have read what I said about the second volume, for at the Canadian Historical Association meeting in 1956 he told me in firm terms that he thought poorly of it. However, later the same day, after a few good cocktails, he expressed a much more charitable view. I always managed to keep on pretty good terms with Donald, but I did so only at the cost of keeping my sense of humour working overtime. He frequently insulted me; but then, I think, he insulted practically everybody.

I have written at some length about the struggle to gain government approval for our history. I have so far said rather less about a perhaps more important matter: the actual writing of the history, and the peculiar problems of human relations which it turned out to involve. These things I must now try to deal with.

Chapter 16

Fables and Foibles:
History and the Human Animal

The first duty of the historian, so it seems to me, is to establish what happened: the facts. After that, if he chooses, he can go on to the perhaps more important tasks of establishing *why* it happened, and philosophizing about its importance in the cosmic scheme of things. But his first job is to find out what actually took place.

The sources he has available for the job come from people, and they fall into two great categories: what people *say*, and what people have *written*. (After all, even the most ponderous official document had an author, or authors; though they may remain severely anonymous.) In assessing the value of both these categories of evidence, the vital element is that of time: *when* did the witness say it, *when* did he write it? The human memory, one soon discovers, is a very frail instrument. Our American opposite numbers, the historians of the European Theatre for the U.S. army, with typical American scientific spirit set out to establish just how long it took a soldier's memory of a battle to begin to fail. Their experiments led them to the conclusion that this happened in *six days*. I shouldn't care to commit myself to this precise formula, but of the general principle there can be no doubt. The validity of a written account of an event, or an interview concerning it, is directly related to the length of time that elapsed between the event and the moment when the account was written or the interview took place. I have no hesitation in saying that one scrap of paper written on the evening of the battle is worth reams of reminiscence written down or spoken into tape recorders after months or years have passed. The best historical evidence is evidence recorded *at the time*.

It is true that it is often necessary to interview people long after the event in order to fill gaps in the story. I did a great deal of this myself. But it is something that should be done only when the contemporary written evidence fails you; and the oral evidence should be checked with care against such contemporary written records as are available. The interviewer, moreover, should prepare himself by reading the written evidence before the interview. In that way he will not only be able to assess the value of what he is being told, but he will be equipped to prompt the person he is interviewing and assist him in reviving his recollections of old times.

On the course of a battle, one document is superior to all others as a source of information: the operations log which is maintained at every headquarters. Here the historian has before him the record of information received and sent out, of orders given and received. Every entry is timed. The record is strictly contemporary; it is almost wholly impersonal; and it is maintained, not for historical purposes, as the unit or formation war diary is, but as an instrument for fighting the battle. (The log, however, in the Second World War was preserved as an appendix to the diary, and was in practice the most important part of it.) If a division's log is available, you can write the history of that division's part in the fight with confidence; if it is missing, you are hamstrung.

At the other end of the scale of evidence are the reminiscences of some captain or colonel or knight in arms twenty or thirty or forty years on, drawn from a memory which becomes increasingly defective with age and which is sometimes coloured by personal or other prejudices of one sort or another. Shakespeare, who knew so much about so many things, knew about this too. When he put into King Harry's mouth those lines about the veteran of Agincourt,

all shall be forgot,

But he'll remember with advantages

  What feats he did that day,

he was putting his finger on the historian's problem. "Old men forget," he said; he might have added that comparatively young men sometimes forget too. And the "advantages" are often much in evidence. Vanity warps people's memories (vanity is an occupational disease of generals, as it certainly is of politicians). Friendship or, more often, unfortunately, hatred, has a similar effect.

While I have been writing this I have experienced a good example of the deficiencies of memory. A London journal, RUSI, the organ of the Royal United Services Institute for Defence Studies, which I have spoken of before, published a review (written, it turned out, by a British retired colonel) of a book on Dieppe. The reviewer, quite ignorantly, blamed General McNaughton for originating the raid. Perhaps foolishly, I wrote a letter pointing out that McNaughton had never heard of the project until approached about it by General Montgomery. The reviewer came back stating that he got his information from a retired British major-general who was "on the Canadian Field Headquarters at the time of the raid." The said major-general wrote a letter supporting him; virtually every statement in it was inaccurate, the most notable (and almost unbelievable) inaccuracy being the assertion that Monty was "at no time . . . asked for advice [about Dieppe] or otherwise involved."[1] I thought of writing again, suggesting that if the general read no other book he might at least look at Monty's memoirs, where the field marshal says of Dieppe, "I was made responsible for the Army side of the planning"; I might also have suggested to the editor that in the interest of the reputation of her journal she might try giving books for review to people who could assess them on the basis of a knowledge of the literature, and not on that of gossip from old service pals. However, I had stated the facts once, and these two old ramblers (who would doubtless call me another old rambler) seemed hardly worth the price of a second stamp. But it would be hard to find a better instance of the decay of memory after nearly forty years — or, it might be added, of the assurance of retired British generals.

This brings me to that great problem of the contemporary historian, the unintentional liar. My experience was that one very seldom encountered a deliberate liar. I don't know how many people I interviewed, but it must have been hundreds; and I don't believe that more than two struck me as lying of set purpose. Some few others, I thought, were perhaps fantasizing a bit, because they were that sort of people. But there were considerable numbers who lied to me while honestly believing that they were telling the absolute truth. In almost all cases this happened when the interview took place years after the events in question. Many of them were returned prisoners of war, who had spent years behind the barbed wire, brooding about their experiences, convincing themselves that things had happened which in fact never took place, and perhaps cherishing grudges against people whom they considered responsible for their plight.* Others were officers who considered they had been hard done by, and who had built up myths in their own minds about those whom they considered the authors of their misfortunes. Others again were people with no special personal complaints, whose memory of events had suffered a sea-change with the passage of the years. Nearly all of them were devoted to their own misconceptions, and refused to be convinced by contrary evidence however overwhelming, whether it took the form of contemporary documents or the evidence of numbers of other people.

The long roster of unintentional liars includes some distinguished generals who have written memoirs. I have already mentioned Lord Montgomery's book. In it there are at least two whoppers which Monty undoubtedly believed to be true. One is the statement about the change in the Dieppe plan which eliminated the use of paratroops and the preliminary bombing from the air: "I should not myself have agreed to either of these changes." Yet the record shows that the field marshal himself presided over the meeting that approved the elimination of the bombing, and there is no indication that he made any objection. The other case relates to the German surrender, and the order ceasing all offensive operations (in order to avoid unnecessary casualties) which he says he issued "on the 3rd May [1945] when the Germans first came to see me." In fact this order was issued only on the evening of 4 May, as part of the message announcing the cease fire; it is reproduced in facsimile in the field marshal's earlier book *Normandy to the Baltic*.[2] Generals, of course, and still more field marshals, are above research; they *know* what happened.

Personalities, on many levels, were the greatest problem we confronted in writing the history of the Canadian army. Nobody gave me any orders or any guidance about this, and I did the best I could. Ours was a small service, almost a family affair, where everybody knew everybody else. I,

---

* That some P.O.W.s should be thus affected by their grim experience is not surprising. But I knew others who emerged from it calm and balanced, capable of taking a remarkably objective view of what they had undergone.

myself, over the years, acquired a large acquaintance, not least among the army's most senior officers. As I have written elsewhere, this was something of an embarrassment when I came to write the history. It is not easy to write pontifical comments about one's friends, especially those who ran risks and carried responsibilities that one did not share. I was so fond of General McNaughton that I should have found it very difficult to tell the story of his dismissal from the command of the army while he was living, especially as I could not have avoided discussing my draft with him. In the end, I told it only in *Arms, Men and Governments*, published after he was dead.

Even on lower levels, and in cases where I had no personal acquaintance with the individual concerned, it was difficult. Many an officer was removed from his command because he had proved unequal to it. But he was probably doing his best, and simply broke under a strain that was too great for him. Should one hold his name up to obloquy for all time on account of that? It was usually possible to carry out without stigmatizing individuals General Foulkes' injunction that we should on no account conceal our failures. I recall Foulkes himself speaking to me of a certain green battalion that came out of action at an undignified speed, "led by the C.O." The episode is in the history, but the commanding officer is not referred to. What good purpose would have been served by mentioning him? Moreover, it is possible that Foulkes, who presumably wasn't actually there, was mistaken.

Between our very senior officers there were many personal tensions which it would scarcely have been proper to attempt to deal with in an official book, the more so as the protagonists in most cases were still living. Today most of them are gone. These difficulties are part of our history, and it may be in order to set down a few facts about them now.

I have already described how Charles Foulkes, and not Guy Simonds, became Chief of the General Staff in 1945. Subsequently, Guy Simonds hated Harry Crerar with a most consuming hatred, and I have little doubt that this was mainly the result of Crerar's part in that affair. I speculate that when Guy finally became Chief he drew his own personal file, found Crerar's cable on it, and hated him forever after. I think he had disliked Crerar and had been jealous of him as Army Commander, feeling — probably not without reason — that he could have done that job better himself. There had been difficulties between the two men in Italy. This hatred, however, was clearly based on something different and deeply personal.

I was made painfully aware of this loathing, for Guy lost no opportunity of impressing on me the crimes of Harry Crerar. Clearly, he wanted these crimes recorded in official print. Since I saw little evidence for these supposed misdoings on the part of the late Army Commander, I was embarrassed. Guy would buttonhole me on social occasions and immediately start on Harry. It was an obsession with him. I remember an afternoon party at the French embassy when he bore down on me and disconcerted not only me but both our wives by launching into an anti-Crerar tirade.

This embarrassment reached a peak after we had both retired from the army and I was writing *Arms, Men and Governments.* Harry Crerar was now dead, but Guy, alas, was carrying the feud beyond the grave. I sent him the portion of my draft dealing with relations with the British military authorities, in which I referred to Montgomery's statement that when General McNaughton wished to visit the 1st Canadian Division in Sicily, Monty consulted Guy, its commander, who said, "For God's sake keep him away." I expected an explosion over this, particularly in the light of my comment (which survives in the published book), "One could wish that the young divisional commander had given a different reply."* But Guy's reaction to this was mild; what he was interested in, to my astonishment, was hanging on General Crerar the responsibility for the Dieppe raid. He recalled that when Crerar was the senior Canadian army officer in England in 1942 in the absence of McNaughton in Canada, he had exerted himself to get opportunities for his browned-off troops to take part in raids. Simonds had been with Crerar during two interviews with Lord Mountbatten, the Chief of Combined Operations, in which Crerar pressed for such opportunities. I was quite sure that Crerar would not have suggested any objective — that he would have considered a strategic matter, and the business of the British; but Guy insisted that he had mentioned Dieppe,

---

* Guy made no attempt to deny Montgomery's story, which is clearly true. He did suggest extenuating circumstances, which are duly noted in the book. I still feel that Guy had reason to be ashamed of this business, and perhaps he was. The whole miserable affair is described in *Arms, Men and Governments*, pages 224-28.

and that this would be found in hand-written memoranda of the conversations which he had himself written. We found the two memoranda and they contained no mention of Dieppe. Guy at once said that there had been a third interview, that he had written a memorandum of it also, and that it mentioned Dieppe; he would find it in his "strongbox" and show it to me. I never heard any more about it. We found nothing about any third interview in Crerar's records, and I feel sure that none ever took place. Simonds' hatred of Crerar had turned him into an unintentional liar; he had convinced himself that Crerar had committed a crime, and he was determined to prove it by hook or by crook.

Inevitably, the Canadian relationship with Lord Montgomery comes into this discussion. After the war, General Crerar told me a story. Taking over the Canadian Corps in Sussex late in 1941, he found that he was going to be under the operational command of Lieutenant-General B. L. Montgomery, then just taking charge of the South-Eastern Command. He had never met this officer; and he asked a British general of his acquaintance, who had had a good deal to do with him, what sort of person Montgomery was. After a moment's reflection, the British general replied, "Well, Harry, all I can tell you about Monty is that he's an efficient little shit." General Crerar, all those years later, clearly felt indisposed to disagree with this assessment.

That Montgomery and McNaughton did not get on is common knowledge, though there is no basis for the belief that Monty was in some way responsible for McNaughton's dismissal. Montgomery and Crerar did not get on either. This may have been due in part to personality clashes, to Montgomery's disagreeable qualities and to Crerar's natural coldness. It cannot be doubted, however, that Montgomery disliked Crerar's insistence on being treated as a national commander and not being content to function as if he were merely any British corps or army commander. In this Crerar was McNaughton's heir; I feel certain that he got his ideas from McNaughton, though he was not, I think, disposed to push them quite as far as McNaughton had. His first encounter with Montgomery in this matter was before Dieppe, when Monty and other British officers had taken the line that no Canadian officer need be present at Headquarters No. 11 Fighter Group, from which in effect the raid would be watched and directed. Crerar explained to Montgomery that a question of responsibility to the Canadian government was involved, and that the matter could not be handled as if the Canadians taking part were British troops. Montgomery fully accepted Crerar's arguments at the time, but he obviously disliked these Canadian pretensions and remembered them.[3]

The difficulties between the two men during the North-West Europe operations of 1944-45 are described in my book *The Victory Campaign*.[4] Late in September 1944 illness obliged Crerar to take leave in England and Simonds took over temporarily as Army Commander. During this period Colonel Ralston, the Canadian Defence Minister, visited the theatre and had a talk with Montgomery which he recorded. The field marshal made quite clear his dislike of Crerar and his preference for Simonds; Ralston's notes run, "He said Crerar adequate but not a ball of fire. Not in same parish with Simmonds [sic] as Army Commander." Montgomery asked the Minister what he would do if Crerar didn't come back and Simonds became a casualty. "He said" (Ralston wrote), "I would have to say 'there's the situation.' There isn't any Canadian in whom I have the necessary confidence. . . . If you said to put in Fowkes [sic] I would have to say it will be necessary to put Canadians in reserve . . . I'd have to suggest as a Comdr. one of the Corps Commanders in 2nd [British] Army. He said I'd like to see Crerar back but don't have him come back till he is in shape. . . ."* Ralston sensibly said he would not decide these matters until he had to. He presumably realized that Montgomery was engaging in his characteristic big talk, and that he would have to accept any commander whom the Canadian government and the Chief of the Imperial General Staff nominated. I remember Crerar saying, "Monty would always go through a yellow light; but when the light turned red, he stopped." It is interesting that Montgomery made it a complaint against Crerar that he had been reluctant, when the 2nd Canadian Corps was widely stretched, to transfer the 2nd Canadian Division, on its far flank, to the adjacent 1st British Corps. "Simonds saw point at once. He was not influenced by national idea. His one idea was to beat the Germans."[5]

This evidence, and what I saw of Guy Simonds myself, leaves no doubt in my mind that he had little of McNaughton's and Crerar's sense of the

---

* Against this, one must put the fact that Charles Foulkes told me in 1948 that during this period when Simonds was acting as Army Commander and Foulkes acting as commander of the 2nd Canadian Corps in his place, Montgomery told him that he could count on remaining as Corps Commander; Crerar wouldn't be coming back. Foulkes' recollection was that Monty said he had "written a letter" to ensure this.

responsibilities of a Canadian national commander; he was quite content to function as the commander of a British formation. This certainly pleased Montgomery. But Monty, I have no doubt, was right when he said that Guy was a more effective army commander than Crerar. A senior staff officer at Army Headquarters at the time told me shortly afterwards that during Simonds' period in command his leadership was much more dynamic than Crerar's; the moment he took over he established a "firm grip" of the operations that had been lacking before. In fairness to Crerar, it must be remembered that he was not a well man at the time. A British officer who was acting as a liaison officer for Simonds during his time at Army Headquarters later gave me a glimpse of Guy's vigorous style. He had, he said, had to deliver two very embarrassing verbal messages from Guy to subordinate commanders; one was to Foulkes at Corps, "to the effect that it was desirable to remember that one of the principles of war was the maintenance of the object"; the other, to a divisional commander, pointed out that "it was usual to keep one brigade in reserve." This cannot have precisely endeared Guy to those subordinates; but it presumably tended to keep them on their toes.

I have already said that Guy Simonds was probably our most genuinely brilliant field commander. I think he was generally recognized as such by the officers of the army. I was impressed by the great number of ex-officers who came to his funeral in Toronto in May 1974. They came not to pay tribute to a man they loved — as might have been the case with McNaughton — but to one they respected as a particularly outstanding soldier. Of any shortcomings he had as a national commander they were not aware, or they didn't care about it.

It is as a national commander that Harry Crerar deserves to be remembered. He was not an inspired or inspiring leader; though I think he was a better general than Montgomery was prepared to admit. I have said that I think he never made a bad mistake. The reason Monty was hostile to him was precisely the fact that he insisted on being treated as a national commander. His position was difficult, as his countrymen, who owe him a considerable debt, should remember. He took command of First Canadian Army without having had battle experience in the war then in progress; there was no Canadian officer of the requisite seniority who had had such experience. The British worshipped battle experience; and Crerar was in the awkward position of commanding British officers who had had it, and who resented being under him. Montgomery, I am sure, preferred Guy Simonds, not merely because Simonds was a first-rate commander, nor because Simonds was prepared to act like an Englishman, but because Monty considered Simonds one of his men; he had written to McNaughton from Sicily, "Simmonds [*sic*] has got to learn the art of command just as his Division has got to learn the art of battle fighting. I shall teach him; and he is learning well. He will be a 1st Class Div. Comd in due course, and he will have a 1st Class Division."[6] All Monty's own work.

Vanity is not limited to generals, it also crops up to make difficulties for us at lower levels. There was, for instance, the case of the brigade major and the Italian general in Sicily. In the early days there the Canadians acquired an Italian divisional commander as a prisoner and this affair got considerable publicity. Who captured the general? A good many people might have claimed the honour, for the general himself insisted on his right to surrender to an officer of his own rank and he was passed back until, finally, he had the satisfaction of making his official submission to General Simonds. But one of our brigade majors was very desirous of being credited with this triumph and was very loath to accept evidence that the first Canadian to make contact with the *generale* was a sergeant in charge of a fighting patrol of Princess Patricia's Canadian Light Infantry. It must be said that the "military probabilities" are much in favour of the sergeant rather than the brigade staff officer. But the brigade major, who was very articulate, subsequently covered many pages with angry argument directed at Jim Conacher and me. One of his particular complaints related to a group photograph which was published with himself cut out! I don't know who committed this crime, but it certainly wasn't the Historical Section. Gerry Nicholson's final version in *The Canadians in Italy* mentions the gallant major but, I am sorry to say, comes down on the whole on the side of the sergeant.

Perhaps the final comment may be the one made to me by a more senior officer of the 1st Division: "Who would want credit for capturing a tame cat?"

The most difficult historical problem I ever confronted was the battle at Hong Kong. Dieppe, I have made clear, was an extraordinarily well documented operation, not least on the German side. Hong Kong was not documented at all.

There were, of course, plenty of papers on the preparatory phase, the events in Canada: the papers that the Duff Commission which investigated the affair mulled over. On the battle itself there were absolutely no contemporary documents except the few brief signals sent out from the colony during the fighting. The so-called war diaries and reports of the Canadian and other components of the defending force were compiled in Japanese prison camps, months or years after the events, almost entirely from memory and under the most difficult conditions. It was nearly four years before our prisoners were liberated and were able to tell their stories. Between different people's stories there were rather wide discrepancies. Members of different national units told different tales. There is always, I suspect, among members of a defeated force a tendency to look for scapegoats and to shift the blame. This tendency was certainly not absent at Hong Kong.

On the enemy side things were no better. There was nothing resembling the magnificent collection of meticulously compiled German war diaries that we had available concerning Dieppe. For a long time we had nothing at all. Japan was under American occupation, and ruled by General Douglas MacArthur. The British historians told us they were having difficulty in extracting anything useful from this regime. They themselves were able to give us some interrogation reports of Japanese officers. There was a Canadian mission in Tokyo headed by the famous and unfortunate Herbert Norman. We asked External Affairs to request help from it. I don't know what the situation there was, but we had to ask a number of times before we got results. Finally, in November 1949, something arrived: not exactly documents, but helpful. It was a narrative of the Hong Kong operations compiled by the "First Demobilization Bureau," a group of Japanese ex-officers working under the American authorities. Stories have been told of this group's relationship to General Charles Willoughby, MacArthur's chief of intelligence, and how Willoughby, if he was displeased with the version of an incident it presented to him, would send the author back to produce one more satisfactory to the conquerors. Fortunately, it seems unlikely that Willoughby had any interest in Hong Kong, and the account of it is probably the best the Japanese could compile. It was pretty clearly based to some extent on contemporary documents.[7] At any rate, it was the best thing we ever got.

Such was the stuff from which I had to create a history of the defence of Hong Kong. I wrote in *Six Years of War*, "Faced with this intractable material, the chronicler can only do his best. The narrative which follows is the writer's own interpretation of evidence which is often unsatisfactory. Some of those who were there will doubtless not agree with it." I said at the beginning of this chapter that the historian's first task is to establish the facts. The Hong Kong battle was the incident where I found this task hardest, and I cannot say with confidence today that I wholly succeeded in it. Things were made worse at the time by the political sensitiveness of the business. Hong Kong had been made the matter of a continuing attack on the government; with George Drew it was a sort of King Charles's head, and anything we wrote was potentially explosive.

In the recriminatory discussions that followed the surrender, in the course of which some nasty things were said,[8] the Canadians were at a disadvantage, simply because their natural spokesmen were dead. Brigadier J. K. Lawson, the force commander, was killed, as was the officer next in rank, Colonel Pat Hennessy; one of the two battalion commanders died in captivity. The dispatch written by the commander at Hong Kong, Major-General C. M. Maltby, was shown us for comment in advance of publication. It seemed to show a tendency to put an undue share of the blame for the failure of the defence on the Canadians, and there were what we thought some errors of fact; so the Department of National Defence asked for some changes, which were made without difficulty. (It was a bit embarrassing for a historian to be involved in what people might call tampering with the facts of history, but my view was that the general, consciously or unconsciously, had tampered with them first.) I don't believe anybody (apart from gallant individuals) had a great deal to be proud of at Hong Kong; but it gave me satisfaction to be able to write that the Japanese accounts indicated that it was in areas where the Canadians were the major units engaged "that the enemy encountered his greatest difficulties and suffered his heaviest losses."

I wrote in the preface to *Arms, Men and Governments*, "I have never been refused access to any document in the possession of the Government of Canada." This was the literal truth. But some important parts of the record of the Canadian war effort were not in the possession of the government. This brings me to the question of ministerial papers.

A cabinet minister may write letters, or file letters he receives in two different ways. He may use his department's filing system, putting his correspondence on official files, which are government property; or he may use a private filing system, separate from the department's, which is his own. Most ministers will use both systems as circumstances may dictate. In the vast majority of cases a minister retiring from office will have a personal file-room full of papers, many of which deal with public business and many of which, almost inevitably, are really government property. But by long-established custom these papers are regarded as the minister's private possessions, to be disposed of as he sees fit. He can leave them with the department; he can take them home and store them; he can make them over to the Public Archives, for preservation and for consultation by historians after the passage of an agreed period of time; if he chooses, he can burn them.

From the point of view of the public interest, this system is abominable. It exposes important parts of the record of our history to loss and makes no provision for their availability to historians. The problem was dealt with by the Canadian Historical Association in its brief to the Massey Commission in 1950; I wrote about it in a paper on archives problems which I wrote for the commission;[9] the commission made suggestions in its report; but there has been, essentially, no change in the system. The reason, of course, is that change requires action by the cabinet, the very people whom change would be likely to discommode. Fortunately, many ministers have been prevailed upon to deposit their papers in the Public Archives in Ottawa, where in due course they become available to historians. Virtually all the prime ministers' papers are to be found there. (An exception, characteristically enough, is those of John Diefenbaker, segregated in distant Saskatoon.)

In my capacity as official historian, this system caused difficulty for me. It was harder to gain access to these important records in private hands than to get at the official records of the cabinet.

It is true that my first contact with the system was fortunate. When Ian Mackenzie, who had been Minister of National Defence in 1935-39, died in 1949, I raised the question of his papers through his former secretary, Norman Senior; and by Senior's good offices and the generosity of Mrs. Mackenzie I obtained custody of the papers. They were to be available to me for purposes of the history, and would subsequently be transferred to the Archives and available to all students after 1975. They were very valuable.

In other cases I was not so lucky. A person of greater importance for my purposes was Colonel J. L. Ralston, Minister of National Defence, 1940-44, and a controversial figure because of his brusque dismissal by Mackenzie King in 1944. Some correspondence with him while he lived produced no results; and after his death in 1948 I had no better fortune with his son Stuart, who was now the custodian of the papers and whom I knew slightly. In April 1949 I spent a day in Montreal fruitlessly discussing access to the papers with Stuart and his law partner J. L. Ilsley, former Minister of Finance and a close friend and associate of Ralston in the King cabinet. It seemed evident to me that Ilsley felt that I had a good case, but he was unwilling to put pressure on his young colleague. Stuart made endless difficulty; he even mentioned security, though as a government servant I had a better right to the papers than he had. Finally, when he spoke of the possibility that he might use them as a basis for some writing of his own, I knew I had lost. He never did this. I made a final approach to him in 1956, and got no further. I have no doubt that the Ralstons felt that in some obscure way I, as an official historian, was an agent of Mackenzie King — even though King had retired in 1948 and died in 1950. His name, I am sure, was anathema to them, and I can't say I blame them. I did, however, ultimately gain access to the papers. After Stuart's early death my former student and officer Jack Granatstein, a person with an uncanny capacity for sniffing out historical sources and getting at them, prevailed upon his widow to let him use the papers and to transfer them to the Public Archives of Canada. After that I could hardly be denied.

There was a great deal of valuable stuff in the Ralston Papers, though much of it merely confirmed evidence already available to me from other sources. The most fascinating single document — a real historical nugget — was the one I have already quoted, Colonel Ralston's notes of his overseas trip before the cabinet crisis of 1944. Ralston did not keep a diary in the usual sense, but on this important journey he apparently took with him a notebook which he held on his knee and in which he made rudimentary notes of his interviews while they actually proceeded. His secretary, Miss Waters, was able to transcribe his hieroglyphics, and it was her transcript that I found and used. This absolutely contemporary record of Ralston's conversations with Montgomery, Simonds and other people at that critical moment is the stuff of history with a capital H. The Ralston Papers made a vital contribution to *Arms, Men and Governments*. The drawback was that when I at last got into them the book was already virtually complete in draft. The result was that large sections of it had to be rewritten, and publication was delayed.

One important collection of ministerial papers I never did get at — those of Angus L. Macdonald, Naval Minister in the King wartime government, friend and ally of Ralston and Ilsley, and certainly as time passed an eminent King-hater. I am sure that what I have said of the Ralstons was at least as true of the Macdonalds: they would have nothing to do with me because I was working officially and was in their eyes tarred with the brush of King. I had the poor satisfaction of stating in the preface to my book that I had been unable to gain access to the Macdonald papers. This made them unique. I had no such difficulty with the former Air Minister, C. G. "Chubby" Power, who talked to me and let me into his records. C. D. Howe's papers were available to me in the Archives.

The most important private archive remains to be spoken of: that of William Lyon Mackenzie King himself. When he died in 1950 he left the control of his voluminous papers in the hands of four literary executors: Norman Robertson; W. Kaye Lamb, the Dominion Archivist; J. W. Pickersgill; and Fred McGregor, one of his former secretaries. Kaye Lamb was a good friend of mine; Jack Pickersgill and I were contemporaries at Oxford; and with Fred MacGregor, in the early days the actual custodian of the King Papers, I was able to establish a very cordial relationship. I had no difficulty in gaining access to the main body of the papers. They were a goldmine, full of official documents, some of which were duplicates of papers in departmental files at External Affairs or elsewhere, while others were certainly to be found nowhere else in Ottawa. They were particularly valuable in connection with relations with Britain and the United States. To give just one example, they enabled me to reconstruct with certainty the events preceding King's Ogdensburg meeting with President Roosevelt in August 1940.

Mackenzie King's celebrated Diary (the capital letter is appropriate) was a separate problem. In the years after King's death it was surrounded with an atmosphere of mystery. It was known to exist; it was known that the official biographer was using it; it was said that there was a possibility of its being destroyed when he was finished with it. It was a holy-of-holies, spoken of almost in whispers. It must have been mentioned in some of my many friendly talks with Kaye Lamb, but nothing was said to embolden me to ask to see it.Then in 1964 something happened to change the situation. Professor James Eayrs published the first volume of his admirable book *In Defence of Canada*. Jim Eayrs had worked as a research assistant to the biographer, MacGregor Dawson. He had had access to the diary and had made good use of his opportunities; his book was full of references to the sacred document. This gave me my own opportunity. I approached the literary executors, pointing out that if the diary was to be used in this way in a purely private book, it was a pity that an official historian should be excluded. The executors kindly accepted the argument, and I was in. (It might be fair to say that I have been in ever since.)

A useful achievement, but more work. I set about reading the diary. It is a colossal as well as an absorbing document, particularly colossal in the second war period, when King might dictate up to twenty pages a day. I ought to have begun in 1935 and read every word of it, but I must admit I didn't; anxious to get on with the long-delayed book, I concentrated on the important conjunctures and on the areas that seemed to me especially in need of illumination. It cast a vast amount of new light for me not only on King but on many events. For a second time the book had to be rewritten; this, combined with the fact that it was a part-time job, was the cause of its not appearing until 1971.

Generals have papers too, and sometimes they can be almost as difficult as politicians about them. Lord Montgomery, one hears, was one of the most difficult. The question of his retaining as his personal property the German surrender document signed at Luneburg Heath in 1945 was raised in Parliament. From the historian's point of view, this is not a particularly serious crime; a good photocopy of a paper like this will serve his turn. What Parliament might have looked into with more reason is the fact that (if I am correctly informed) Monty kept the records of Tactical Headquarters 21 Army Group at his place in Hampshire and allowed no access to them to anybody, including the British official historians. One of the few people who came close was Chester Wilmot, the author of *The Struggle for Europe*; but from what Wilmot told me, Monty did not allow him to poke about freely among the papers; instead, he would produce one paper and say, "Ah, Wilmot, now here's something very interesting." The first person to have free run of the papers, I gather, was the official biographer designated by Monty.

Our two Canadian army commanders, McNaughton and Crerar, were liberal in their approach. I have described how Andy McNaughton handed his overseas papers over to me when he went back to Canada in 1943; later he gave me for custody both his prewar and postwar papers, and the whole boiling rested at the Army Historical Section in Ottawa until in due time they went to the Public Archives. I assisted the McNaughton family in making arrangements with the Archives under which the papers would be opened to researchers twenty years after the general's death, that is, in 1986. In fact, I believe, considerable portions of the papers, those particularly of early dates, have already been opened. The papers were, of course, a great resource to me in my historical task, just as the general's countenance and friendship had been in his lifetime.

General Crerar likewise made his papers fully available to me. Before his death he handed them over to my office and asked me to take the responsibility for controlling access to them. When he died I helped Mrs. Crerar with the business of arranging for their permanent future custody at the Public Archives of Canada, again on a basis of general closure for twenty years. General Crerar always laid special stress on the importance of making certain that no information that might embarrass "any living officer" found its way to the public from his papers, and I did my best to ensure this.

Neither Crerar nor McNaughton wrote memoirs. General McNaughton designated John Swettenham, one of my officers, as his biographer, and had many talks with him. Swettenham's three-volume biography is a valuable book. One general who did think of writing an account of his military life was Guy Simonds; indeed, he did produce a manuscript soon after the war, but ran into the roadblock interposed by the regulation requiring serving officers to obtain permission to publish material on military subjects. Charles Foulkes told me, "We've told him he can't publish it." After his retirement Simonds mentioned to me that he was working on memoirs. I know that he had a long-standing contract with Macmillan of Canada, but no book ever appeared. I gather that death interrupted him before the manuscript go to the war period. General Simonds' papers, so far as I know, have never reached any public repository. It is a pity that they should not be beside those of two other great military servants of Canada, McNaughton and Crerar, in the Archives at Ottawa.

The wheels of government publishing grind slowly, and although the imprint on *Arms, Men and Governments* is 1970, the book was not actually published until April 1971. My file of reviews of it is rather thin. This may owe something to the fact that the volume was so enormous, with 35 pages of references and 74 of appendices. Even academic reviewers blanched. However, there were some appreciative notices. My friend Dick Preston wrote in the *American Historical Review* that the book would serve more effectively than some others "the purpose for which general staff histories are written, to record experience for future use." It was in fact intended to be useful, in the event of another great emergency, not only to military men but also to diplomatists and even politicians. We may have another great war, but it certainly will not be much like that of 1939-45. Even so, I hoped, the book's presentation of national problems and attempts at solution might have some value. On the basis of experience, however, I feel pretty certain that when and if the emergency comes nobody in authority will think of consulting it. They will learn the old lessons over again and make the old mistakes.

I had retired from the army in 1959, having worn the uniform for nineteen years and, by and large, loved it. I had reached the age limit for colonels (53); and though the powers that were would probably have been willing to "extend" me, many things made me feel that it was time to go. The army history was finished (though *The Victory Campaign* did not actually appear until 1960); the volume on policy I could write elsewhere; and a competent successor was available in the person of Gerry

Nicholson, who had certainly earned a promotion. Moreover, Doris's parents in Toronto were very old and needed her, and my own mother, also in Toronto, was likewise old and unwell. And we had both come to feel that fourteen years in Ottawa was, on the whole, enough.

Everything pointed to our old home, Toronto. Since we obviously could hardly live on my $5,000 pension, I proceeded to negotiate with my old university there. The chairman of the History Department was now Donald Creighton. Donald's appointment a few years before had been something of an earthquake shock. He was probably the university's most eminent historian, but all the senior members of the department disliked him cordially. Frank Underhill, who hated his insides, resigned on the instant (a highly unprofessional action at the moment when there was no time to find a replacement before the beginning of the next term). As I have made clear, I could get on with Don after a fashion, and we worked out an arrangement. He said that I couldn't be made a "full" professor; "the young men," he explained, wouldn't stand for it. (I don't think he really had the faintest idea what the young men thought.) This didn't worry me. I recalled that there had once been what were called "special lecturers"; this would suit me, and it turned out to suit the university. Salary? My pay and allowances as a colonel had been about $12,000 a year. If the university would pay me $8,000 for working two-thirds time, I would have a little more than I had been getting and would be happy. The university agreed with what I now think was suspicious alacrity, and I worked for $8,000 for years. I began teaching again in the autumn of 1959, and, what with one thing and another, had a feeling that I had come home.

Chapter 17

Back to the Don

T he University of Toronto that I returned to in 1959 was of course a very different place from the institution I had graduated from in 1927. Academically, however, it was still basically the same; it was during the next decade or so that revolutionary changes were to take place.

The Faculty of Arts in 1959 still had its specialized honour courses, not yet swept away by bright young activists hypnotized by the charm of freedom of choice. The annual spring examinations were still enormously important — too important, I must say — and at the end of the academic year lists were still published grading the students in the various courses into first, second and third classes and ranking individuals within those classes. This time-honoured practice was shortly to be abandoned, presumably because it was considered hard on the characters in the lower brackets and fostered an undesirable spirit of competition. Students had always (naturally and inevitably) disliked examinations. In the sixties they found that they could influence, if not dictate, university policy; so exams, though never absolutely abolished, very nearly faded away.

Social atmosphere and customs underwent a similar revolution. In 1959 women students always wore skirts to classes, not because of any official requirement, but because they thought it fitting. In the sixties, Unisex came in and both sexes adopted the universal jeans. Sexual segregation in residences went by the board. In my day, women's residences had been convents; and anyone caught introducing a woman into a men's residence would have been very drastically dealt with. I remember my mild surprise in (perhaps) 1965 when a colleague in charge of a residence told me that the only remaining rule was that your proceedings should not disturb your room-mate.

Of all these developments I was an interested but rather passive spectator. I got on well with my own students and almost always liked them. Practically all my teaching was in small tutorial or seminar groups (the "young men" preferred to do the lecturing themselves, and when I gave a lecture it was usually for a colleague at his request). People were tending more and more to offer courses dealing with their own limited specialties, and the most constant element in my own little curriculum was a seminar course on Canada in the Second World War which, for a considerable time, was open both to senior undergraduates and graduate students. I also offered (at the suggestion of the departmental chairman) a graduate seminar on Canadian external policies which fitted well with my research on war policy and ultimately resulted in a two-volume history of external matters called *Canada and the Age of Conflict*. Writing this was in a sense a new career. I might mention that at an early stage, in spite of the alleged views of the "young men," I acquired the status of a full professor; this was the result of an inquiry from the University of Alberta as to whether I would be interested in the job of chairman of its history department. I didn't particularly want to go to Alberta, and in any case my family circumstances made it impossible; but in the time-honoured academic manner I used the offer as a lever.

One circumstance brought me briefly into touch with the main stream of student political life. I let myself be talked into becoming honorary president of the "U.C. Lit," the University College Literary and Athletic Society, the central student organization of my old college. The constitution required the honorary president to preside at meetings, and I found the task a bit demanding but also enlightening. Remembering my own student days, in my simplicity I assumed that the proceedings would be conducted in a spirit, if not of levity, at any rate of a certain jocundity, and I approached them accordingly. I couldn't have been more wrong. Nothing could have exceeded the seriousness with which these student politicians took themselves and their organization. They acted as if they were transacting the business of the nation; indeed, I have never seen the House of Commons approach its business with such grim devotion. I felt out of my depth, and I am afraid my presiding left something to be desired. Indeed, one of the honourable members said so in a letter to *The Varsity*; he accused me of undue deference to the views of the elected student president.

One thing these young people certainly didn't want from me was advice. I think they probably knew rather more about the world than my contemporaries and I did in the twenties, but they *thought* they knew everything; it is literally true that they thought they knew everything. They were engaged, among other things, in the task of drawing up a new constitution for the Lit. Remembering the function of "faculty advisers" in days past, it occurred to me that they might like me to sit in on the discussions and make what contribution I could. Without anything being actually said, it became clear that nothing was further from their thoughts. All things taken together, I was glad that the fact that I was taking a sabbatical in the following year gave me an excuse for declining the second year of service as honorary president which would have been normal. Just what the nature of the constitution they made was I don't now remember, if I ever knew; but I rather think it eliminated the office of honorary president, in which case I was the last honorary president of the U.C. Lit. Thereafter my contacts with the student body were largely limited to teaching; and if the young men and women in my seminars thought they knew more history than I did, they were polite enough to conceal it.

I mentioned *The Varsity*. It still existed, but it was very different from the days when I was editor. It was no longer a daily; and it was no longer a newspaper. It was a *cahier de doléances*, a schedule of grievances; and it was a poor day when it could not muster a total of at least five grievances on the front page. The old distinction between editorials and news stories had vanished; all stories were now full of editorial comment. I have a feeling that most people, including I think most students, stopped reading it.

Although Donald Creighton had hired me, by the time I reported for duty he was no longer chairman of the History Department. He had, I think, hated the job, and he had not been a popular chairman. I was told that he looked after the interests of the younger members of the staff better than they knew; but he got no credit for good deeds done by stealth. He was succeeded by Maurice Careless, a younger Canadian historian but with a growing reputation in the field. Where Donald had had a genius for getting people's backs up, Maurice was a confirmed conciliator. If Donald had been the department's Diefenbaker, Maurice was its Mackenzie King.

The department when I joined it was still small, and full of old friends of mine. Two of my former officers, Jim Conacher and Bob Spencer, were members of it, as at the time of writing they still are. But in the next few years it grew greatly to meet the needs of a growing student body. The new recruits were found largely in the United States, and a department whose practice and traditions had largely been formed on English models had some difficulty in assimilating them. It had been a small family with family feelings; its fights, when they happened, were family fights. Now things were rather different. The pursuit of private specialization, the cultivation of new and exotic fields of history, was another complication. Nevertheless, looking back, I think the community coped surprisingly well with the great expansion and transformation. The department maintained its reputation for scholarship and good teaching; and at the same time the family feeling, though undeniably diluted, never wholly disappeared. It was always, I felt, a pleasure to be a member of the Toronto historical fellowship.

The year I arrived at Toronto I published three books, each dealing with a different century: for me, at least, a record. One was *The Victory Campaign*, the last volume of the army history, which I have told about. The second went back to the nineteenth century. It was *Records of the Nile Voyageurs*, the documents concerning one of the strangest and most fascinating episodes in Canadian military history, the participation of Canadian boatmen in the Nile Expedition of 1884-85, the unsuccessful attempt to rescue General Gordon from Khartoum. The boatmen were a microcosm of Canadian society, French and English, red men and white; and they were commanded by Frederick Denison, a Toronto militia officer who was also an alderman, who went off to the other side of the world, on no notice at all, at the call of his old commander, Lord Wolseley, whom he had served under in the Red River Expedition. The book was published by the venerable Champlain Society, which since 1905 has been making available to readers rare or unpublished documents of Canadian history. To have one of the society's beautifully produced volumes with my name on it gave me great satisfaction. I have been a fairly active member of that respectable and rather curious organization ever since.

The third book carried me back to the beginnings of British rule in Canada. As the bicentenary of the Battle of the Plains of Abraham approached, I had a discussion with John Gray, the president of the Macmillan Company of Canada, whose brother Bob had been a member of our historical team in North-West Europe. He wanted to put out some book in observance of the occasion, and inquired what I would think of a new edition of Hawkins' *Picture of Quebec*. This didn't strike me as a particularly good idea, and I was moved to suggest that I might perhaps try my hand at writing a short book about the campaign of 1759. John agreed, and in spare time I set to work. I had a good deal of spare time, I was still in Ottawa at the time, but Doris had been obliged to go to Toronto to look after her aged parents, and we saw each other only at weekends. I took to spending my evenings in the Public Archives, where virtually all the basic sources on the famous clash between Wolfe and Montcalm were available either as original documents or copies.

When I began the task I had only general ideas about the happenings at Quebec in 1759. However, since so much had been written on the subject I simple-mindedly assumed that I could read the works of my predecessors and produce on that basis a sort of easy gentlemanly essay, a commentary on the familiar facts. I hadn't done much reading before I put that plan aside. I came to the conclusion that a great deal of what had been written was, to put it bluntly, nonsense. Historians had approached the subject, not in the spirit of investigators reading the records in order to discover what happened, but with preconceptions and closed minds. In particular, many British writers had begun with the assumption that James Wolfe was a military genius and had written in the light of that assumption. I felt obliged to start from the ground up, reading the papers left behind them by the people who were there and reconstructing the events on that basis. I wrote in my introduction, perhaps a bit priggishly, "I have made a conscious effort to rise above prejudice and to put forward a new and independent interpretation based on a careful re-examination of the contemporary documents of both sides and on the 'military probabilities'." I went over the ground carefully, visiting Quebec and climbing the cliff that Colonel William Howe's light infantry scaled on the night of that incredibly romantic encounter two centuries ago.

To a person putting the finishing touches to an account of operations in the Second World War this was a fascinating avocation. I had an overwhelming feeling of having been here before. "The weapons of war," I wrote, "have changed beyond all recognition since the time of Wolfe and Montcalm; the men who wield them have changed, like the rest of mankind, remarkably little." Clashes of personality, conflicts of ambition, inter-service antagonisms, discord between "colonial" forces and those from the mother country — all these were present in 1759 and turned up again in 1939-45. Two centuries had changed little about the human animal at war.

About the two famous rival leaders, incidentally, this was my final, highly personal conclusion: "Montcalm and Wolfe, though in many ways dissimilar, had much in common. Both were exceptionally gallant fighting soldiers. Both had defects of temperament and personality which affected their dealings with other men in a manner damaging to their military usefulness. Both had some military talent. And the abilities of both have been grossly exaggerated by partial and sentimental historians, writing under the spell of the romantic circumstances in which the two generals fought and died in that extraordinary campaign on the St. Lawrence two hundred years ago."

My little book, called *Quebec 1759: The Siege and the Battle*, had a kind reception (though so many people wrote books on the same subject that year that none of the authors made much money out of them, and I might add that the Governor General's Awards Board went on record to the effect that no non-fiction book of sufficient merit to warrant an award was published that year in Canada). Macmillans, under John Gray's inspiration, produced it in a very agreeable form; and fourteen years later, when Pan Books brought it out as a paperback in their British Battles series, giving it a wider audience, I was delighted, though the paperback About the two famous rival leaders, incidentally, this was my final,

It was John Gray who brought me on to the Toronto Historical Board. This organization (originally called the Toronto Historical Committee) had been set up to administer and protect the great and growing city's few historic sites and advise the city government on historical matters. It had lately emerged from the battle to save the Old Fort (Fort York) from the vandals who wanted to "move" this unique and priceless civic and national possession, the centre of a bloody battle in 1813, in order to avoid putting a curve in an expressway. I had been able to play a silent and anonymous part in the defence. In Ottawa I was following the progress of the fight in the newspapers. The legal situation was that any change in the situation of the fort required the consent of the Department of National Defence. Checking with my friend Freddie Johns, who was in charge of properties, I found that some civil servant, on being applied to by the civic authorities, had written giving the required permission without checking with anyone who knew anything about the matter. Freddie had the letter withdrawn. So there was a line of defence in Ottawa if all else had failed. However, the fight was won locally and the retreat to prepared positions was not necessary.

I was a member of the Historical Board for some years, and then went on to its Advisory Council (now the Museums Committee) where I still remain. Over two decades the board's activities have steadily expanded and it has been assiduous in defending the old buildings of Toronto against would-be destroyers. Largely as a result of its work, renovation has tended to replace demolition. Fortunately, it has had increasing public support; Canadians, including Torontonians, are more conscious of their historical heritage (and its architectural expressions) than they were a quarter of a century ago, and people like the gentleman who burned down a Rosedale mansion which he owned and which the Board (and the provincial heritage law) were hindering him from demolishing are not very numerous. Owners are more and more disposed to take pride in the historical value of their properties.

Incidentally, I remember another service which Freddie Johns rendered the country in this department. On a visit to the Collège Militaire Royal at St. Jean, Quebec, I heard that the authorities were gaily preparing to tear down the three barrack buildings there built in or about 1838, in the days when the border troubles following the rebellions of 1837 led the British authorities to increase the garrison of Canada. I alerted Freddie, and he again took action. I have no recent information, but I trust that the old barracks are still ornamenting the ancient military station of St. Johns (as the place was generally known when they were built). I recall another visit to an old military site, this time Halifax. I went to York Redoubt, a magnificent late-Victorian coast-defence battery with its enormous "Woolwich Infant"-type guns, shaped like old-fashioned milk bottles, still standing on their original carriages. Again I was told that it was proposed to demolish it. I wrote a letter of protest, and while I should not care to take the credit, I am glad to hear that York Redoubt still exists and is being restored.

In 1965-66 I made a temporary return to Ottawa. Paul Hellyer was now Minister of National Defence. "Integration" of the forces was the order of the day. Few people believed that Hellyer and his colleagues would really be so silly as to attempt actual unification, but it was generally admitted that at the Ottawa level a considerable degree of integration made sense. It seemed to me that it made sense in the historical department, and in the hope of ensuring the survival of a historical organization I offered my services to see the integration through in that area. I spent about fifteen months in Ottawa, having made a financial arrangement that was just enough to cover my out-of-pocket expenses while ensuring that I didn't lose money by comparison with my university salary. I went home to Toronto at weekends.

Thanks to what the army used to call "goodwill and the desire to cooperate" on the part of all concerned, the amalgamation went smoothly. My worst problem was accommodation. Gerry Nicholson had not stayed long as director of the Army Historical Section, and had been succeeded by a non-historian colonel whose chief accomplishment was allowing the higher authorities to move the section into premises below a pool-room in Eastview (now Vanier). The place's only recommendation was the neighbours, the nice French-Canadian people of Eastview. The worst of its many disadvantages was the fact that our invaluable records were largely stored in a basement which was subject to flooding. After considerable pulling and hauling I obtained space for the combined directorate in a building housing a department store's furniture department, which put us on a somewhat higher social level than the pool-room's and was also dry.

I was fortunate in being supported during this time in Ottawa by some very good friends and colleagues. I cannot mention them all. But I must speak of Lieutenant-Colonel Donald Goodspeed, who must have been one of the most genuinely brilliant people who ever graduated from Queen's University. He was also a person of colossal industry and a very skilful writer. One of the tasks we were saddled with was producing as a departmental celebration of the centennial of Canadian Confederation a volume telling the story of the Canadian forces during the century since 1867. Don carried the main burden of editing the book, and it was published under his name as editor. *The Armed Forces of Canada, 1867-1967: A Record of Achievement* was in great part a picture book, very handsomely produced; but it also contained more solid history than some reviewers were disposed to admit. As of 1983, its account of the RCAF in the Second World War is still, I think, the best available. The book ended with the forces still in the "integration" stage, and quoted the then Chief of the Defence Staff, Air Chief Marshal Frank Miller, as saying in 1965 that what was contemplated was the integration of "management and command" rather than of "the fighting elements themselves." But by the time the book was published in 1967 the government had plunged into that once unbelievable piece of stupidity. One reviewer reviled us for not assailing this nonsense. Since it had not been embarked upon when the book was written, we could hardly have done so, even in the improbable event of the Minister of National Defence being prepared to finance and publish an attack upon his policies. And after all, what we were writing was a celebration of a hundred years of service, and it would have been sad to turn the celebration into a wake.

Another tower of strength was Mrs. (formerly Lieutenant-Colonel) Alice Sorby. During the war she was the senior officer of the Canadian Women's Army Corps overseas and ran the corps, so far as an outsider could judge, to the complete satisfaction both of the girls in it and the army staff — no mean achievement. In 1959 she was a widow and interested in a civil service job. The last thing I did before I left was to hire her for the directorate, and she was the best legacy I could have given it. Equipped with a good education, sound military knowledge and boundless common sense, she dealt with the sticky business of answering historical inquiries from government departments and the public (one never knew what was going to be asked next — it could be anything) to the Queen's taste. Alice died, to the sorrow of many people, in 1982.

I have already said that I got authority for the production of a history of the Royal Canadian Air Force. This would fill a thoroughly disgraceful gap in the national historiography; and it provided a core job for the new Directorate of History which has kept it busy ever since. I didn't anticipate that it would take nearly fifteen years to roll out the first volume; but better late than never. The plan for the history has grown beyond anything I ever anticipated, and it will be interesting to see how long it takes to complete it.

During these months in Ottawa I was a spectator of the process of unifying the three Canadian fighting services, which had so distinguished themselves in the war, into a single force. It was a sad business to watch, and for one who had worn the army's British-type uniform for many years it was painful to see it replaced by the green costume whose cut and colour suggested bus conductors or gas-station attendants. (The best thing the people who were forced to wear it — thank heaven I was not one of them — had to say for this outfit was that it was "good for office work." Incidentally, one of the changes of the period was the abandonment of the civilized old British tradition that officers of the armed forces employed at a static headquarters wore civilian clothes.)

The precise origins of unification are interesting to speculate about. As I have said, tendencies in this direction had appeared as early as Brooke Claxton's time. One might have thought that a program of such vital national importance as a proposal to unify the fighting forces would not have been undertaken without very thoughtful professional examination, including perhaps consideration by a high-level inter-service committee. So far as I know no such examination was made. The decision to proceed with unification was apparently essentially Paul Hellyer's, taken after consultation only with a small group of private advisers.

Hellyer was probably influenced by his own war experience, which was rather unusual. He was only 16 when war broke out, and spent the early part of the war in the United States. After returning to Canada he worked in an aircraft plant until 1944, when he joined the RCAF. He was one of the men who in 1945 were, in effect, compulsorily transferred to the army as a result of the fact that the army was short of manpower while the RCAF was overstocked with it. He never served overseas.

I have a strong impression that it was in the air force that the origins of, and the support for, unification were largely found. *Arms, Men and Governments* points out that the manner in which the British Commonwealth Air Training Plan was set up in 1939 "broke the back" of the RCAF and militated against its putting in the field a national air force comparable to the First Canadian Army. The BCATP operated largely as an aircrew recruiting scheme for the Royal Air Force, and at the end of the war the majority of Canadian aircrew overseas were still in RAF rather than RCAF units. Opportunities for RCAF officers to exercise senior field command were limited. There was only one RCAF air vice-marshal in an operational command overseas — the commander of No. 6 Bomber Group — whereas in First Canadian Army there were five major-generals commanding divisions plus three lieutenant-generals for the army and the two corps. This situation certainly produced feelings of resentment and frustration among RCAF officers, particularly in the senior ranks (there is a good deal of evidence that many Canadian aircrew in the squadrons had no quarrel with the wartime arrangements).

After the war the RCAF was thrown into close relations with the United States Air Force under the North Atlantic Treaty Organization in Europe (where the Canadian Air Division worked under U.S. higher command), and nearer home in the North American Air Defence Command. I conjecture that RCAF officers who had resented the supposedly "colonial" relationship with the RAF were gratified to find themselves treated by the USAF as allies and became disposed to copy U.S. methods. (The American inability to understand RAF ranks was notorious, and I have no doubt that this made RCAF officers inclined to favour converting air vice-marshals into major-generals.)

There were other feelings of frustration current among RCAF senior officers. One of Hellyer's chief advisers on his program was Air Vice-Marshal/Major-General F. S. Carpenter. I had a conversation with General Carpenter when I went to give a lecture at the National Defence College while he was commandant there, and he told me, to my considerable astonishment, that he was largely moved in the advice he gave by his recollection of the situation when he joined the service, when the Royal Canadian Air Force was subordinated to the army's Chief of the General Staff. This situation had ended as long ago as 1938, when the director of the Royal Canadian Air Force was redesignated as Chief of the Air Staff; but the resentment against it lingered long enough to affect Carpenter's thinking in the 1960s. It seems rather illogical — just how do you relate this to unification of the services? — but I am reporting what Carpenter told me. The other person reported as especially influential with Hellyer was Group Captain Bill Lee, a public relations man. Perhaps he viewed the matter as a PR project, believing that unification as an "innovative" idea would have some popular appeal and bring his minister into public prominence.

My own impression was that unification had little support professionally in the services except the air force, and that even there it was far from universal. The navy hated it: blue, not green, was the universal naval colour all around the world, and the idea of a colonel instead of a captain walking the quarterdeck was ludicrous. (On these points, in fact, the government had to make concessions.) Only in the navy did a senior officer find the courage to make an outspoken public protest against the plan. On the other hand, one remembers with no particular respect the naval type whose support for the Hellyer program was rewarded with a promotion straight from commodore to vice-admiral, jumping the rank of rear-admiral on the way. Some generals retired silently; others made the best of things, perhaps trying to convince themselves that the system could be made to work; after all, the service was their bread and butter.

One aspect that seemed to me important got surprisingly little attention during the controversy. Canada has never fought a war on her own, and probably never will. She has always fought as a junior partner in a large alliance. This surely ought to be taken into account in planning her military organization. Her forces must be able to fit into large international bodies, and an organization different from everybody else's is bound to make this difficult. I think the naïve people who planned Canadian unification actually expected other nations to rush to copy us. Of course, they have not done so; integration elsewhere has been limited to the highest echelons of direction and command, and no important country has imitated the Canadian one-force concept. In another great war, circumstances would press very strong for a return to the old tri-service organization.

The scheme had some appeal to extreme nationalists, and of course to anglophobes, of whom there were some, not all in the air force. These nationalistic feelings sometimes took rather ludicrous forms. I was asked whether I could devise a "distinctively Canadian" ceremonial to replace the enormously popular Changing of the Guard by the two Guards militia regiments, wearing scarlet and bearskins, which delighted the tourists on Parliament Hill in the summertime. I told the questioner that I thought following this line would probably result in a pageant of Indians, voyageurs, canoes, war dances and peace pipes, with tourists staying away in droves. Apparently other people felt the same, for at last report the

Guards (or, at any rate, high school students, male and female, wearing their uniforms) were still performing on Parliament's lawn, to the great edification of visitors from Michigan and Arkansas, and I am sure the chagrin of many Canadian nationalists.

On another occasion I was asked whether I could suggest a design for a "distinctively Canadian" sword to replace the British patterns which Canadian officers had worn from time immemorial. I forget just what I said in reply, but I think it contained some reference to tomahawks, and was otherwise unprintable. It was a long time before the distinctively Canadian sword finally appeared, but in 1981 I had the displeasure of reading in the "magazine of the Canadian Forces" an illustrated account of "the first CF ceremonial combined services sword," created by Wilkinsons. The article stated, "The 12.7 cm ceremonial sword, designed in the style of the 16th century knightly Royal Oakley sword, was used by Christian forces during the Crusades." (There's history for you.) Photographs showed a cross-hilted affair with a "polished rosewood hand-grip." Notably lacking was the Royal Cypher of the reigning Sovereign which former swords had always carried.[1]

The sword forcibly reminded me of the objects carried by certain fraternal organizations. I was also reminded of the sergeant-major who drilled the U.T.S. cadet corps, ages ago. On mornings when we were particularly awful, he used to say, "You look like the Knights of Pythi-ass." The new sword would, I think, be eminently suited to the purposes of the Knights of Pythi-ass. It certainly suggests nothing military — and nothing Canadian.

It will be gathered that I was not sorry to shake the dust of Ottawa off my feet for a second time. Having recruited a very suitable person to head the new Directorate of History (Sydney Wise, a wartime airman and a competent military scholar) I returned to Toronto and my students. At this point, incidentally, I for the first time suggested to the university an increase in my salary; which was graciously conceded.

The fact that I was still struggling with the book called *Arms, Men and Governments* brings me to my literary association with the late Mr. Mackenzie King.

I have described how writing this book brought me access to the great man's remarkable diary. At this stage I was, of course, dealing with the war and immediate prewar period, and hardly concerned myself at all with

King's personal life, which was not particularly relevant to an official history. And in these later years of King's life those personal peculiarities that help to make his career so fascinating were not so much in evidence as when he was younger. Even so, there was plenty in the diary to surprise and titillate the reader. In particular, there were the dreams — King's usual word for them was "visions." Almost every day's entry began with an account of the overnight vision, and often it was very peculiar indeed. I came across few direct references to the Prime Minister's spiritualistic beliefs and activities. Later I was to discover that he swore off spiritualism at the very moment of the outbreak of war.

My study of the diary advanced a stage further when I undertook to write my book on Canadian external policies. In this connection I read the diary for the years immediately after the First World War, seeking to discover whether King's later policies in external matters were foreshadowed in his early days as Liberal party leader. I did not find a very great deal about external affairs, though what I found was important and helpful; but I was set back on my heels by discovering that the diary at this point was concerned at greater length with King's relations with women. In particular, this was the time of the beginning of his relationship with Joan Patteson, and of the extraordinary triangular connection with her and her husband which lasted until King's death. Subsequently, of course, I found that this was the second triangle in King's life: when much younger, he had had a not dissimilar involvement with the Very Reverend W. T. Herridge and his wife Marjorie, Herridge being the minister of St. Andrew's Presbyterian Church in Ottawa, which King attended. As the picture expanded, I was more and more astonished: it was clear that King, the solid, stolid, stodgy figure, the dullest personality in modern Canadian history, had unsuspected depths — depths which his first official biographer, MacGregor Dawson, had not explored or at any rate not revealed. (In justice to Dawson, it must be said that this could hardly have been done in a book published in 1958.)*

---

* When King's literary executors were searching for a biographer, Fred McGregor asked me whether I thought Dawson would be suitable. I didn't then know Dawson, but on the basis of his reputation as a scholar in political science and the fact that he was thought to be generally sympathetic to King (which seemd to me desirable) I assented. Later I was to regret giving this advice. When I mentioned the matter to Donald Creighton, he exploded, "Of course, they wouldn't think of appointing the one person who has written a modern Canadian political biography!" Donald as Mackenzie King's official biographer: imagination boggles.

When I first looked into the earliest portion of the diary (King began it in 1893, when he was entering his third year as an undergraduate at the University of Toronto) I had further surprises. The youngster described relations with a vast number of females, respectable and not so respectable. That he should explore the Toronto sub-world inhabited by prostitutes is really not extraordinary when one comes to think of it; it is pretty clear that this was fairly common form among the students of his time. What *was* remarkable was that King recorded these encounters in his diary. Further research revealed that they were succeeded by similar business in Chicago, Boston and abroad. It was by now becoming clear to me that there was a book to be written about the aspects of King's personal life that Dawson had left severely alone; and the conviction grew that I had to write it.

As I continued to explore the diary, it seemed apparent that King's private life was largely dominated by three friendships: those with Bert Harper (the young associate of his early days in Ottawa who was drowned in 1901), Marjorie Herridge, and Joan Patteson. There were other close friends, but these three were the constant companions of his daily life, filling the need which I think King felt from the time when he left the parental roof in 1896 for some kind of surrogate family circle that would provide him with a cocoon of ever-present friendly confidence and support. It was the same sort of need, the urgent desire to have contact with the dead members of his family and particularly his mother, that ultimately pushed him into spiritualism, a pursuit in which his associate, devoted but never I think entirely free from scepticism, was Joan Patteson. Piecing together the story of King's movement into (and, temporarily at least, out of) spiritualism was a fascinating task, to which the growing conviction that the records the Prime Minister kept of his "conversations" with the spirits told one a good deal about his mind and ideas lent a special piquancy. (No use is made of these records in the official biography; and the typewritten transcript of King's difficult handwritten originals which the literary executors arranged to prepare for the biographers' use omits them.)

The essay in biography which I was now proposing to attempt raised questions. I was setting about describing the private — and to a considerable extent, the secret — life of a public man, including his sexual adventures. At an earlier day this simply would have been "not done."

Twenty years before, I should not have dreamed of doing it myself. But times, and public taste, had changed. Such books as Michael Holroyd's life of Lytton Strachey had dealt frankly with the sexual lives of eminent people on the basis of the authentic records they had left behind them. In King's case the record was unusually complete; the most surprising parts of it were already in the public domain, available to any researcher, and the whole of the diary would very shortly be opened. If I didn't write the book somebody else was going to, and I was vain enough to think that I might do it more acceptably than some other people. No conspiracy of silence was going to last long, and in any case it seemed to me that conspiracies of silence were out of date. The first volume of King's official biography was markedly incomplete and inadequate. Finally — one might as well be frank — here was a subject which might have sufficient public appeal that a little money might be made out of it, a rare event in the life of a Canadian historian.

In 1974 I read to the Canadian Historical Association a long paper based on my findings; and its reception encouraged me to proceed. In the spring of 1976 Macmillan of Canada published the result, a book of a little over 250 pages called *A Very Double Life*, a phrase of King's own from the diary. The publication was accompanied by rather curious incidents. Macmillans had arranged for the book to be "excerpted" by the *Toronto Star* and other papers across Canada. In an evil hour for myself I agreed to this (moved, of course, by the fact that there was a fair bit of cash involved) without insisting on seeing the excerpts in advance of publication. Just before the book came out I delivered, by invitation, the first Joanne Goodman lectures at the University of Western Ontario. The subject, arising out of my recent studies, was "Mackenzie King and the Atlantic Triangle." As a result I got caught in a feud between the *Star* and the *Globe and Mail*, arising out of the fact that although the *Star* had purchased the "excerpting" rights on the first volume of John Diefenbaker's memoirs (also published by Macmillan) the *Globe* had got hold of an advance copy of the book and scooped it. The *Globe* sent a reporter to my lectures and all three were reported on its front page (treatment not often accorded an academic lecturer, and I was under no illusions as to any connection with the lectures' intrinsic quality). The *Star* took alarm after the first report, and I got a telephone call saying that they were advancing the publication of the excerpts of my book. I told them they needn't worry, that there was little in the following lectures that in any way duplicated the book, but they went ahead, and I suspect that the "excerpting" was more hastily and carelessly done than would otherwise have been the case.[2]

At any rate, the book as presented by the *Star* and the other papers that published the extracts was a highly sensationalized job. Needless to say, King's dealings with the female sex were the main topic, and the presentation was, to say the least, crude. I am sure that it did the book's reputation, and probably mine too, permanent harm. Some time later I discovered that an old friend of mine who had known King well had not seen the book. I sent him a copy, and received a letter of acknowledgment saying that the newspaper version had shocked him: this, as he put it, was not the Charles Stacey he knew. But the actual book, when he read it, had made an utterly different impression. He even remarked that he thought it well written — something no one could have gathered from the excerpts.

The book's reception was certainly affected by the newspaper treatment. The *Canadian Historical Review*, I was told, offered it to four reviewers before one accepted; and the notice it finally published might have been written by a Victorian grandmother. It was evident that many respectable Canadians felt that the conspiracy of silence should have continued. Some seemed inclined to accuse me of fabricating the whole thing (the book was very fully documented, but naturally there was no documentation in the newspapers). A lady from Cannington, Ontario, my mother's home town, who wrote to the *Star*, doubtless spoke for a multitude: "I lived through all of King's public life and never heard or read any scandal connected with it, something that would be impossible to hide when one held the highest position in the country."[3] John Evans, the president of the University of Toronto at the time, told me later that I had made a lot of trouble for him; he received angry letters from alumni (often doubtless good Liberals) demanding that I should be fired or deprived of my tenure (which I had never had). He said he had a simple answer: "Nothing can be done, he's just retired." An interesting phenomenon is the continuing unwillingness of many people, in the face of the evidence provided by King himself, to believe that he can possibly have patronized prostitutes.

There has been a rather marked reluctance to accept *A Very Double Life* as a serious contribution to biography, which it was intended to be and I think is. I decline to be ashamed of it; on the contrary, I am not ill pleased with it, and I think its status will improve with time.[4]

Chapter 18

Past and Present

H istory — as read, written or taught — has undergone a good many changes in my time. I really believe that, in the English-speaking world at least, more history is being read today than ever before. That is a large statement and, like most large statements, incapable of proof; but when one looks at the last generation and considers the number of readers achieved by, say, Barbara Tuchman, the late Winston Churchill (a super-human phenomenon who perhaps should be regarded as *hors concours*) or, in Canada, Pierre Berton, one is forced to take it seriously. Of course, none of these is a "professional" historian; and for each of the popular writers of the sort I have named there are a myriad of academic delvers whose sales are numbered in hundreds rather than in thousands. There are also, however, a fair number of professionals who have respectable followings among readers at large.

When I was young there was still some controversy between those who regarded history austerely as a research science and those who thought of it as in some sort an art. "Scientific" history was largely a German invention of the late nineteenth century, taken up with enthusiasm by the new American graduate schools and with somewhat less conviction in the old British universities. The great J. B. Bury, appointed Regius Professor of Modern History at Cambridge in 1901, announced that history was "a science, no more and no less." His successor in that chair, the not less great George Macaulay Trevelyan, took a very different view, arguing that history was both a science and an art, "that the discovery of historical facts should be scientific in method, but that the exposition of them for the reader partook of the nature of art, the art of written words commonly called literature."[1] The debate still goes on, though usually in different and rather more mundane terms. In academic circles, it takes the form of the question, is history to be classed among the social sciences or the humanities? It is a curious fact that the same historian will sometimes be found on both sides of this question. The reason is that for some reason grants (magic word!) come more easily to the so-called social sciences than to the humanities; the mere word "science" seems to appeal to people who control purse strings. Thus, though almost every historian worthy of the name thinks of himself, within himself, as a humanist, he puts his pride in his pocket and is willing to be classed as a social scientist when the time comes for pay parade.

The fact is, however, that history is a branch of literature or it is next to nothing. The most indefatigable researcher in the world is like a dumb man if he cannot communicate his results. Inability to communicate, indeed, is what keeps so many academic historians mute and inglorious; nobody reads the works of the semi-literate, which is what some of them are close to being. Learning requires literary skill if it is to gain the audience it deserves. Trevelyan was a great scholar; but there is more than scholarship in the passage where he describes the heyday of the stagecoach, "from those proud summer mornings when, hung with laurels, it left behind the news of fresh victories in Spain, as it careered without a halt through cheering villages, to the time when its daily message on the fortunes of the Reform Bill were no less eagerly awaited by assembled multitudes, staring down the road for its coming." I often think of Samuel Eliot Morison as the American Trevelyan; and although he too was a profound scholar, it is not scholarship that charms the reader in his famous description of the American clipper ship, "stately as a cathedral, beautiful as a terraced cloud."[2] Neither of these writers, I think, is as much read by students as he once was; so much the worse for the students. In Canada, our nearest equivalent was Donald Creighton; and I think his star too is sinking. But it will be a poor day for Canadian history, and Canadian literature, when people cease to read the passages where his *Macdonald* rises to its peaks, and

particularly perhaps the description of the first Dominion Day with which
the first volume concludes.

Since the Second World War, in historical studies as in other matters,
there has been what the *Times Literary Supplement* has called "a ferment of
fashion." When I was a student there was a great vogue for constitutional
history: William Stubbs at Oxford, the so-called "struggle for responsible
government" in Canada. In Canada at least this topic is now almost
unheard of; and I rather sympathize with those students who will some
day strive to unravel the constitutional developments of the last decade.
Political history, once the core of any curriculum, has been fighting for its
life; social history in its various manifestations has long held the field, and
many younger historians in particular have had little use for anything else.
There has been a rush to study what popular jargon calls the "disadvan-
taged" elements in society, and it has been a standing joke among the older
generation that to be anybody nowadays you must work on women, North
American Indians or blacks: preferably all three. Women's history in
particular has had a tremendous vogue. Certainly it was too long neglected; now it seems to be in danger of drowning in its own popularity.
Labour history is another very active field, and the current fashion is to
denigrate those who tend to equate labour with trade unionism. Here-
abouts, of course, the Marxists are highly visible. The urban historians are
likewise very numerous, and are to be found holding conferences on every
side. Ethnic history, and Jewish history in particular, is much in vogue.
And the students of the history of ideas (intellectual history) naturally tend
to consider themselves the aristocrats of the profession. Which may
prompt the final reflection that historians as a class, and Canadians not
least, could do with a little more sense of humour.

I have already mentioned one trend that seems to run contrary to the
stream: the tremendous boom in military history during the past generation, so utterly at odds with the expectations of my friend Brooke Claxton.
Books on the two world wars have continued to flow from the presses in a
river that shows no sign of drying up; and earlier wars receive only slightly
less attention. The current academic fashion is reflected however in the
attempt to study war as a social institution; it is a thoroughly intelligent
approach, but I sometimes think that if I see the phrase "war and society"
once more I shall scream. The technical and the secret aspects of war
particularly appeal to the current imagination, and popular writers have

exploited these to the full. A curious phenomenon has been the success of the book *A Man Called Intrepid*, which has been condemned as almost utterly worthless by every expert who has commented on it, but which is reported to have sold two million copies. One English critic referred to the school of authors that produce books like this as "the Intrepid Bodyguard of Liars." The serious military student wishes he could achieve their circulation.

The newest generation of historians have sought to be innovators in methods as well as in themes. The advent of the computer has produced the quantification school. Extreme claims have been made for the statistical approach. Obviously much can be done with it, especially on social and economic questions; obviously also it has limitations. Though the British had more tanks than the Germans in North Africa, for a long period the Germans had the upper hand there; computers can hardly explain why. Nor could a computer analyse the change that came to the North African scene when Lord Montgomery took over the Eighth Army in 1942. There has also been a vogue of psycho-history, which seeks to use the tools of psychoanalysis to explain the behaviour of historical personalities. This has not gained wide acceptance, particularly as some of the practitioners of the art are neither trained psychologists nor trained historians. Oral history, based upon human memory, had had a good many followers, who have even organized themselves in societies. I have said something about my own experience with oral history; I have seen a good deal of it, and my conclusion, I have made clear, is that normally it is something to be resorted to when the written records fail you.

Fads and fashions pass, but the solid realities remain. People will always study and read history, and I think they will recognize again, as time goes by, that the core of history is politics and government, including foreign relations. History will not be read because it will solve the problems of today, for it will do no such thing; nevertheless, people who know nothing of their past will make a poor fist of dealing with the present. I used to tell young officers at the staff college that there was little hope for the man who, when the enemy came over the hill, asked himself, "Now, what would Napoleon do?" But the soldier who has studied the campaigns of Napoleon, or of other men who did well on the battlefield, is more likely to make sound decisions in a crisis than one who has not bothered his head with the history of his profession.

And people will go on reading history, not for any practical or professional benefit, but simply because the stuff is so fascinating. Geography, a high authority once said, is about maps; but biography is about chaps. History also is about chaps; and chaps are endlessly interesting, especially to other chaps.*

You don't as a rule make much money out of writing history, especially Canadian history; your satisfaction comes in other ways. I mentioned that I thought I might make a little filthy lucre out of *A Very Double Life*, it being considered a mildly scandalous work. So I did — far more than out of anything else I have ever written. If anyone is interested, my take from the book was about $17,000 — over six years. Nobody gets rich that way. Out of my more solemnly scholarly writings I have made about enough to pay expenses, with a little bit over. My history of Canadian external policies has had some sale as a university textbook, but in Canada that field is very small and the returns are smaller.

Over the years I have had the opportunity of seeing something of the Canadian book publishing industry, as it passed through what can only be called a process of decline and fall. I was fortunate in having an association with the Macmillan Company of Canada when it was under the direction of John Gray, whom I have already mentioned. It was a highly autonomous subsidiary of Macmillans of London. So far as I know, John never put his publishing philosophy on paper; it was tragic that death put a period to his delightful autobiography at the end of the first volume (entitled *Fun Tomorrow*), at the point where he took over Macmillans after the second war. But my contacts with him, and what I saw of his practice, lead me to think that his scheme of things boiled down to this: first, to publish good Canadian books — books of some merit, not merely books that would sell; and secondly, to earn if possible a modest return for the owners of the company. It is my impression that this policy was quite acceptable to the parent firm in England, and it certainly produced a significant contribution to Canadian literature, and not least to Canadian history.

The government of Canada was largely responsible for putting an end to this admirable situation. In February 1972 the Secretary of State, Gérard Pelletier, announced a program of subsidies for the book publishing industry. From these subsidies firms owned abroad — the largest and most important of which was Macmillans — were to be excluded. I was

---

* To avoid any implication of sexism, it must of course be understood that "chaps" comprehends female chaps as well as males.

moved to write the *Globe and Mail* a letter of protest calling attention to the injustice to Macmillans in particular:

> Macmillans have been a major Canadian publisher since 1905. The books they have published in Canadian history, biography and related subjects would fill a small library. Decades ago they published the works of George M. Wrong when he was laying the foundations of a new school of Canadian historical writing. More recently they have produced Donald Creighton's famous life of Sir John A. Macdonald, J.M.S. Careless's "Brown of the Globe", Joseph Schull's biography of Laurier, and dozens of other original and important contributions to Canadian studies. They have encouraged Canadian authors and given employment to large numbers of Canadian workmen. At the moment, I believe, they have in print more Canadian-manufactured titles than any other publisher except the University of Toronto Press, and most of them are by Canadian writers. In so far as British capital has contributed to these results, we have no reason to be anything but grateful to it.[3]

I suggested that in applying its policy the government should take careful account of the past record and contributions of individual firms like Macmillans. My protest and others had no effect whatever; and the result was disastrous.

Finding themselves faced with this sort of government discrimination, Macmillans in London felt that they had no choice but to divest themselves of their Canadian operation; and it was sold to Maclean-Hunter Limited, an enormous Canadian concern which had long been involved in publishing, but not book publishing (I think it was Kildare Dobbs who remarked that they had been chiefly known as the producers of *Canadian Bus and Truck*). John Gray, having made the best terms he could in the hope (which proved illusory) of ensuring the continuance of the efficient organization to which he had given the best years of his life, retired; at a dinner in his honour in the spring of 1973 I had the pleasure of being one of a succession of people who paid tribute to him. It seems apparent in retrospect that Gray's retirement was a milestone on the downward path of Canadian book publishing.

My own further experiences with the industry I don't propose to narrate, though some of them were painful enough. They leave me rather pessimistic about the prospects for the future publication of serious books in Canada. Money and the mass market are increasingly what people in the business are interested in; the modest returns that I have suggested seem to have satisfied the old Macmillans are not enough. If present trends continue, serious book publishing in Canada — and I am thinking mainly of Canadian history — seems likely to become a monopoly of the university presses, which means in practice largely the University of Toronto Press. We are fortunate that that institution exists. Of course, the other side of the government policy coin is that the UTP and other serious publishers would not be able to produce these books without the subsidies they receive from agencies financed by government.

This modest memoir may end as it began, with personal and family affairs. I lost Doris in 1969, Since I left the army and returned to Toronto we had been camping in an upper duplex on Avenue Road. In 1967 (as our Canadian centennial project, we said) we bought a small house on Tranmer Avenue, only a block or so from our flat. (I also celebrated the centennial year by developing rheumatoid arthritis, my constant companion since.) Doris enjoyed the house, but she had only two years in it. She had long been in poor health, but the appearance of bowel cancer was a terrible shock, the more so as her two younger sisters had both died of it, painfully. There was an operation which was supposed to be "exploratory"; when it was over the surgeon telephoned me that it was indeed cancer, and that he had not been able to "get it all out." It was a sentence of death. It seemed however that we might still expect a few months together, which we hoped might be tranquil. But during another spell in hospital there was a sudden pneumonic attack, and she died quickly and peacefully. Hard as the blow was at the moment, I realized almost at once that it was for the best; she was spared the grim experience her sisters had had, which we had both feared.

My mother had died in 1964. I stayed on in the little house, my life centring more and more on the university. When in 1973 I was made a University Professor I was given an office in Massey College, and some time later I was elected a Senior Fellow of the College. I have been involved with it since that time.

Massey College, basically a residence for graduate students, was the last great benefaction of the Massey Foundation (and more specifically, of

Vincent Massey) to the University of Toronto. I think Vincent's view of education, at bottom, was that it had stopped short in Balliol College, Oxford, about 1911, when he himself went up to Balliol. This conception, inevitably, was reflected in his new college. Uncultured persons accused it of being sham Oxbridge, which of course it was. (One local wit dubbed it "Half Soles College.") Sham Oxbridge didn't bother me; after all, I had lived for a dozen years in the Princeton Graduate College, which I believe was Vincent's specific model for his own foundation. Dean West's Gothic structure at Princeton was larger and more magnificent — one of Massey's bad features was that it could accommodate only a small minority of the university's graduate students — but the idea was the same, a "collegial" atmosphere, with the inmates dining together in hall in gowns.

Massey College's architecture is reputed to have won many awards from architectural organizations. It has won few from the people who live and work in it. The architect, who evidently had never been to college, failed to appreciate the importance of light to the process of study. The college's fenestration is designed to exclude as much of the natural light of heaven as possible; while the electric fixtures the architect provided were clearly intended to ensure a state of almost total darkness. To the approaching stranger Massey presents fortress-like blank walls, suggesting a desire to isolate this outpost of the republic of learning from the common people outside: not a concept that I find attractive. However, if the visitor persists and penetrates to the interior, he finds himself in a pleasant and welcoming little quadrangle; for this at least the architect deserves thanks.

Massey College's first Master, who was appointed by the founder and presided over the place for nineteen years after it opened in 1962, did nothing to diminish the Oxbridge atmosphere. He was Robertson Davies, the eminent novelist and playwright. By statute the college was governed by the "Master and Fellows," but in Rob's time it was rather more the Master than the Fellows. Massey had recruited him from the newspaper world. Though a very well-read man, he was a creative artist rather than a scholar. He ran the place somewhat as if it had been a theatrical production; in fact he was rarely seen outside his lodging except on quasi-theatrical occasions like high-table nights or Gaudies. The latter, the Christmas parties, largely attended by eminent guests from outside the college, had as their high point the annual College Ghost Story, written and read by the Master, and as one would expect frequently very funny.

These stories have now been made available to a wider world in a book called *High Spirits*. Rob's administration had a certain style; it was elegant and amusing, and he was a good figurehead for the college in its beginning years.

Vincent Massey wrote of Balliol that it was "what a college ought to be — a community." In spite of the Oxbridge frippery, I think his own young foundation has not done badly in this respect. I hope and believe that its Junior Fellows, the graduate students, have found it a pleasant place to live and work in, a place where scholarship and friendship can grow agreeably together. The Senior Fellows, mainly senior people from the university faculty, have been an interesting, compatible and clubby group. Luncheon at Massey is a cheerful experience and sometimes an intellectual treat. It is a pleasure I give myself regularly. The University of Toronto is the better for Vincent's college; though it has given it very little practical encouragement.

I did a little teaching at the university after my official retirement in 1975; the last course I actually taught was in 1978. I did not stand for re-election as a Senior Fellow at Massey when my five-year term was up, preferring to become an Associate (now Emeritus) Fellow. In this capacity I continue to infest the college. Since my retirement I have inscribed my occupation on my income tax return as "writer"; and this has been my chief activity, though not, as I have explained, one that generates vast amounts of income.

Fate was very good to me in one respect. After eleven years as a widower, I married Helen Allen in October 1980. The reader may remember her from Chapter Two, as the girl who went on from University College to a distinguished career, first in newspaper work, later as a pioneer in the field of child adoption; also, perhaps, as the girl who played Aline in *The Sorcerer*. We were good friends, but as people do, we drifted in different directions, I to distant parts, marriage, and the army, while her concerns kept her in Toronto (with a few excursions in the line of duty to such places as Hong Kong and Saigon). Occasionally we sent each other distant signals; I wrote congratulating her on being appointed to the Order of Canada, she wrote congratulating me when some generous colleagues published a *Festschrift* in my honour.[4] We met again at a reunion of the staff of *The Varsity*, on which we had been colleagues so long ago. It was a rainy night; I ferried one of Helen's party to their car, and Helen's umbrella got left in *my* car. It had to be returned. Thereafter one thing gradually led to another. We met again at an Order of Canada party. Helen was alone, it transpired, in the lovely house on the Scarborough cliffs she had shared with her mother and Phyllis Griffiths, both of whom were now gone; I was alone in my house on Tranmer Avenue; and we began to find our way, I to her house, she to mine. Age and arthritis made me doubtful about raising the question of marriage, but finally I ventured, and Helen was brave enough to take me on. We were married by the Very Reverend DeCourcy Rayner, another former editor of *The Varsity*, in St. Andrew's Church on King Street. (Helen's father, who lost his life in the First War, had been a Presbyterian minister.) We kept the enterprise very dark. The church was celebrating its 150th anniversary that year, and we boasted that ours was the smallest wedding that had ever taken place in it. I suspect it was also one of the most fortunate in its results. I may say, as Winston Churchill did, in a phrase not I think entirely original with him, that I have lived happily ever after.

That is perhaps a good note on which to end. Looking back over it all, I think I have been on the whole a lucky fellow. I have been allowed to devote myself to things that interested me, and my lot has been cast among interesting people. Fascinated by history, I have been able to make a career of writing and teaching it. I had an affection for the army, and I found myself an army historian. Soldiers often observed with amazement that in my case the army used a person with special qualifications in the job for which he was qualified; normally, they observed acidly, it would have used a pork butcher to write history and a historian to butcher hogs. The credit for this unusual achievement, I suppose, is due to General Harry Crerar. I have had the good luck to meet important and sometimes famous people, and — what is perhaps more genuinely worthwhile — to work among agreeable people both in the universities and the army.

At seventy-six, I feel no powerful disposition to terminate my date with history. I think I may still have something to say about Canada. The politics of the Trudeau era do not attract me as those of the day of my old friend Mackenzie King did, but there is no lack of subject matter. I even discover that I still find excitement in the business of book-making, just as I did when I first encountered it back in 1936. There is still a thrill in receiving the first proofs, a thrill in getting the first bound copy, a thrill in waiting for the reviews, and wondering whether they will be warm, lukewarm, waspish or just plain hostile. All this no doubt is childish, but I suspect that no author, young or old, is wholly exempt from it. It is the literary equivalent of the first-night sensations in the theatre, and the academic historian is no more free from it than the novelist or the poet. If he is worth his salt, he too is a literary artist, and suffers the same labour pains as do those people commonly considered more creative.

History continues to unfold. Revolutions explode, wars are lost and won, statesmen are assassinated. Conferences great and small are held around the world. The records accumulate inexorably in the file-rooms and the archives. One's fellow historians publish brilliant books which cry out to be read. Occasionally I am asked to review one of them, and then I really have to read it. Duty calls. Up and at it. But, at the age of seventy-six, not too vigorously, not too zealously. There is still time to spare.

References

Chapter One

And Quiet Flows the Don

1. Mr. A. G. Rankin, the University's Vice-President, Business Affairs, reported in University of Toronto *Bulletin*, 11 July 1975.
2. *The Twig*, III, (December 1922).

Chapter Two

Undergraduate

1. *Globe*, Toronto, 26 October 1923.
2. *Torontonensis. The Year Book of the University of Toronto*, 1927, pp. 262-63.
3. King Diary, 12 June and 21 August 1927. Bickersteth's file on the affair, Massey College, Toronto. See also J. R. Mallory, "Mackenzie King and the origins of the cabinet secretariat," *Canadian Public Administration*, 19 (Summer 1976), pp. 254-66.
4. King Diary, 9 May 1929.

5. *The Canadian Army, 1939–1945: An Official Historical Summary* (Ottawa, 1948), p. 3.
6. *The Varsity*, 25 October 1927.

Chapter Three

Oxford, and Some Other Places

1. *The Times* (London), September 3 and 4, 1941.
2. First published 1907; reprinted Toronto, 1974, with introduction by Robert Hill.
3. "The Abbé Groulx: Particularist" and "Henri Bourassa," in E. K. Brown, *Responses and Evaluations: Essays on Canada*, ed. David Staines (Toronto, 1977), pp. 24-33.
4. William Stubbs, *The Constitutional History of England*, 5th ed., 3 vols. (Oxford, 1891), I:235-36.

Chapter Four

A New Country

1. Article on Andrew Fleming West by Lawrence R. Veysey, *Dictionary of American Biography*, Supplement Three.
2. *New York Times*, April 24, 1939.

Chapter Five

Consequences of Hitler

1. Order-in-Council P.C. 1652, 27 May 1921, cites dates of Cruikshank's appointment and retirement. *The Macmillan Dictionary of Canadian Biography*, 4th ed., p. 185. I would be prepared to produce examples of inaccurate inscriptions.
2. Order-in-Council P.C. 1652.
3. *Official History of the Canadian Forces in the Great War, General Series*, Vol. 1 (with appendix volume). Duguid's account of his terms of reference, p. viii.
4. "Canada's Last War — and the Next," *University of Toronto Quarterly* (April 1939).

Chapter Six

Cockspur Street

1. *Soldiers and Politicians: The Memoirs of Lt.-Gen. Maurice A. Pope, C.B., M.C.* (Toronto, 1962), p. 71.
2. See my official volume *Arms, Men and Governments: The Military Policies of Canada, 1939–1945* (Ottawa, 1970), pp. 215-16, 226.
3. Ibid., p. 96*n*.
4. I made careful notes of these conversations at the time; subsequently, after doing some research in the relevant documents, I incorporated them in "Memorandum on 'Victor' Exercise, January, 1941," 24 May 41. A bit absurdly, perhaps, I allowed McNaughton's injunction of secrecy to prevent me from sending this to Ottawa. I published the substance of it in *Arms, Men and Governments*. I still have the original.
5. "The Life and Hard Times of an Official Historian," *Canadian Historical Review* (March 1970).
6. "The New Canadian Corps," *Canadian Geographical Journal*, 23, (July 1941), pp. 2-49.
7. The various versions and correspondence are in CMHQ file 6 Historical 1, Public Archives Canada, R.G. 24, Vol. 12, p. 485.
8. The story of this phase of the German air offensive is well outlined in the contemporary British official booklet, *Front Line, 1940–41: The Official Story of the Civil Defence of Britain* (London: His Majesty's Stationery Office, 1942). For Canadian aspects, see our booklet *The Canadians in Britain, 1939–1944* ("The Canadian Army at War," 2nd ed., Ottawa, 1946).

Chapter Seven

Aftermath of a Dress Rehearsal

1. I preserved my draft with COHQ's marks on it, and Lawrence's revised version. They are on CMHQ file 3/Dieppe/1 in Record Group 24, Vol. 12, p. 300, Public Archives of Canada.
2. See C. P. Stacey, *Six Years of War* (Ottawa, 1955), pp. 381-82.
3. Earl Mountbatten of Burma, "Operation Jubilee: The Place of the Dieppe Raid in History," *RUSI: Journal of the Royal United Services Institute for Defence Studies* (March 1974). Correspondence, ibid. (December 1974). Letters in the author's hands.

4. *Six Years of War*, pp. 331-32.
5. William Whitehead and Terence Macartney-Filgate, *Dieppe 1942: Echoes of Disaster* (Toronto, 1979), p. 174.
6. Ibid., Introduction.
7. *Six Years of War*, p. 337, and cf. *Arms, Men and Governments*, p. 217. See also Lord Mountbatten's account in "Operation Jubilee."
8. Ronald Atkin, *Dieppe 1942: The Jubilee Disaster* (London, 1980).

Chapter Eight

Getting on with It

1. *Six Years of War*, pp. 249-51; *Arms, Men and Governments*, pp. 232-47.

Chapter Nine

Battles in Italy, Intrigues in England

1. Stacey, *Arms, Men and Governments*, pp. 230-31.
2. Ibid., pp. 231-47.
3. The Toronto *Globe and Mail* of 3 February 1942 noted without comment the fact that Mrs. McNaughton had accompanied the general to Canada and would be returning with him.
4. Interview with Lieutenant-General Charles Foulkes, Chief of the General Staff, 27 June 1947.
5. *Arms, Men and Governments*, pp. 241-46.
6. Interview with Lieutenant-General K. Stuart, 6 February 1944.
7. In Douglas LePan, *Bright Glass of Memory* (Toronto, 1979).

Chapter Ten

Fair Stood the Wind for France

1. G.W.L. Nicholson, *The Canadians in Italy* (Ottawa, 1956), p. 451*n*.
2. C.P. Stacey, *The Victory Campaign* (Ottawa, 1960), p. 367 *n*.

Chapter Eleven

The End of the Affair

1. *Arms, Men and Governments*, p. 455.
2. Ibid., pp. 474-78.
3. J.W. Pickersgill and D.F. Forster, *The Mackenzie King Record*, 4 vols (Toronto, 1960-70), I, p. 588; IV, p. 427.
4. *The Victory Campaign*, p. 545.

Chapter Twelve

Launching a History

1. I have described this period of my affairs in "The Life and Hard Times of an Official Historian."
2. *The Mackenzie King Record*, I, p. 689.
3. Major-General George Kitching, "General Guy Simonds — in appreciation," *Canadian Defence Quarterly* (Autumn 1974).
4. In "The Life and Hard Times of an Official Historian."

Chapter Thirteen

Swanning with Rex

1. Arnold Heeney, *The Things that are Caesar's: Memoirs of a Canadian Public Servant* (Toronto, 1972), p. 88.
2. *The Mackenzie King Record*, III, p. 300.
3. Ibid., p. 309.
4. Ibid., p. 312.

Chapter Fourteen

The Fight for the History: Phase One

1. *The Mackenzie King Record*, II, p. 218.
2. I owe this reference to Robert Bothwell.

3. *The Canadian Army, 1939–1945*, p. 17.
4. Sir Lyman Duff, *Report on the Canadian Expeditionary Force to the Crown Colony of Hong Kong* (Ottawa, 1942), p. 4.
5. *Six Years of War*, p. 453.
6. Public Record Office, file DO 127/81. Most of the papers referred to in the account that follows are in this file. Some are from the equivalent Department of External Affairs file, 4596-40.

Chapter Fifteen

The Fight for the History: Phase Two

1. Part A, Supplement to Canadian Army Orders, No. 33-1, 10 September 1956.
2. "The Canadian-American Permanent Joint Board on Defence, 1940–1945," *International Journal* (Spring 1954).
3. "Cabinet Government in Canada: Some Recent Developments in the Machinery of the Central Executive" (August 1946).

Chapter Sixteen

Fables and Foibles: History and the Human Animal

1. RUSI, March 1981.
2. *Six Years of War*, p. 336; *The Victory Campaign*, p. 610.
3. *Six Years of War*, p. 338.
4. See particularly pp. 196-98 and 303-306.
5. Notes of conversation, "8/10/44, Eindhoven, F.M.M." [Field-Marshal Montgomery], Ralston Papers, Public Archives Canada; see *Arms, Men and Governments*, p. 224.
6. *Arms, Men and Governments*, p. 228. On the difficulties of Crerar's position, see *Six Years of War*, p. 416, and *The Victory Campaign*, pp. 196-98.
7. See the description in *Six Years of War*, pp. 462-63.
8. For an example, see Oliver Lindsay, *The Lasting Honour: The Fall of Hong Kong, 1941* (London, 1978), pp. 147-48.
9. "Canadian Archives," Ottawa, 1951; published in *Royal Commission Studies*, printed for the Massey Commission (Ottawa, 1951).

Chapter Seventeen

Back to the Don

1. *Sentinel*, 17, no. 2 (1981/2).
2. Five excerpts, *Toronto Star*, 6-11 March 1976.
3. *Toronto Star*, 17 March 1976.
4. An indication of more serious consideration is Donald Swainson's article, "Trends in Canadian Biography: Recent Historical Writing," *Queen's Quarterly* (Autumn 1980).

Chapter Eighteen

Past and Present

1. G.M. Trevelyan, *History and the Reader* (London, 1945), p. 1.
2. G.M. Trevelyan, *British History in the Nineteenth Century (1782-1901)* (London 1922), p. 167. Samuel Eliot Morison, *The Oxford History of the United States, 1783-1917* (2 vols., 1927), II, pp. 116-19. This book was later expanded into a collaborative work with Henry Steele Commager, *The Growht of the American Republic*, in various editions.
3. *Globe and Mail*, 17 February 1972.
4. Michael Cross and Robert Bothwell, eds., *Policy by Other Means* (Toronto, 1972).

Index